CLOTHED WITH THE SUN

CLOTHED
WITH THE SUN

Biblical Women,
Social Justice,
and Us

JOYCE HOLLYDAY

WESTMINSTER JOHN KNOX PRESS
LOUISVILLE, KENTUCKY

To Fay, Judith, Kay, Lynne,
Marie, Mary, Mary Etta,
and Savannah

for helping me through

Book and Cover design by Drew Stevens
Cover illustration: Africa: Madonna *by Betty LaDuke, from* Multi-Cultural Images: The Paintings of Betty LaDuke, 1972–1992 *by Gloria Orenstein*

First edition

Published by Westminster John Knox Press
Louisville, Kentucky

This book is printed on acid-free paper that meets the American National Standards Institute Z39.48 standard. ∞

PRINTED IN THE UNITED STATES OF AMERICA

96 97 98 99 00 01 02 03 04 — 10 9 8 7 6 5 4 3

Library of Congress Cataloging-in-Publication Data

Hollyday, Joyce.
    Clothed with the sun : biblical women, social justice, and us /
Joyce Hollyday. — 1st ed.
        p.   cm.
    ISBN 0-664-25538-8 (alk. paper)
    1. Women in the Bible—Meditations. 2. Devotional calendars.
I. Title.
BS575.H65 1994
220.9′2′082—dc20   94-15670

Contents

PART 10. WITNESSES TO LIFE AND RESURRECTION

Suggestions for Using This Book

Clothed with the Sun is designed to be read throughout a year. It includes an Introduction, an Epilogue, and fifty meditations divided into ten sections with five in each section. Scripture texts listed should be read with each meditation.

FOR INDIVIDUAL USE

1. Read the Introduction in week one.

2. Every week, read one meditation and the scripture identified at the beginning of the meditation. Take the week to ponder and reflect on the material in that week's reading.

3. After completing each section, use the reflection questions in prayer time or to spark personal writing in a journal.

4. Read the Epilogue on week fifty-two to conclude the year's reading.

FOR GROUP USE

1. Read the Introduction for week one. Meet to discuss structure, facilitation, and expectations of group members. Plan to meet every five weeks, after the completion of each section.

2. Read one meditation and the related scripture each week, reflecting on it throughout a week.

3. Use the reflection questions at the end of each section to structure discussion time as the group meets. Participants may also wish to use the questions to guide individual prayer time and to write their reflections based on the questions ahead of time and bring them to the group to share.

4. Conclude the reading on week fifty-two with the Epilogue.

5. Meet to close the year with the ritual found at the end of the book.

Introduction

A great portent appeared in heaven: a woman clothed with the
sun, with the moon under her feet, and on her head a crown of
twelve stars. (Rev. 12:1)

What an image of the glory and power of womanhood we
have in the Bible's last book! Woman as *portent*, an indication of things
momentous and marvelous about to occur. Standing at the end of the
path, the Woman Clothed with the Sun invites us forward, beckoning
us toward the courage that she possesses. She will be there at the end,
welcoming us into the light of her glory.

This book, intended to be read as a yearlong journey, contains fifty
meditations grounded in the lives of women of the Bible. During the
course of its writing, when I mentioned to people in a variety of set-
tings what I was working on, more than one asked in all earnestness,
"*Are* there fifty women in the Bible?"

That response speaks to our need to know these women better.
Edith Deen, who in 1955 wrote a book titled *All of the Women of the
Bible*, mentions 189 women by name. She also writes of scores of others known simply as "the wife of," "the mother of," or "the daughter
of" some well-known man (not to mention a throng of women listed
under such titles as "Women with Tabrets"—an ancient version of
tambourine—and "Women Who Sew Pillows to Armholes"—see
Ezek. 13:18 KJV if your curiosity is piqued about the latter). And that, of
course, speaks to the dilemma. Many of these women were not considered important enough even to be named by the patriarchal recorders
of their time.

Most of us grew up knowing few of the female heroes of the Bible. If
pressed, we could name Deborah and Esther, perhaps Priscilla, and of
course Mary. But our difficulty is certainly not that there are too few
women in the Bible, as I once thought. The truth is that we were simply
not properly introduced. And from my perspective as a writer forced to
choose among them, there are, indeed, too many marvelous women in
the pages of scripture; I regret that I couldn't include them all.

They are judges and prophets, caregivers and teachers; prominent
matriarchs of large clans or quiet disciples; women who suffered alone
or sang joyous praises to God amid the crowds. Like all of us, they are
blendings of sin and goodness, fear and courage, bondage and freedom.

Each had to confront patriarchal power. Some were primarily victims of that power. Others used their shrewdness to work within the rules of patriarchy to claim their rights and secure their lives. A few boldly broke all the rules and paid the price.

Their stories are not always easy to read. But even in their suffering, they teach us about dignity and courage. They are an amazing company of women, a "cloud of witnesses" that goes before us and invites us to follow on the journey. They are witnesses to faith and justice, to persistence and hope, and most of all, to resurrection. They stand by the empty tomb and call us to life.

Some of the women represented in this book are historically real; others are considered myths or archetypes of female humanity. A few have entire chapters of the Bible devoted to them; some appear in only a verse. But each has a pearl of wisdom to reveal to us. From Eve to the Woman Clothed with the Sun—from the first creative impulse to the close of time—female energy is a river of life and wisdom.

That river flows in our midst now, as women of faith continue to claim life in the face of the forces of destruction. Their stories are woven in throughout these pages: today's trend of the "feminization of poverty" with the economic vulnerability of the biblical widows Ruth and Naomi; the growing awareness about sexual harassment with the attempted exploitation of Vashti and Esther; the current epidemic of sexual violence with the rape of Tamar and Dinah.

Grounding all the stories is a persistent hope. Included are the Deborahs and Priscillas of today, who are carving out their places in church and society; the mothers in places such as South Africa, Nicaragua, and the inner cities of America, who—like the Hebrew midwives Puah and Shiphrah or the five daughters of Zelophehad—courageously defy wrongful authority and band together to demand justice and uphold life.

Today, as they did generations ago, women insert the valor and vigor of womanhood into history. Their stories are intertwined by the power of the word of God, shedding light on one another and bringing ancient stories to life. That word continues to be revealed, adding new stories and strength to the river of life and wisdom.

Wisdom (in the Greek, *Sophia*) is God personified in the feminine. She is the beloved daughter who existed at the creation of the world, appearing later in the form of the Holy Spirit. In ancient traditions, wisdom was viewed as the daughter of the sun god, embodying divine justice. So, from the very beginning, feminine energy came "clothed with the sun."

Does not wisdom call,
and does not understanding raise her voice?

. . . .

"The Lord created me at the beginning of his work,
    the first of his acts of long ago.

. . . .

When he established the heavens, I was there,
    when he drew a circle on the face of the deep,
    when he made firm the skies above,
    when he established the fountains of the deep,

. . . .

    when he marked out the foundations of the earth,
    then I was beside him, . . .
    and I was daily his delight.

. . . .

Whoever finds me finds life." (Prov. 8:1, 22–30, 35)

The one who finds wisdom finds life. To find wisdom, we need to
look toward women clothed with the sun, who shine their light on our
path and beckon us forward. They are in the Bible. They are among us
as modern witnesses to the resurrection. And they are each of us; for
we all carry a pearl of wisdom to add to life's treasure.

There is a rich journey ahead; the women of the scriptures provide
strong and witty and wonderful companionship. I hope that you will
find living with each of them for a week an experience to savor and
cherish, as I have. And I pray that this year might be one of blessing as
you walk, hand in hand with sisters in the faith, toward the light of
wisdom and glory.

PART 1
Women of Patriarchy

Examining patriarchy and its effects is essential grounding for understanding the women of the Bible. Patriarchal beliefs and structures accorded women second-class status, severely limiting both their rights and opportunities.

Beginning with a glimpse at the creation of Eve, Part 1 offers a progression of responses to patriarchy. Sarah and Hagar were tormented and trapped by patriarchy's crueler aspects, as were sisters Rachel and Leah. Ruth and Naomi shrewdly worked the system to ensure their survival. The five sisters Mahlah, Noah, Hoglah, Milcah, and Tirzah confronted the patriarchal system at its roots, challenging and eventually effecting change in the law that kept women landless and without inheritance.

The lives of these women, as with all the women in the Bible, offer helpful clues about how to live under a system that denies equality. They invite us to share a journey that they began, learning from their courage as well as their fears.

1 Eve: Created in God's Image

SCRIPTURE: Genesis 1—3

Then God said, "Let us make humankind in our image, according to our likeness. . . . " So . . . male and female he created them. (Gen. 1:26, 27)

Every religious tradition has its creation stories; the Judeo-Christian tradition has two. The first—from Genesis 1—has humanity as the culmination of creation; the other—found in Genesis 2 and 3—has humanity as its starting point. The first views humankind as the blessed crowning achievement in a world that is continually pronounced good; the second pins the advent of evil on human weakness.

The second story, from an older tradition, is the perfect creation myth for patriarchal Christianity. Man was created first and was therefore superior (notwithstanding feminism's tongue-in-cheek declaration that "Adam was a rough draft"). Man is at the center, and all else—woman as well as beasts and birds—exists to help and support him.

In a great reversal of nature, man gives life to woman. Woman is derivative, a secondary creation. And of course, she is the weak one, the tempted one, the one whose deficiency gave sin a toehold in the world. The implication is that all would have been perfect had woman not come along and spoiled it.

With the fall from grace came an awareness of sexual differences. And with the power of that recognition came upheaval and shame—but perhaps nothing more shameful than the ironclad subjugation of women that followed. For centuries, this version of creation was used by the church to deny women access to ministry and authority, confining them to the "fit helper" roles of parish and family.

Interestingly, those who have condemned Eve for listening to the serpent have not similarly attacked Adam for listening to Eve. God was not so easy on him. Meting out punishment, God dismissed Adam's effort to pass the buck to both Eve and God ("The woman whom *you* gave to me made me do it"). Had Adam been simply an unwitting victim, ignorant of the fruit he was eating—as some have argued—God would have dealt with him differently.

But indeed, the point here is that no one was an innocent bystander. From the beginning, man and woman wanted to know, to love, to flourish. To the extent that they desired to be godly, reflecting the goodness of the Creator, they were blessed. Trouble came when they wanted to be *God*. Idolatry, that pesky and pervasive sin, raised its ugly head right there in the garden. Humanity wanted knowledge and power that only God possesses.

The creation account in Genesis 1—from a later, Priestly tradition—paints a different picture. God is referred to as both "he" and "us." Humanity being created male and female "in the image of God" makes clear that womankind is not some blighted, subordinate part of creation but an equal partner in reflecting the goodness of the Creator. And God is more than just Father.

The feminine part of the divine creative force was banned centuries ago in the Judeo-Christian tradition, in reaction to the fertility cults with pagan goddesses that surrounded the early Israelites. Because "heathens" worshiped female divinity—and were always tempting the Israelites away from worship of their God—the God of Israel became male: "the God of Abraham, Isaac and Jacob," as this Father God is often referred to in the Old Testament.

Sadly, our tradition often overlooks the mother eagle of Deut. 32:11; the midwife of Ps. 22:9; the womb-endowed Creator in Job 38:29; the birthing, nursing, and comforting mother of Isa. 42:14; 49:15; 66:13—all images of the maternal provision of God. And incredibly, the God who comes to us as rock and refuge and fortress and shepherd and light is forbidden in most of our churches from appearing in any female guise. When the church forgets that women, too, were created in God's image, it limits not only women but also God.

Eve was an original. In that sense, she is all of us. She was there at the dawn of creation, with all her hopes and strengths, frailties and fears. She is womanhood at its best—and its worst. She reflects back to the Creator the glory of the choice to create humanity male and female, with all its mystery, joy, and pain. Surely, God danced in celebration of this beautiful crown of creation—and then had to rest up for a day from the frenzied festivity.

Today, God dances with us still, bidding us to live in all the glory and giftedness with which we have been bestowed. The Creator is still smiling, still proclaiming over and over, "This is very good."

2 Sarah and Hagar: Trapped Rivals

SCRIPTURE: Gen. 12:1–5a, 10–20; 16:1–15; 17:1–17; 18:1–15; 21:1–21

> And Sarai said to Abram, "You see that the Lord has prevented me from bearing children; go in to my slave-girl; it may be that I shall obtain children by her." (Gen. 16:2)

The saga of Sarah and Hagar provides a revealing view of the life of women of the Bible. Their story took place in the nineteenth or twentieth century B.C.E. Foundational to it were patterns and assumptions that affected all the women to come after them.

At the heart of the faith of the Israelites was God's covenant with them. But only half of the people could participate in the sign of the covenant. Women were excluded from a ritual of faithfulness that was based on circumcision.

In ancient Israel, women were considered property, first of their fathers and then of their husbands. Thus it was not surprising that Sarah could be handed over to pharaoh in order to safeguard Abraham's life. The violation of her body was of less concern in the situation than his safety. The event repeated itself with Abimelech, king of the Philistines, who also "took" Sarah when Abraham told him she was his sister (Genesis 20). Though in fact Sarah and Abraham had the same father, his declaration about her was a deceit to protect himself. He explained to Abimelech, "When God caused me to wander from my father's house, I said to her, 'This is the kindness you must do me: at every place to which we come, say of me, He is my brother'" (20:13). This "kindness" placed Sarah in an extremely vulnerable position as she and Abraham wandered through foreign lands.

But Sarah was expected to obey Abraham in all things. Women were expected to be submissive toward their husbands. Sarah was praised centuries later in the writings of the early church: "Holy women who hoped in God used to adorn themselves by accepting the authority of their husbands. Thus Sarah obeyed Abraham and called him lord" (1 Peter 3:5–6).

The worth of women was judged by their capacity to produce heirs for their husbands, meaning sons. Inability to conceive was viewed as a sign of divine disfavor—and always the fault of the woman. Sarah was

5

only the first of many women in the Bible who were "barren." Barrenness, a theme that arises again and again in the Old Testament, set the stage for the enmity that arose between her and Hagar.

Desperate for a son, Sarah turned over to Abraham her maid Hagar, whose offspring Sarah had a right to claim as her own. That gesture reveals much about the differences between the two women. Sarah enjoyed the privileges and security that came from being the wife of a wealthy and prominent herdsman. Hagar was an Egyptian, a slave; she had no say in the decision to have her body used for surrogate motherhood. Sarah's action launched a drama undergirded by the interplay of oppressions based on gender, class, and race.

The exploited Hagar, having gained some standing in the situation by conceiving Abraham's child, turned her contempt toward Sarah. As often happens, exploited women turned into rivals, rather than allies against the system and people that kept them enslaved. Each grasped her piece of power and used it against the other.

Ultimately, Sarah's power won out. As the protected wife, she had the authority to make life miserable for her slave. Finding the situation intolerable, Hagar ran away into the wilderness. But an angel of God, according to the writer of the story, told her to go back and submit to Sarah.

Years later, as they were each closing in on a century of living, Abraham and Sarah (who was well past menopause) received word from divine messengers that she would conceive. The message seemed laughable. Abraham, in fact, fell down laughing. Sarah laughed to herself—and the angels chastised her for it. When a son was born, they named him Isaac, "He laughs."

Sarah immediately became protective of her new status as a mother. Now that Abraham had an heir by her, the presence of Hagar and her son, Ishmael, was threatening. Hagar and Ishmael were sent out into the wilderness with nothing but a skin of water and a little bread. They were saved only by the mercy of God.

Sarah lived to the ripe old age of 127. The history of the faith was carried on through the record of her son Isaac and his descendants. Believing the truth of God's promise long after it seemed possible to come true, she became the mother of many heirs—"as many as the stars of heaven and as the innumerable grains of sand by the seashore," according to Heb. 11:12.

We are not told what happened to Hagar. As with too much of history, a voice outside of the mainstream has been lost. Yet this bold woman probably had an inspiring story to tell—of her days in the wilderness, her anguish at the thought of losing her child, her new-found freedom, and the grace and mercy of God. Hagar was, after all, the first person in the Bible to receive a divine messenger and the only one who dared to name God. Hagar called God "Elroi"—"God who sees." Her son's name, Ishmael, means "God hears." Her gift to faith history is the reminder of God's faithfulness to those who are despised, exploited, or lonely. She reminds us that God doesn't distinguish by race, class, or gender. The covenant of faith is available to all.

Hagar is the homeless woman, the single mother, the cast-off wife, the exploited worker. She stands in the wilderness, on the margins, with an invitation. This invitation was given voice centuries later by Lilla Watson, an Australian aboriginal woman: "If you have come to help me, you are wasting your time. But if you have come because your liberation is bound up with mine, then let us walk together."[1]

NOTES

1. Barbara Tamialis, "Ten Years of Keeping the Faith," *Sojourners* 22, no. 8 (October 1993): 17.

3 Rachel and Leah: Pawns in a Game of Love

SCRIPTURE: Gen. 29:1–30:25; 31:4, 14–26, 34–36, 43; 33:1–4

When morning came, it was Leah! And Jacob said to Laban, "What is this you have done to me? Did I not serve with you for Rachel? Why then have you deceived me?" (Gen. 29:25)

It began as a great love story. Jacob, far from home, came upon a beautiful young woman who was kin to him. So great was his feeling on seeing her that he wept. In the presence of her and her family, he was at home again.

In the first month of his stay, Jacob was overcome with his adoration for Rachel. He was willing to work seven years to earn her as his wife. What discipline, what devotion, what love! Finally, the wedding day arrived. After the feast, husband and wife consummated the marriage. But deception and betrayal crept in. The woman in Jacob's bed was not Rachel at all but her older sister, Leah.

Poor Leah was plain to the eye, and her father thought that her chances for marriage were dim. Jacob himself must have been lacking something in the eyesight department or in intuition to have been so easily tricked. With unsurpassed desire and devotion, Jacob agreed to work another seven years to earn Rachel. In the meantime, they married, creating an impossible situation for the two sisters.

Rachel was cherished by her husband, but she was barren. Leah was unloved, but she was fertile, producing son after son. Her escalating refrain rends the heart: "Surely now my husband will love me"; "Now this time my husband will be joined to me." Few shreds of dignity or self-esteem were left to her; she had only her sons to make her happy.

Rachel's desperation is equally wrenching: "Give me children, or I shall die!" Both sisters were locked in a tragic drama. Like Sarah and Hagar, they became bitter rivals under this oppressive arrangement.

Jacob's response to Rachel's despair was to get angry and blame her. She then handed her maid Bilhah over to him, hoping, as Sarah had, to acquire a son this way. When Leah stopped bearing children, she did the same with her maid Zilpah. Thus five lives were enmeshed in a complicated web of sex and family.

Repressed anger and envy erupted in the scene over the mandrakes, roots of a potato-like plant that were considered to have aphrodisiac qualities that aided conception. Jacob had apparently stopped sleeping with Leah, who traded the mandrakes for a night in his bed. Thus she "hired" her own husband, whom she accused Rachel of stealing from her. And either the mandrakes, or prayer, enabled Rachel finally to conceive.

The birth of Joseph, Jacob's first son by Rachel, prompted his desire to return to his own people. Before leaving, Rachel stole her father's household gods. This was no small rebellion on Rachel's part; as long as she lived in her father's household, she was considered his property, as Laban tried to assert. The theft was an act of taking power—and her destiny—into her own hands.

Using her wits and her understanding of the Levitical purity codes, Rachel guarded the gods by claiming that she couldn't get up from her camel; the "way of women" was upon her. This was enough to deter her father from searching her camel. Under Levitical law, a menstruating woman was "unclean," as was anything she touched. Thus Rachel's father could not have searched the camel or saddle on which she sat without polluting himself. Rachel took the power of an oppressive taboo and turned it into a positive force.

Blood, considered the seat of life in early Israel, was both powerful and mysterious. It was to be revered in religious ritual but otherwise shunned as a source of contamination. The blood taboo, outlined in Leviticus, was a cornerstone of Jewish patriarchal society: "When a woman has a discharge of blood that is her regular discharge from her body, she shall be in her impurity for seven days, and whoever touches her shall be unclean until the evening. Everything upon which she lies during her impurity shall be unclean; everything upon which she sits shall be unclean" (Lev. 15:19–20).

These two verses had a tremendous stigmatizing and confining impact on women. They were destined to live from month to month—and childbirth to childbirth—considered impure and untouchable, adhering to strict practices of purification and sin offerings (Lev. 15:30). Because impurity had no place in the temple, women were regularly denied entrance. Menstruation was seen as a reason for deeming women unfit to be priests and strengthened the notion that women were aberrant humans.

The four women in this story all suffered as a result of the patriarchy that enshrouded them. Zilpah and Bilhah were concubines. Their worth to Jacob was made clear when he set them in front of the rest of his family. Expecting an attack from Esau, his brother from whom he had stolen a birthright and a blessing, Jacob placed all his women in reverse order of their personal value to him.

Leah and her children came next. Leah could be considered the Hagar of the pair of sisters. Her marginalization was not racial or economic but physical. Her looks were her destiny, her sons her redemption. From her son Judah descended David, an ancestor of Jesus.

Rachel remained beloved to the end. She died in childbirth while on a journey, and Jacob set up a pillar to mark her grave (Gen. 35:16–20). Years later, when he was in his last days, Jacob sadly recalled her death (Gen. 48:7).

From these two sisters came Israel's twelve tribes: "Together [they] built up the house of Israel" (Ruth 4:11). Unfortunately, it was not as a result of affection and cooperation that the house of Israel was built. The bondage of patriarchy made it impossible for these two sisters to view each other as anything but rivals.

In contrast is a pair of sisters from our own era, whose love for each other matches in strength the contention that marked the relationship between Rachel and Leah. Sarah "Sadie" Delany is 104 years old. Elizabeth "Bessie" Delany is 102. The sisters share the distinction of being among the few people on earth who can make the observation that Halley's comet was disappointing the second time around. But they have seen much more in their century apiece of living. In the sweep of their lives, they experienced the birth of legalized segregation, the Harlem Renaissance, the Great Depression, and the civil rights movement.

Their father, who was born a slave in Georgia, became the first black bishop of the Episcopal Church, U.S.A. Close ties and faith were at the heart of a family life that included ten children. Bessie became a dentist and Sadie an educator. Though both had many suitors, they decided not to marry so that they could focus on their careers. Bessie was particularly determined not to be bossed around by a man.

In their bestselling book, *Having Our Say: The Delany Sisters' First 100 Years*, the sisters speak affectionately of each other and of the differences between them that bring balance to their life together. They talk of themselves as "molasses and vinegar"—"Sweet Sadie" and "Queen Bess."

When Bessie was only five, she drank from a water fountain labeled "Whites Only," in protest of newly instituted Jim Crow laws. When white missionaries gave her and Sadie expensive china dolls, Bessie mixed paint until she got a color that matched her own skin and painted her doll's face. In later life, she never backed away from an opportunity to challenge injustice. She was almost lynched once for confronting a white man who harassed her while she was waiting for a train. "We loved our country," says Bessie, "even though it didn't love us back."[1]

Sadie operated more subtly. When she knew she would be turned down for a teaching position at a white high school because of her race, she skipped an interview and sent a letter explaining that there had been a mix-up. She simply showed up for the first day of classes. Her plan worked: "Once I was in, they couldn't figure out how to get rid of me."[2]

As a black female dentist, Bessie faced both racism and sexism. She was an activist, willing to give "life or limb," she says, for the cause of freedom. She comments on the importance of voting: "If you don't vote, you don't have the right to complain. And, honey, I surely do not want to give up my right to complain, no, sir!"[3] She says now, "It took me a hundred years to figure out I can't change the world. I can only change Bessie. And, honey, that ain't easy, either. . . . I don't know how Sadie's put up with this old flabbermouth for the past one hundred years."[4] Sadie believes that she and Bessie probably know each other better than any other two people on earth.

As young women, the Delany sisters decided to dabble in the stock market. People laughed at them, because women weren't supposed to do such things. One of Bessie's dental patients suggested Creole Petroleum Company, and the sisters bought two and a half shares each. When Exxon bought out the company, they were "bullied," according to Sadie, into selling their shares. Bessie predicted that Exxon would be in for "some big trouble, someday" for running roughshod over them. "That's why Bessie and I weren't the least bit surprised when Exxon went and spilled all that oil up in Alaska and everyone in the whole world was just disgusted with them," says Sadie. "Bessie said to me, 'See, I told you so'."[5]

The sisters do yoga and eat a clove of garlic every day. They usually avoid liquor, although Bessie confesses to making Jell-O with wine instead of water occasionally. They still observe their father's birthday sixty-five years after his death, making his favorite meal of chicken and gravy, as well as a birthday cake. They pray twice a day for everyone, dead or alive, in their large extended family. Sadie explains that the ones whom Bessie doesn't approve of get extra prayers. Bessie is concerned that the aggressive and forthright way in which she has lived her life may keep her out of heaven.

Recently, the New York City Board of Education wanted to cut off Sadie's pension. They demanded she prove that she was still alive. "That is the type of thing you have to deal with when you get to be our age," reflects Sadie. "They think we're sitting around in rocking chairs, which isn't at all true. Why, we don't even own a rocking chair."[6]

"When people ask me how we've lived past one hundred," says Bessie, "I say, 'Honey, we never married. We never had husbands to worry us to death!'"[7] The sisters consider it justice that they have outlived "those old rebby boys," the white southern men who harassed and discriminated against them during their many years in Raleigh, North Carolina.

According to Sadie, Bessie plans to live as long as Moses: "And when Bessie says she's going to do something, she does it. . . . So I told Bessie that if she lives to 120, then I'll just have to live to 122 so I can take care of her."[8]

Bessie says she knows that Sadie will get into heaven because of her compassionate and gentle ways. She adds, "I just might get into Heaven. I may have to hang on to Sadie's heels, but I'll get there."[9]

No doubt they will both get there. In the meantime, we have the great gift of two pillars of living history in our midst.

NOTES

1. Sarah Delany and A. Elizabeth Delany, *Having Our Say: The Delany Sisters' First 100 Years* (New York: Kodansha International, 1993), 60.
2. Ibid., 120.
3. Ibid., 141.
4. Ibid., 85, 115.
5. Ibid., 135.
6. Ibid., 168.
7. Ibid., 13.
8. Ibid., 5.
9. Ibid., 210.

4 Ruth and Naomi: Vulnerable Survivors

SCRIPTURE: The Book of Ruth

Ruth said, "Do not press me to leave you or to turn back from following you! Where you go, I will go; Where you lodge, I will lodge; your people shall be my people, and your God my God." (Ruth 1:16)

The status of women in ancient Israel changed overnight when their husbands died. Women on their own had no rights and no stable means of survival. Widows were often blamed for their own state, considered a disgrace, harshly treated, and sometimes enslaved. The phrase "widows and orphans"—meaning women and children without men—appears throughout the scriptures as the paradigmatic example of victimization and powerlessness.

The beautiful story of Ruth and Naomi makes clear the realities of such vulnerability. But it is also a celebration of the feminine instincts for survival and care that preserved the lives of two remarkable women.

Under the Hebrew law of levirate marriage, a childless widow became the wife of her late husband's brother, with the intent that she would bear a son in her dead husband's name. The law presented a double bind for women. On the one hand, the woman had no choice; she was passed on like property from one brother to another, or to another relative if there was no brother. On the other hand, if her brother-in-law refused to marry her, she was left without security. Then she was allowed to go with him before the elders, pull his sandal off his foot, spit in his face, and declare, "This is what is done to the man who does not build up his brother's house" (Deut. 25:5–10)!

Naomi, recognizing the absurdity of marrying again in her old age and producing sons that would be many years younger than Orpah and Ruth, realized that this law was of little help to her daughters-in-law. She encouraged them to return to the homes of their families.

But Ruth was rare in her devotion to her mother-in-law. In a poignant declaration, she pledged her loyalty and promised to stay with Naomi until death. In contrast to the bitter rivalries between Sarah and Hagar and between Rachel and Leah, Ruth and Naomi shared a bond based on each putting the needs of the other ahead of her own.

13

So the young and compassionate Ruth and the old and wise Naomi began an arduous journey together. Tackling mountains and valleys, crossing rivers and deserts, they clung to each other and slowly made their way back to Bethlehem. They made an impression when they arrived. So great was their care for each other, "the whole town was stirred because of them" (Ruth 1:19).

Bereft, uprooted, and on their own, Ruth and Naomi were consigned to the life of the poor. Ruth gleaned in the fields among the grain that had been left by the harvesters, subsisting with Naomi on the leftovers of the rich. Ruth eventually appeared in the field of Boaz, a relative of her late husband. His first question was "To whom does this young woman belong?" Every woman belonged to someone.

Ruth needed Boaz's protection. A woman alone out in the fields was likely to be harassed or sexually violated. Boaz, moved by Ruth's devotion to Naomi and her tireless work, treated her kindly, inviting her to his table, commanding his workers not to bother her, ordering them to leave grain within easy reach for her.

Ruth and Naomi managed to create a life of survival this way but not one of security. Without a man, there would be no security. So Naomi conceived a plan, and Ruth carried it out. Appealing to the law of levirate marriage, Ruth asked Boaz to fulfill his obligation. Because her late husband had no remaining brothers, the obligation passed to his next of kin.

Boaz knew of another relative who was next in line to fulfill the obligation of marriage. He found him and made a business transaction with him. With the removal of his sandal, the man handed over to Boaz his right to all of the property of Elimelech, Mahlon, and Chilion, including Ruth.

Ruth and Naomi could not destroy the laws of patriarchy that defined them as property. But with courage and savvy, they worked the system to secure their own survival. At the heart of their success was a deep love and devotion to each other, an unbreakable bond of sisterhood. When one suffered, both suffered. When one was blessed, both were blessed. And so it was that the neighbor women could say, "A son has been born to Naomi," and she could take Ruth's child to her breast as her own. By faithfulness, the sorrow that Ruth and Naomi bore together was turned to joy—sorrow halved, joy doubled, as the old adage says of friendship.

The women around Ruth and Naomi understood the richness that they were blessed to witness. Challenging the Hebrew value placed on sons, they declared Ruth to be worth more than seven sons to Naomi.

Contrary to custom, the women named Ruth's special child, who preserved the heritage of the community and was a link to the future. Obed became the grandfather of a king. From the lineage of that king came another miraculous birth in Bethlehem. Blessing upon blessing was given to Ruth and Naomi.

Ancient Israel's phrase "widows and orphans" has been replaced with today's "feminization of poverty." Women on their own or solely responsible for the care of their children are slipping into poverty in enormous numbers. A recent U.S. Census Bureau study reported that when a marriage breaks up, an astounding three out of four mothers and their children who were, until then, above the poverty line fall below it. In the United States, one of every five children lives in poverty, and one out of four homeless persons is a child.

At the other end of life's spectrum are the widows. A recent *New York Times* news service article declared that "the great mass of women are still only a man or a misstep away from penury in retirement."[1] The article reported that nearly half of women over age sixty-five are widows; three-quarters of the elderly poor are female; and the median income for women over sixty-five is only slightly more than half of what men of that age receive from Social Security, pensions, and investments.

Twice a week during my year in seminary, I traveled to a senior center and housing project for low-income elderly residents in New Haven, Connecticut. True to the statistics, the overwhelming number of residents were women. My job as chaplain included everything from visiting the sick to doing apartment maintenance checks, from leading Bible studies to overseeing a flu vaccination program. Most of the 110 residents bore the triple anguish of poverty, illness, and isolation. Their husbands were gone, their children had abandoned them, and their days were marked by the pain of growing old alone.

That winter, city funds for the Visiting Nurse Association, Meals on Wheels, and maintenance services were drastically cut. I had to tell a disabled woman that her nurse would not be coming back to care for her; another who could not leave her apartment that she could no longer receive meals at home; and tenants who already struggled to pay their rent that they would now also have to pay for all repairs.

The brokenness and despair swelled, and it was my job to pick up the pieces. I could not reinstate the services, but I was mandated to "bring hope" to the place. The residents knew they were a low priority in everybody's budget, and their sense of powerlessness was profound.

I devoted much of my energy the second half of the year toward trying to foster a caring community among them. But tough facades and longstanding suspicions born out of years of feeling neglected and unwanted were not easily dropped. One resident didn't like her neighbor because she kept too many plants, and another claimed that the woman next door was "stealing her electricity." The day I walked into Hilda's apartment and found her lying on the floor, unconscious from an overdose of sleeping pills, I felt overcome by a sense of futility.

Many other tragic stories were lived or recalled between the walls. Mrs. P. spoke of her life as a concert pianist in Poland; newspaper clippings, concert programs, and photographs plastered all over her walls attested to the truth of her claim. I never learned what had brought her to this place—a flight from communism, perhaps, or a personal scandal or family tragedy that had led to a mental breakdown. She lived in a world all her own. I was her only visitor. A large piano took up most of the space in her small living room. "It won't be long now until you'll be ready for a concert—we'll do one together!" she proclaimed as I sat behind the keys, awkwardly pounding out "Turkey in the Straw," the only song I seemed to remember from my years of piano lessons. She thumped on my back with her arm like a metronome, shouting, "But you'll never be famous unless you get your time down!"

Mrs. P. would not talk to me unless we went through this ritual every week, and she never gave up believing that I was a pupil arriving for my piano lesson. When I was through, she would sit down at the piano, and her still-nimble, eighty-two-year-old fingers would glide over the keys, moving from a delicate sonata to a beautiful rhapsody. Always, when she finished and I got ready to leave, she wept.

There were some unexpected joys—and a few laughs. Spring brought the annual garden contest. Tenants walked around the cottages as judges and awarded a prize for the prettiest garden out front. When I stopped to congratulate the winner, she leaned over and whispered, "I've won it three years in a row now. The flowers are plastic. I bring 'em in every fall and stick 'em in the ground every spring—and the judges are too blind to notice."

The greatest source of joy was two women who evidenced a rare kind of gracious care for each other. Jean Abbot and Elisa Garcia found in their friendship the kind of ministering community I had hoped to see take root among the others. They never left each other alone to wallow in grief or isolation. Every visit with them was a guaranteed lift to the spirits.

Jean was from Scotland and had a delightful accent, as well as an infectious smile, with or without her teeth. She always welcomed me with cakelike Scottish scones and butter cookies and a special blend of Scottish tea, which she kept warm in her silver teapot covered with a colorful tea cozy that bore her family's coat of arms.

Elisa was paralyzed from her neck down. She spent her days painting beautiful watercolor landscapes, using a brush held between her teeth. The painting she gave me one day remains a precious treasure.

The two women could often be seen together taking a walk, Jean slowly but steadily pushing Elisa's wheelchair. She would pause occasionally to adjust the blanket that swathed her friend or to tighten the scarf around Elisa's neck. With each stop, a smile passed between them.

As I picture them making their way together with quiet determination, I see the strength of Ruth and Naomi. Tackling the mountains and deserts of urban life, Jean and Elisa found survival in their bond of mutual devotion. And beyond survival, they offer a stellar example of life lived in joyful appreciation.

NOTES

1. "Pension Benefits: Old Age Is No Place for Sissies," *New York Times* news service, February 6, 1994.

5 Mahlah, Noah, Hoglah, Milcah, and Tirzah: Challenging the Law

SCRIPTURE: Num. 27:1–11; 36:1–12

And the Lord spoke to Moses, saying: The daughters of Zelophehad are right in what they are saying; you shall indeed let them possess an inheritance among their father's brothers and pass the inheritance of their father on to them. (Num. 27:6–7)

Five sisters—Mahlah, Noah, Hoglah, Milcah, and Tirzah—publicly challenged tradition and the law. With audacious and unprecedented boldness, they stood before the entire assembly—Moses, the priest, the leaders, the people—and declared the injustice of the system of inheritance. Asserting that they should not suffer discrimination simply on the basis of their gender, they claimed a right to their father's land.

Their claim was a new idea to Moses, so he took it to God. And on this occasion, according to the recorder of the story, God took the side of women. "The daughters of Zelophehad are right," said God. Apparently, God's mind could be changed.

It was surprising enough that these five feisty young women confronted the law. Even more astounding is that they won. By empowering themselves, they not only changed their own situation but also rewrote a statute and thus altered conditions for women who would come after them. Not only were women granted legal property rights in certain circumstances, but pressure was lifted from all women who had been obligated to produce sons in order for their husbands to have heirs.

The claim of the five daughters of Zelophehad is one of the earliest lawsuits on record. Amazingly enough, lawyers still turn to it. It has been declared the oldest legal case "that is still cited as an authority."[1]

Of course, women couldn't be given too much freedom or power. Land was a primary source of security and an indicator of wealth. If there was a son in a family, he remained sole heir. And if a daughter with land married, her land passed into the possession of her husband. Thus the command that Mahlah, Noah, Hoglah, Milcah, and Tirzah

18

had to marry within their own tribe—the tribal leaders didn't want to lose the goods just because a woman fell in love with a man of another clan.

The five daughters of Zelophehad didn't bring patriarchy to a screeching halt. But they did move their society a few steps forward toward justice.

Today, on the Sea Islands off the coast of South Carolina, modern-day daughters of Zelophehad are challenging the law and claiming their inheritance. Two centuries ago, ships brought slaves from the coast of West Africa to these islands. Now only the ruins of the slave quarters stand. But if you rub your hand over the crumbling, lichen-covered walls made of "tabby"—a mixture of oyster shells, lime, sand, and water—you can still hear the echoes of another time.

You can hear the lilting cadence known as Gullah, the creolized language that melded the richness of African dialects and the tongue of the master. You can hear the "trickster tales" being told around the fire to wide-eyed children, the stories of Bruh Rabbit who always outwitted Bruh Bear. You can hear the hushed tones of new parents giving their children "basket names" in the African tradition—names such as Rain or Hardtimes, Boney or Handful—that reflected a trait of the child or conditions at the time of the birth. You can hear the "shouts," the rhythmic clapping and movement that accompanied the singing of the spirituals and the soaring of ecstatic prayers, that went on, sometimes all night long, in the "praise houses."

These are the reverberations of resistance. A unique language, stories that symbolized the undermining of the powerful by the cunning, a ritual of naming that refused the power of slave names, and prayers to a liberating God forged a courageous and strong African-American culture—a culture not only of survival but of artistry, beauty, and hope.

After the Civil War, northern industrialists confiscated island rice and cotton plantations. Freed slaves worked in return for wages that they used to buy parcels of land. Recurrent hurricanes and the boll weevil's arrival in 1916 eventually sent the northerners back home, and the Sea Islands became an isolated haven for a flourishing culture.

But today that culture is in serious jeopardy. Developers have bought up the best of the island land. They have constructed an apartheid system that offers rich whites golf courses, marinas, and tennis clubs while native islanders are consigned to seasonal, minimum-wage jobs cleaning and serving in the upscale hotels and private residential communities called "plantations." The encroachment is an assault on a way of life. "Land is probably the most important element of black

American life," Sea Islander Emory Campbell told me. "It symbolizes freedom."

Only forty-five natives are left on Daufuskie Island, described by the late author Alex Haley as the last survivor of the historic Sea Islands. Back when a thousand people lived there, "everybody was like one big family," native Yvonne Wilson said to me. "Anybody who caught a fish or planted a field shared everything. If you had, I had."

Older Daufuskie residents remember when boats from Savannah, Georgia, carried people over for picnics on the beach and the sharing of communion on Sundays, as well as baptisms on the shore. Many made a living from harvesting famous Daufuskie oysters, until pollution from the Savannah River tainted the oyster beds. The whole island was also once a big pasture for cows. The animals were tethered until November 1, after the last sweet potatoes had been dug up. Then they roamed free until April 1, when the gardens were planted again.

But in the mid-1980s, International Paper Corporation bought 1,040 acres of Daufuskie for $8.5 million and developed Haig Point, a private residential community whose promotional literature boasts one of the country's top golf courses and "a lifestyle enjoyed by only a few." When the Haig Point golf course was completed, the cows headed straight for the lush, green grass. Islanders could not afford the fines imposed or winter feed for the animals, so the cows were carried off the island on a barge.

About the same time, Melrose Corporation bought up 720 acres of Daufuskie for $6.5 million. With the arrival of the Melrose Plantation resort—whose memberships begin at $50,000—came fences, "Members Only" signs, and the takeover of the road leading to Daufuskie's nicest beach. Property taxes skyrocketed (more than 400 percent one year), and many natives were forced to move from their homes. Developers, meanwhile, were taking advantage of an "agricultural exemption" and paying a fraction of their taxes on their prime oceanfront property.

But the most outrageous affront to the native islanders was the fact that Melrose Plantation built its "welcome center" on top of the islanders' Cooper River Cemetery. Yvonne Wilson's infant son is buried there. Inadequate medical care on the island and lack of access to transportation to the mainland contributed to his tragic death. He was buried according to the tradition that was carried on from Yvonne's ancestors from Africa. She placed his spoon and plate in his tiny casket and his bottle and clothes on the grave, so that he would have these items for the afterlife and Yvonne's grandmother could take care of him there. The cemetery, like all the graveyards of her people, is near water, Yvonne explained, so that it can carry the spirits of the dead back to Africa and on to heaven.

In 1990, Yvonne Wilson and her mother, Louise Wilson, became plaintiffs with several others in a lawsuit against Melrose Corporation, demanding that the company move its welcome center off the site of the cemetery. Louise wrote a letter to the developers who were taking over her island and to their clients:

Dear Neighbors,

My name is Louise Wilson. I am 72 years old and am a fifth-generation Daufuskie native and resident. I was born on Daufuskie in the days of horses and buggies, clean air and water, when beaches and roads were open to everyone, and concern for one another was a heartfelt expression of our common status as God's children. . . .

Our way of life was certainly not luxurious, but there is value in a simple life. We worked hard, raised our own food, sewed our own clothes, raised our children to be self-sufficient, productive, and caring members of the community. We were, and are, proud of our unique culture, which we preserved through the horrors of abduction and slavery, and which kept us together as a people for over 300 years.

My mother, father, grandparents, great-grandparents, countless aunts, uncles, and other relatives are buried on Daufuskie. Their resting places are not sacred, however. Melrose and Haig Point Plantations are building resorts for your pleasure all over the island without regard for my history, my culture, and my feelings.

Many of you make provisions for your children and grandchildren to have the benefit of your life and labor. I am poor in money, yet rich in heritage, but what have I to leave my daughter and grandchildren except a landscape of golf courses and plantation homes? Doesn't my past and their future count? . . .

Please don't let the notions of exclusive, private, and separate blind you to doing the right, just thing. Help us in our struggle to hold on to our history.

Their lawsuit was considered by many to be a virtually hopeless, "David versus Goliath" battle. But they persisted. Yvonne said she was doing it for her children, so that they might have a future. "If we younger ones don't do this now, our whole way of life will be lost," she told me. "It's a survival thing now. We have to survive this plague in the midst of paradise."

"It may be a losing battle," said Louise Wilson, "but you gotta show some people you're not scared. You got to fight back and let them know you were here when they came." She added, "I'm gonna stay here 'til the Good Master carry me. It's the only way I'll go."

In the summer of 1993, Melrose Corporation returned the half-acre of the cemetery that was being contested and agreed to move its welcome center. It also paid damages to the plaintiffs. In the battle to preserve a culture and curtail encroaching development, it was only a small victory, but it was a victory nonetheless. A tiny plot of sacred history was reclaimed as an inheritance that will be passed on to Louise and Yvonne Wilson's descendants.

NOTES

1. Edith Deen, *All of the Women of the Bible* (New York: Harper & Row, 1955), 63.

Part 1. Questions for Reflection

1. When did you become aware of the reality of patriarchy?

2. Do you feel limited or trapped by patriarchy? How?

3. When and how have you challenged limits or assumptions about the place of women? Do you see a progression in your life in your efforts to understand and confront inequalities between women and men?

4. Are there examples from your life when sisterhood meant strength, security, or survival?

5. Who has been a model for you of someone living in freedom, beyond the bonds of patriarchy? Have you been or could you be a model for someone else?

PART 2
Victims of Male Abuse

Current feminist sensitivities would have us call the women who appear in this section "survivors" rather than "victims." But, in fact, not all of them survived the violence that was done to them.

Extremes of brutality always appear when part of humanity is considered less than equal. The stories of these women are heart-wrenching and difficult to read. But it is crucial that we face the reality of the abuses that were done to them.

By remembering Dinah and Tamar, the Levite's concubine and Jephthah's daughter, Samson's wife and the women of Midian, we honor them. And as we grieve the multiple forms of abuse committed against women, we draw strength from their stories for confronting the epidemic of sexual violence that plagues our own world today.

6 Dinah and Tamar: No Safe Place

SCRIPTURE: Genesis 34; 2 Sam. 13:1–22

When Shechem son of Hamor the Hivite, prince of the region, saw [Dinah], he seized her and lay with her by force. (Gen. 34:2)

But [Amnon] would not listen to [Tamar]; and being stronger than she, he forced her and lay with her. (2 Sam. 13:14)

The disturbing lesson of the stories of Dinah and Tamar is that no place is safe—not the unfamiliar road on the way to visit women friends; not the familiar home of a brother. Women are vulnerable to the physical power of men wherever they are.

Dinah, with no sisters of her own, was likely about fourteen or fifteen when she went out to share the company of other young women. Some RSV Bibles title her story "The seduction of Dinah," apparently attempting to place part of the blame for what happened to her on Dinah herself. But the text makes clear that Dinah was seized by Shechem and raped.

Though his father is described as a "prince," Shechem surely was not. It is a bit outrageous for us to be asked to believe that his "soul was drawn to Dinah." It was not his soul that was in need of satisfaction. This young man, in an act of blatant sexual violence, overpowered Dinah. Then, suddenly changing his tune, he "spoke tenderly to her" and asked for her to be his wife.

The story of Dinah reveals much about the place of women in Israel. Dinah is the first daughter in the Bible whose name is mentioned at birth (Gen. 30:21). But she was not included in the number of Jacob's children who crossed the Jabbok River; only her eleven brothers counted (32:22). Even in the story in which she is the central figure, there is no mention of her thoughts or feelings. There is great detail about Shechem's desires, her brothers' anger, and her father's apprehension—not to mention much ado about flocks and herds. But we never hear from Dinah.

Her brothers likely felt guilty that they had failed to protect their younger sister's virginity, thus ruining her chances for an honorable marriage. Their revenge was motivated, however, by the fact that her rape was an "outrage against Israel," not by the violation that had been done to her personally.

Dinah became a pawn in their deceit—and an excuse for a massacre. Shechem made a deal for her, as he might for any other piece of property. So much did he want her to be his wife, he told her father and brothers to set any price. Seeing an opportunity to take advantage, and under the guise of religious purity, Jacob's sons asked for the circumcision of all the men in Hamor's tribe. Moved by greed and the opportunity to acquire livestock and property, Hamor and Shechem agreed to the deal. While all the men were still in pain from the procedure, Dinah's brothers Simeon and Levi struck.

Her brothers rescued Dinah from Shechem's house, where she apparently had been taken even though she and Shechem had not yet married, much contrary to the laws of Israel. All the men the sons of Jacob killed. All the women and children "they captured and made their prey." One woman's defilement was met with the defilement of the women of an entire tribe.

Dinah had been ambushed, raped, bargained for, taken captive, and made a pawn of her brothers' vengeance. Nowhere do we hear of her anguish, her fear, or her tears. Nowhere is there mention of a despair that must have been beyond consolation. After this, she simply disappears from scripture.

Tamar's story is devastatingly similar. Amnon made himself sick with lust for her and made her the victim of a devious scheme. Feigning illness, he took advantage of her concern and care for him. With every reason to trust her half-brother and an obligation to obey her father's command, Tamar attended to Amnon's needs. With generosity and compassion, she baked and brought him the cakes he requested.

When Amnon grabbed Tamar and declared his intentions toward her, she pleaded on her own behalf. Thinking quickly, she tried to reason with him, pointing out not only the shame that would come to her but the fact that all of Israel would think him a scoundrel for forcing her. In a disturbing indication that she knew the limits of her power over her own life, she even agreed to marry him if he would refrain from raping her and ask their father for her. But Amnon wasn't interested in her reasoning or her dignity. He raped her. Then, in contrast to Shechem, he projected his repulsion at his own action onto Tamar, loathing her after the act more than he had lusted for her before. He cast her out, ignoring her pleas that he behave decently toward her.

We know Tamar's feelings. She rent her clothes and put ashes on her head. With a gesture of anguish, she went away wailing for what had been done to her—for the violation and the shame and for the fact that she was now "damaged goods" in the eyes of Israel, unmarriageable. With one reprehensible act, her life had been changed forever.

Her brother Absalom compounded the misery, offering advice that is all too common to survivors of incest: keep quiet; don't take it personally; he didn't really mean any harm; don't compound his shame—or yours—by telling; no point in upsetting the family. Her father, the king, was angry; but there is no indication that he mourned over the violation of his daughter. He refused to punish Amnon because he loved his eldest son. And perhaps the situation was a little too close for comfort: David himself had lusted after Bathsheba and been punished by God for taking her.

Revenge was finally Absalom's two years later when he had Amnon killed. Afterward, he fled, and King David "mourned for his son day after day" for three years (2 Sam. 13:37–38). David eventually forgave Absalom, who succeeded him on the throne.

As for Tamar, one sentence says it all: "So Tamar remained, a desolate woman, in her brother Absalom's house" (13:20). There was for her perhaps one consolation, a tiny footnote in history: "There were born to Absalom three sons, and one daughter whose name was Tamar; she was a beautiful woman" (14:27).

In a rare reversal, only the daughter is named here, a namesake of her aunt. One hopes that her beauty did not arouse the lustful violence of an unscrupulous stranger or relative, as her aunt's did.

Today, sexual violence has reached epidemic proportions. Rape has been called the fastest growing, most underreported, and least convicted crime in the world. Every ten seconds, on average, a woman is a victim of rape or attempted rape in the United States. At current rates, one in three women can expect to be a victim of sexual assault in her lifetime.

The battlefields of this war against women are everywhere—the home, the workplace, parking lots, college dormitories, next door, upstairs. In several recent studies, 100 percent of the women surveyed indicated a fear of sexual violence. As long as some men rape, all women live with the threat of rape.

University of Pennsylvania anthropologist Peggy Reeves Sanday conducted a 1981 study on the phenomenon of rape within different cultures. Surveying ninety-five societies, she discovered that 47 percent were virtually rape-free, 17 percent were rape-prone, and the remaining 36 percent indicated some incidence of rape.[1]

In cultures with little or no rape, women are respected and influential in all areas of life. The religions in those cultures emphasize the equality of women, with women taking an active role in religious life and ritual, and maintain that God is female as well as male. People tend to live in cooperative systems, with both women and men involved in decision making. Fertility, nurturance, and child rearing are highly regarded, and there is little distinction between men's and women's work.

In societies with a high incidence of rape, women have little or no part in governance and religious leadership, and men are more removed from child rearing. Boys are encouraged to be tough and competitive, while girls are taught to be nurturing and dependent. These roles are modeled by adults who live out prescribed masculine and feminine roles, perpetuating structures and symbols of dominance and submission.

It is disturbing to realize that our own culture is among those that are most rape-prone. According to Sanday's study, women in the United States are several hundred times more likely to be raped than women in a number of other cultures. Recent strides toward equality for women have been met by a violent backlash and an explosion in sexual crimes.

But the good news is that survivors of rape and other forms of sexual violence do not have to suffer alone. They are finding one another in rape crisis centers and support groups. They no longer have to live with the isolation and desolation that devastated Dinah and Tamar.

In January 1993, I attended a daylong program given by Roberta Nobleman. Introduced as "an actress, storyteller, teacher, and spiritual pilgrim," Nobleman spoke to a packed house. A white curtain hung at the right of the stage. On it were written in large letters the words "For thine especial safety." The phrase remained a mystery until Nobleman began to tell her story.

She fell in love with the theater as a child in England. She remembers sitting in the highest balcony with others who could not afford seats closer to the stage. The footlights generated a great deal of heat and occasionally caught fire. A fireproof curtain ringed the stage. Written on the curtain were the words "For thine especial safety."

That curtain came to represent Nobleman's feeling when she was in the theater. Here was a place that was safe. She had hidden under tables during the bombing raids of World War II and walked through bomb-scarred neighborhoods. Those fearful memories fled as she lost herself in the theater's world of imagination.

But there was another reason why the theater represented safety for her: her home did not. She carried another fear, a more intimate one. Her soldier father had returned from the war when she was seven years old. That was when the sexual abuse began. It continued until she was thirteen.

Nobleman's program began with a one-woman drama called "Masks and Mirrors." Through poetry, music, and masks, Nobleman invited her audience along on her compelling journey, which she described as movement "from incest victim, to courageous survivor, to joyous celebrant." She linked her childhood experiences to those of British novelist Virginia Woolf, carrying us on a tide of emotion that spanned quiet tears and boisterous laughter.

In the afternoon, she invited each of us to connect with her props. She had a creative array, including a chain of gloves signifying the generation-to-generation nature of sexual abuse; a mirror constructed with symbols of the stages of her remembering and healing; and the apron of "Cleopatra, Queen of Denial," representing the person who refuses to accept evidence of sexual abuse.

We formed ourselves into groups based on the props. Deep sharing and healing happened in those groups, as incest survivors, friends, and supporters shared some of the pain and the loneliness of the journey to recovery. Each group was invited to share with the regathered audience. Songs were sung, and dramatic presentations were offered. Individuals gave testimony to the hope they had discovered in the day or rose to confess their failure in relationship to a family member or friend.

In a gesture that was simple but profoundly moving, the group dealing with issues of trust formed a circle on the stage. One member of the group offered her hand to the woman next to her and said, "I am a survivor, and I offer you my hand." That woman took it, responding, "I am a survivor, and I take your hand." She then offered her other hand to the person next to her. The relaying of trust continued in turn around the circle, with each person declaring her- or himself a survivor, spouse, or friend.

The audience was invited to form similar circles of trust. As hands connected in circles all around the auditorium, the murmur of the declaration "I am a survivor" reached a rumble. It was a graced moment, electrified with empowerment.

At the end of the day, as Roberta Nobleman packed her props and costumes into two huge suitcases, I thanked her. We spoke of the depth of what had been shared on the stage from the audience. She smiled and nodded toward the curtain at the right of the stage. "All it takes is a safe place," she said.

NOTES

1. Ginny Earnest Soley, "Our Lives at Stake," *Sojourners* 13, no. 10 (November 1984): 14.

7　The Levite's Concubine: Seized and Tortured

SCRIPTURE: Judges 19

> They wantonly raped her, and abused her all through the night until the morning. . . . As morning appeared, the woman came and fell down at the door of the man's house where her master was, until it was light. (Judg. 19:25–26)

The first sentence of this story betrays the difference between its two central figures. He was a Levite, of a priestly class regarded above other men; she was a concubine, considered of an inferior status and below other women. It was his privilege to "take her" and own her. And it was this difference in power between them that opened the door for the torrent of abuses that followed.

Concubinage was common in ancient Israel, either as sexual slavery or as a way for a man to acquire a son if his wife did not produce one. Wives had the status of property; concubines were wives with the status of slaves. It was a tremendous act of courage for the young woman in this story to leave her master and return to her father's house. She is the main character in the story, yet at no time does she speak or is she named. She comes across as a voiceless, anonymous victim of all the men around her.

The account does not reveal why the young woman was angry with her husband, but it is not hard to imagine that he had abused her or in some way made her life unsafe or intolerable. We have no indication of how her father received her, although when her husband appeared four months later, her father "came with joy to meet him" (Judg. 19:3). And we have no record of what she felt on seeing her husband again after four months. Like Shechem in the story of Dinah, he came to "speak tenderly to her," which in both stories comes across as a deceptive form of sweet talk designed to appease a woman's legitimate anger—all too common among men who batter and violate.

The father and son-in-law develop a camaraderie, bonding through eating and drinking together, while the woman disappears from the story for a while. Much is made of the father's insistence—in almost comic repetition—that his son-in-law spend another night. Yet there is no intimation of the heart of the matter: what the woman felt about returning with her husband-master, what transpired in their conversations, and what might have changed in him to make her want to go back. All we have is a vision of two men getting drunk together well into the night.

Perhaps her master made tender promises to her and regained her trust. Perhaps she had been taught to believe, like so many of us, that anger is an inappropriate emotion for women and that she needed to push it away and go back with him. Maybe her father commanded her to return. Whatever the case, the Levite and his concubine started out on their return to the remote hill country at the end of a day. They soon found themselves in foreign territory well after dark, with only the city square as a sleeping place until an old man happened by. With the promise of taking care of all their wants, the man took them into his home.

Their enjoyment was interrupted by pounding at the door. The men of the city had surrounded the house, demanding that the old man hand over his male guest for their sexual pleasure. The man's words in response are hard to forget. He offered them his own virgin daughter and the man's concubine, saying, "Ravish them and do whatever you want to them" (19:24).

It would have been a "vile thing" for the men of the city to rape another man, but the rape of young women was considered negligible damage. The conflict could be resolved with no man violated and even the wicked men satisfied; all it took was the sacrifice of women.

The Levite seized his concubine and pushed her out the door in order to save himself. The men of the city "wantonly raped her, and abused her all through the night until the morning." We are told nothing of her cries, her struggle, her terror, her shame. Both the carousing and deliberations of the men are treated in far more depth than this brutal crime against a woman and the anguish it caused her.

By dawn, all the young woman could do was collapse at the door of the house, broken and alone—a woman abandoned by her father, betrayed by her husband, and tortured by a mob. It is one of the most heart-rending scenes in scripture.

In the morning, as if nothing had happened, her master glibly told her to get up from the threshold where her hands clung limply for safety. Receiving no answer, he put her on his donkey. It was time to go. There was no thought of letting her bruised and battered body recover, no thought of pausing to comfort or mourn.

When he got home, he dismembered her. At what point she died—

whether at the hands of her attackers, on the difficult ride back, or at the end of his knife blade—is unclear. But she was torn apart like some sacrificial animal, the pieces of her body sent throughout Israel. There was no honoring of her body, no sacred burial. She became an object lesson, a victim in her master's need to make a point. And indeed, that point was made; his actions sparked a war against the Benjamites. But his outrage was a bit misplaced. He was, after all, the one who had put her out to the mob.

Ironically, from his mouth came words that should be remembered and heeded: "Consider it, take counsel, and speak out." The woman with no voice needs those of us who are outraged to speak for her— and to join our voices with all our sisters who are victims of sexual abuse.

A survivor of incest once told me that the image of dismemberment was a particularly disturbing one for her. Before she was aware of the sexual abuse she had suffered as a child, she felt "dismembered," bearing a sense of physical brokenness and distance from her body. She had begun to sense that it carried secrets she didn't want to know.

One Sunday during Communion, as this survivor's pastor consecrated the bread, he spoke the words "This is my body broken for you; eat this, and remember." She had a vision of "re-membering," bringing the parts of her body back into a sense of wholeness. The words opened a floodgate of memories that put her on the long and difficult path toward healing. She began to see that shame was not the same as guilt, that she needed no forgiveness for the violations done to her body. And she knew that the broken body being offered to her—the one that had been stripped and tortured—had carried her pain to the cross.

Another friend, a survivor of rape, spoke with me on an Easter morning. She shared a nightmare she had had the night before. In it, she was on a stage. In one corner she was raped, then thrown to another corner and raped again. The violations happened repeatedly, and she woke up sobbing and shaking with terror.

But a feeling of deep reassurance enveloped her as she identified the message of the dream. It came to her that she was experiencing the Stations of the Cross, the agonies and humiliations that Jesus experienced in the moments before his crucifixion. The horror began to melt as she understood that Jesus, too, was a victim of her rape two years earlier. She felt Jesus' bearing of her suffering in a way she never had before. Through the scars, resurrection was breaking through.

The Levite's concubine suffered alone, voiceless and without power.

Today, women—and men—are empowering themselves to speak out about sexual abuse in all its forms. Augustine once said, "Hope has two beautiful daughters, anger and courage; anger at the way things are, and courage to work to make things other than they are."[1] These are the qualities that are enabling women to find their voices and demand an end to the violence.

NOTES

1. Denise Lardner Carmody, *Biblical Woman* (New York: Crossroad, 1988), 148.

8   Jephthah's Daughter:
A Sacrificial Offering

SCRIPTURE: Judg. 11:1–6, 29–40

At the end of two months, she returned to her father, who did with her according to the vow he had made. (Judg. 11:39)

A warrior makes a vow to God: he will sacrifice the life of the first person who greets him when he returns home in exchange for victory in battle. It is a rash and reckless promise from a man who feels he has much to prove.

A psychological profile of Jephthah might reveal a man with a severe inferiority complex. He was the son of a prostitute and had been thrown out of his family. In his exile, he became the leader of a band of criminals who gravitated toward his strengths as a fighter and leader.

When the Ammonites attacked Israel, his brothers suddenly changed their tune and wooed him back. They needed a fierce commander to crush the enemy. Jephthah was their man. This was his chance, and he bargained with God for a victory. His triumph was great: twenty cities vanquished. He was a hero, and his only daughter was proud. Unaware of the tragic irony about to unfold, she ran anxiously to meet him, dancing with timbrel in hand, ready to throw her arms around his neck—and she sealed her own death.

What a look her father must have given her when he saw her approaching. Her joyful, innocent, welcoming smile slowly transformed into a countenance of confusion, then fright as her father rent his clothes in agony. Whom had he expected? A servant? Someone whose loss he could bear?

In a classic case of blaming the victim, Jephthah lamented, "Alas, my daughter! You have brought me very low; you have become the cause of great trouble to me. . . . I cannot take back my vow" (Judg. 11:35). He offered her neither comfort nor release.

A young woman had no power to contradict a man's vow to God. She knew it was her duty as a good daughter to submit. But she did not acquiesce completely. She bargained for two months of her life, to grieve her fate in the company of her friends—not only dying but dying childless, which in her culture meant to die unfulfilled.

What anguish this young woman must have felt as she wandered the mountains, disconsolate. She had no recourse, no power to appeal to that her life might be spared; it had already been determined by her father that God would be honored by her death. But within the limits of the inevitable, she claimed meaning for her life. She spent her last days in the loving presence of faithful women, in the wilderness, far from the laws of men.

Womanist theologian Renita J. Weems describes the power of her grieving: "There is a sorrow known only to women; a sorrow so profound and so bottomless, it can only be shared with a woman; a sorrow that only another woman can help you bear. It comes from the feeling of having been violated, betrayed, and abandoned by a force much stronger than yourself. And when the force is someone you trusted, the sorrow can be unbearable."[1]

Many tears were shed upon those mountains. The women wept for the injustice and the loss, for their powerlessness and their vulnerability. They wept at the realization that their lives were worth less than the reckless words of men and for the fact that this is ultimately a father's story, not a daughter's.

After two months, Jephthah's daughter returned home to die. With one short phrase—her father "did with her according to the vow he had made"—her life was over. But once again, much is missing from the story. What did she feel as her father tied her to the wood of the altar? Did she tremble with fear or hold her head high with courage garnered from the mountains? Did he light the fire or was it too much for him? Did he watch her die or leave her to face this ultimate tragedy alone? Were friends by her side?

Jephthah's daughter could not have known of all the women throughout the ages who would join her as burnt offerings, sacrificed on the altars of male-regulated religion. She has sisters from all faith traditions and all corners of the globe.

Hinduism created suttee. This ritual forced a widow to immolate herself on her husband's funeral pyre, in order to "spare" her from temptations to impurity.

In Europe from the fifteenth to the seventeenth century, and to a lesser extent in the United States, witch hunts were carried out. Large numbers of single or widowed women were publicly stripped, raped, tortured, and burned at the Christian stake or hanged. The primary accusation leveled against them was sexual impurity; but in truth, their "crime" was being outside traditional male control.

Confucianism, which combined principles based on ancient

Buddhist-Hindu beliefs and was the state religion of China for more than two thousand years, initiated the foot binding of young girls. The ritual was a way of curtailing their mobility and forcing them as women into total dependence. It left women grotesquely crippled from early childhood. Concubinage, the selling of girl children, and female infanticide were also widely practiced.

Japan's Shintoism instructed a young woman in the practice of suicide, in case her chastity was violated or her relationship with her husband threatened his loyalty to his lord. The unwritten code of discipline known as Bushido upheld a social order in which wives were for managing households and producing children, while other women were for pleasure. All women were second-class citizens in a world where harmony depended on "rational" men dominating the "demonic power" of women.

Islam enforced veiling of women and purdah, or seclusion. Totally marginalizing women in their societies, these rites were created to protect men from the sexual danger that females represented. Muslim husbands were in absolute control of their wives, who could be imprisoned or even killed for disobedience.

In continental Africa, more than seventy-four million women have undergone clitoridectomies. The ritual was designed to "purify" a woman by removing her center of sexual sensitivity. In some countries, female genital mutilation has become big business for the medical establishment. It is often accompanied by infibulation, the sewing together of the vaginal opening. Infibulated women must be cut open for intercourse or childbirth and then resewn, guaranteeing a husband's total control. A European version of the same concept was the chastity belt, a source of not only discomfort but often infection. Author Joan Chittister writes:

> Religion names God, but religion names us as well. It is my belief that religion's name for woman is negative and that this diminishment of half the human race legitimates multiple forms of violence. . . . In every major world religion, though the feminine is part of the creative principle, women are nevertheless defined as the blighted and inferior part of the human race. Religious writings by men have said so, and the structures they have built to the honor and glory of their gods reflect that proposition.[2]

Control and subjugation of women have been foundational to religious practice around the globe and throughout history. Jephthah's daughter is just one more loss. No angel intervenes to save her on the altar, as one did to save Abraham's son Isaac. No ram appears, caught by its horns in a thicket. The horrible deed is done. An innocent daughter pays for her conqueror-father's chilling promise. Jephthah joins the roll call of the faithful given in the book of Hebrews—those "who through faith conquered kingdoms, administered justice, obtained promises, shut the mouths of lions, quenched raging fire, escaped the edge of the sword, won strength out of weakness, became mighty in war, put foreign armies to flight" (Heb. 11:32–34). His daughter remains unnamed. She conquered nothing, got no justice, received no promises. She could not stop the madness, quench the fire, escape her death.

Jephthah's daughter is doomed to the margins of history—except for the actions of the women who knew her. They were with her those two months in the mountains, where they witnessed a rare courage and faith in this young woman. They knew that she was a daughter of God before she was Jephthah's daughter.

"So there arose an Israelite custom that for four days every year the daughters of Israel would go to lament the daughter of Jephthah the Gileadite" (Judg. 11:39–40). Horror and hope drove them back to the mountains to weep once more. Likely they returned to a place where they had cradled and comforted their now-dead sister. They wept, they sang, they danced, mourning and celebrating the vulnerability and strength of womanhood. Perhaps they built an altar and turned their prayers to a Mother God, consecrating their bond as her daughters. Year in and year out they commemorated the tragedy, never forgetting. They kept their ritual, acknowledging that this daughter of God was not the first woman to be a victim; nor would she be the last.

They had the last word. A story that began with a man's unwavering vow ended with women's undying devotion—to God, to a sister, to one another, and ultimately, to the truth. Claiming the power of their sisterhood, they made sure that the memory of Jephthah's brave and faithful daughter—and the story of what had been done to her—were not snuffed out with her life.

NOTES

1. Renita J. Weems, *Just a Sister Away* (San Digeo: Luramedia, 1988), 58.
2. Joan Chittister, "Divinely Ordained?" *Sojourners* 13, no. 10 (November 1984): 16.

9 Samson's Wife: Emotional Assault and Physical Battery

SCRIPTURE: Judg. 14:1–15:8

> They said to Samson's wife, "Coax your husband to explain the riddle to us, or we will burn you and your father's house with fire." (Judg. 14:15)

I have vivid recollections of strong and courageous Samson tearing a lion apart with his bare hands and of foxes with their tails on fire running through wheat fields, images that implanted themselves in my memory when I was a young child in Sunday school. What I have no remembrance of is the nameless woman who was the victim of Samson's power.

This "man of steel" always got what he wanted. He saw a woman he desired for his wife and simply said to his parents, "Get her for me, because she pleases me." She may have been pleasing to Samson's eye, but as a Philistine, she also gave him a pretext to act against her people. From the beginning, the marriage was founded on Samson's desire and deceit.

His "riddle" amounted to emotional torture of his wife. Thirty Philistines threatened to burn down her and her father's house if she didn't convince Samson to tell her the answer. Desperate and in tears, she begged Samson for seven days. Before finally revealing the answer—because she "nagged him"!—Samson had allowed his wife and her family to live under threat of death for an entire week.

When he found out that she had told her people the riddle's answer, he flew into a hot rage and killed thirty Philistines. He made the uncomplimentary comparison that talking to his wife was like "plowing with his heifer." Her father got her away from him—and handed her over to the best man at the wedding! But after a time, Samson came in search of her again, bringing a kid, considered a sign of his intention to have sex with her. Her father wisely refused to allow Samson to go in to her. But then he added insult to injury by trying to hand over his younger and "prettier" daughter to Samson. Indignant at the suggestion, Samson did his fox trick.

Now the Philistines were enraged. But instead of striking back at

Samson or his people, a mob grabbed his wife and her father and burned them to death. And in one more cycle of vengeance, Samson launched a great slaughter of the Philistines, which culminated with him killing a thousand men with the jawbone of a donkey (Judg. 15:15).

This story is in the annals of faith as a showcase for Samson's strength and ingenuity. But the cries of the woman who was taken, tormented, passed around, threatened, and finally murdered are muffled by history.

Only in very recent years have women who are emotionally or physically abused by their husbands found their voices and raised a thunderous chorus for change. According to the Women's Legal Defense Fund, an estimated six million women are physically abused by their husbands or partners each year in the United States; between two thousand and four thousand are beaten to death. Experts estimate that one out of every six households experiences domestic violence, 95 percent of it from husbands toward wives.

Battery is the single most common cause of injury to women. Nearly half of the women who need emergency surgery have been battered, and two of every three pregnant patients seen in emergency rooms are victims of abuse. Between one-quarter and one-third of all abused women suffer "serial victimization," with many beaten as often as once a week. So widespread has battery become that the American Medical Association recently recommended that all physicians inquire about battery as part of routine medical care for women. The nation's police spend one-third of their time responding to domestic violence calls. According to the Federal Bureau of Investigation, 31 percent of female murder victims have been killed by their husbands or partners. It has been noted that the most dangerous place for women is in the home.

The inequality of women was institutionalized in the traditional marriage vow of obedience, opening the way for domination and abuse. The common phrase "rule of thumb" derived from an early colonial law that a husband could beat his wife with a stick no thicker than his thumb—a law designed as protection for women who had taken much worse.

Female inferiority was considered part of "natural law," in much the same way that slavery was justified. In fact, in the nineteenth century, the laws governing the rights of women in society served as the model for laws regulating slaves. From our nation's founding, legislation established the inferiority of women and enforced their dependence on men by denying women property, education, economic advancement, and credit. While recent years have brought significant progress toward equality, today women are still denied economic parity, earning on average only seventy-one cents for every dollar earned by men.

As in situations of domestic violence today, the power differential between Samson and his wife set the stage for the abuse that followed. Samson, in many ways, was a classic stereotype of a battering husband. He believed that he had a right to dominate and control his wife, a pattern that apparently was established from his first glimpse of her. His fury over external circumstances of powerlessness—in this case, the Philistines' dominion over Israel—was played out in his most intimate relationship, claiming his wife as a victim. He experienced cycles of rage and equated power and aggression with masculinity.

His arrival at his wife's home with a kid fits the pattern that battered women everywhere experience. He makes her a target of his rage, through verbal or physical attack, then cools off. He shows remorse, promises to change, showers her with affection and gifts. Many batterers demand sex immediately after they've attacked their wives, some by forcing them as an act of violence, some by convincing them that this will reinforce the batterer's love for the wife and seal his promise not to hurt her again.

Samson's wife was removed from the situation before his emotional torment of her escalated into battery. But his callousness had the same effect. She was sacrificed in a game of revenge that he initiated.

This woman likely fit the profile of a battered wife. Many women stay in abusive situations out of fear of their husband's retaliation toward them or their children if they try to leave. Most are economically dependent, lacking the education, skills, or self-confidence necessary to get work that would provide a livable income. Many dread the humiliation they would bear if their abuse was exposed and the guilt they would feel if their marriage failed. Often they live for the peaceful "honeymoon" times when the husband is attentive and loving, clinging to a belief that he will change and the brutality will stop. Most disturbing of all is that battered women often begin to believe that they deserve the abuse, taking on the role of victim, unable to break their emotional dependency on a violent husband.

Charlotte Fedders stayed married for nineteen years to John Fedders, the former enforcement chief of the federal government's Securities and Exchange Commission. He resigned in 1985 amid widely publicized allegations about his repeated abuse of her. John Fedders admitted during divorce proceedings that he had battered Charlotte but stated that she should share the blame for his violent outbursts because she had denied him emotional support. A circuit court judge ruled that "excessive vicious and cruel conduct" by John had caused the breakup of the marriage.

Charlotte Fedders has been hailed as the woman who blew the whistle on white-collar wife abuse. She wrote a book about her marriage called *Shattered Dreams*. In October 1987, in an outrageous decision, a court-appointed official awarded John Fedders a 25 percent share of the royalties from the book.

In telling her own story, Charlotte Fedders gave many women across the economic spectrum the courage to come forward and tell theirs. No longer content to live with abuse as their silent shame, women are finding their voices. And they are being heard. Shelters, telephone hotlines, and other services for battered women are mushrooming across the country. In many cities within the last decade, police and prosecutors, who have historically viewed domestic violence situations as private matters to be worked out between the conflicting parties, are beginning to charge batterers with criminal offenses. Changing guidelines on the handling of such cases are an indication of a national trend toward strengthening protection for survivors of domestic abuse.

Every abused woman must live with the shattered dreams and the nightmares. There are many who will not write a book, who will struggle with few resources to build a new life from the broken and damaged pieces. But as they are finding one another, their chorus is swelling. And they are creating a movement that is spreading across the country—like wildfire on the tails of foxes amid dry grain.

10 Women of Midian: Spoils of War

Scripture: Num. 31:1–35

The booty remaining from the spoil that the troops had taken totaled six hundred seventy-five thousand sheep, seventy-two thousand oxen, sixty-one thousand donkeys, and thirty-two thousand persons in all, women who had not known a man by sleeping with him. (Num. 31:32)

Her name is Mary. She is physically weak now. But when she is able, she wants to give her testimony publicly that God has helped her to overcome.

She spent several months in a "rape camp" in Bosnia, sharing a room with seventy other women. She witnessed barbaric tortures: soldiers cutting the breasts off of women, ramming weapons up their bodies. Women were killed before her eyes because they tried to resist. Daughters were raped in view of their mothers and mothers in sight of their daughters. And the screams and cries went on all night.

A sixteen-year-old from Petrina watched as her father, mother, and grandparents were murdered. She was spared to be raped. After her long days and nights in a camp, she spent six months in a clinic suffering from deep psychological trauma. Now she awakes at about 1 A.M. every morning and screams until 7 or 8. A thirty-five-year-old Muslim woman from Mostar pulls out her hair and hits her head against a wall, crying out to God for mercy. A fifteen-year-old suffered broken pelvic bones as a result of being raped fifteen or twenty times a day for five months; whenever she sees a man, she shakes uncontrollably. Others suffer from spontaneous abortions, infections, and sexually transmitted diseases. They are as young as seven and as old as sixty.

They were kept in outdoor pens ringed with barbed wire, in animal stalls, in concrete cells no larger than closets. The sexual torture was systematic, and some of it was videotaped for the viewing of soldiers. Private humiliation became pornography under the glare of lights on blood-stained beds.

"Rape is used as a political and military weapon," says Sister Ancilla Vujkovic, a Sister of Mercy of the Franciscan order. "It is a wound of the whole nation."[1] Sister Ancilla, a nurse, works in Zagreb. In November 1991, after the fall of Vukovar, she organized prayer meetings for refugees. She soon began hearing stories of the widescale rape of women. She tried to locate these women, but many had scattered, ashamed, fearful, and traumatized. Most were unable to speak of their experience. It wasn't until the summer of 1992 that word of specialized camps for women and systematic sexual abuse reached the world.

"Our women now are really martyrs," says Sister Ancilla, "because there is no crime to compare with rape; it's worse than to kill someone."[2] She says the scale of the trauma these women have witnessed and experienced cannot be measured. Estimates of the number of women who have been raped range from thirty thousand to fifty thousand; most of the women are Muslim.

An impassioned Bosnian appeal called the Serbian rapes "unprecedented in the history of war crimes," an organized attempt "to destroy a whole Muslim population, to destroy a society's cultural, traditional, and religious integrity."[3] But unfortunately, there is nothing unprecedented about mass rape as an instrument of war.

The immensity of the suffering in Bosnia boggles the mind and rends the heart. The historical weight of the tragedy of rape overwhelms the soul. In this century alone, German troops raped Russian women, Japanese fighters raped Chinese women, U.S. soldiers raped Vietnamese women—and on and on. "Rapists," according to feminist author Susan Brownmiller, "are the shock troops of patriarchy."[4]

Throughout the ages and across the globe, rape has been an instrument of terror and conquest of "enemy" populations. Women have been just one more enemy possession to steal or violate. But when the national terror is over, the personal anguish remains, as raped women become a sign of a nation's dishonor, the ultimate "damaged property."

The biblical story of the women of Midian disturbs deeply. The young women were seized as the spoils of war—thirty-two thousand rounded up, like animals, mentioned in the scripture after the sheep and the donkeys. Only the virgins were spared, prizes to be handed over to the men of Israel. And all this was done, according to the biblical writer, not only with God's blessing but at God's command—at least, that's how Moses understood it.

To what God could the women of Midian cry out for mercy? Did they beg to be killed rather than violated in this way? Did their screams fill the night?

As those young women clung together in terror, they could not have known how many sisters through the ages would share their fate. But perhaps they discovered some of the same courage that visited a woman named Mary centuries later in Zagreb.

In a Bosnian rape camp, Mary became pregnant with the child of a Serbian soldier. Like most of the women, she was kept in the camp until she was past five months of pregnancy, then sent by bus to Zagreb. She arrived bruised and weak. She visited Sister Ancilla regularly for the next few months. On her last visit, she told Ancilla that she was willing to forgive. She said that she was going to give birth to the child that she carried to show everyone that she can, with God's help, overcome her suffering.

When she is stronger, Mary explained, she will make a public statement, holding her baby in her arms. She will do it, she said, "as a sign to the world that love conquers evil."

NOTES

1. Elizabeth Holler, "Grief Upon the Earth," *Sojourners* 22, no. 3 (April 1993): 25.
2. Ibid.
3. Susan Brownmiller, "Making Female Bodies the Battlefield," *Newsweek* (January 4, 1993): 37.
4. Ibid.

Part 2. Questions for Reflection

1. Which story in this section was the most difficult for you to read? Why?

2. In what ways have you encountered sexual abuse?

3. Have you or has someone you know experienced healing from sexual violence?

4. What are your feelings about living in a society so plagued by violence against women?

5. What steps, both as an individual and within your church or community, do you believe could be taken to confront and change the epidemic of sexual violence?

PART 3
Women of Treachery and Guile

This book would be less than honest if it did not look at biblical women who themselves operated less than honestly. Rebekah, Tamar, and the daughters of Lot manipulated circumstances to get their way. Potiphar's wife, Delilah, Jezebel, and Herodias chose deceit and violence.

Their stories stand as a corrective to those who would claim that aggression and corruption reside solely in men, that goodness is the essence of womanhood. They remind us of the capacity within each of us for sin, betrayal, and inhumanity.

Women have always had a choice about how to react to our oppression. While the biblical women of this section opted to compromise their integrity or surrender to evil impulses, women such as Wilma Mankiller, who is paired with Rebekah, offer an example of a different choice out of comparable circumstances. Although none of us can change the abuses or wounds that we have experienced, it is in our power to choose either anger and hatred or healing and transformation.

11   Rebekah: A Deceptive Blessing

SCRIPTURE: Genesis 24; 25:20–28; 27:1–35, 41–45

Rebekah said to her son Jacob, " . . . Go to the flock, and get me two choice kids, so that I may prepare from them savory food for your father, such as he likes . . . so that he may bless you before he dies." (Gen. 27:6–10)

When Abraham was very old, he sent a servant back to his homeland to find a wife for his son Isaac. Setting out with camels and gifts, the servant made the journey and waited by a well one evening at twilight. Soon Rebekah arrived with a water jar on her shoulder. When this kind and beautiful young woman offered him a drink—and then made several more trips to the well to water his camels—he knew that she was the one. He gave her a nose ring and two bracelets and went home with her to meet her family.

Rebekah, young and enthralled by the servant's promises, agreed to go off with him to a far land to become the wife of Isaac, her second cousin. Her mother and brother asked the servant to allow her ten days to remain with her family, but the servant insisted that there be no delay. Rebekah agreed to leave right away. Days later, when Isaac, out walking in a field, and Rebekah, sitting on a camel, caught a glimpse of each other from afar, it was love at first sight.

The story of Isaac and Rebekah begins like a romantic adventure. But before long, real-life struggles set in. Rebekah was barren and remained so for twenty years. Famine struck, and Isaac, like his father before him, went to Gerar to speak with King Abimelech. Also like his father, Isaac told Abimelech that the beautiful woman at his side was his sister, and the king fell for it again (Gen. 26:1–11).

Rebekah, like her mother-in-law Sarah, eventually conceived. The twins she bore were as different as night and day. Rugged Esau was a skillful hunter, Jacob a quiet man more comfortable in his tent than in the wilderness. Isaac loved Esau, according to the scripture, "because he was fond of game." But Rebekah had a special love for Jacob.

One afternoon, Esau, the elder brother, came in from his work in the fields, famished, and begged Jacob to give him some of the lentil stew he was cooking. Jacob agreed to give him some if Esau would sell him his birthright, his right as Isaac's heir. Esau, fearing he would die without some food, relinquished it (25:29–34). But Jacob still needed his father's blessing to make the transaction official. Thus the stage was set for the deceptive procurement of the blessing.

Esau had married Hittite wives and "made life bitter" for Isaac and Rebekah (26:34–35). Rebekah believed that her younger son was kinder, more devout, and better able to uphold the covenant with God. Taking advantage of her husband's blindness, she intervened to manipulate a blessing for her favored son. Was Rebekah a daring and clever matriarch who refused to be submissive and got what she wanted? Or was she a deceptive and manipulative wife and mother? Perhaps a little of both. She nevertheless paid a price. She had to bid good-bye to her favorite son and never saw him again. She spent her last years with a husband and son who felt betrayed by her.

Like Rebekah, Wilma Mankiller journeyed far from her homeland, and she is a consistent advocate for the "birthright and blessing" of her people. Unlike Rebekah, she is a woman without guile. Her integrity has earned her great honor.

Wilma Mankiller is the principal chief of the Cherokee Nation of Oklahoma, the first woman to lead a major Native American tribe. A century and a half ago, her people were forced from their homelands in the southeastern United States and marched west as a result of the federal Indian Removal Act of 1830. Cherokees were first rounded up and placed in stockades, where some froze and others starved. Women and girls were raped. Homes were looted and crops burned. More than four thousand Cherokees died on the brutal twelve-hundred-mile "Trail of Tears."

In the West they confronted a form of "ethnic cleansing." Native Americans were hunted like wild game, and bounties were paid for Indian scalps or severed heads. In the 1850s, a thousand American Indian women in California were raped so brutally that they died. Thousands of others were forced to become concubines for white men, and almost four thousand children were kidnapped and sold into slavery.

A hundred years later, in 1956, a month before Mankiller's eleventh birthday, she herself experienced the pain of government relocation. Poverty forced her family to leave their homeland in Oklahoma and participate in a relocation program in California. Leaving behind wide, open spaces and the comforting sounds of nature, they were dumped amid the sirens, gaudy neon lights, and chaos of San Francisco's Tenderloin District. A popular sign in city restaurants then proclaimed, "No Dogs, No Indians." Wilma Mankiller speaks about how she survived:

Remembering those Cherokees and others who were forced to move to Indian Territory and how they persisted brings me at least some relief whenever I feel distressed or afraid. Through the years, I have learned to use my memory and the historical memory of my people to help me endure the most difficult and trying periods of my life. That is why I continue to think about the past and to circle back to my tribal history for doses of comfort. . . . The experiences of those who made that journey to Indian Territory remain an unrivaled lesson in courage and hope.[1]

Wilma Mankiller has indeed had difficult and trying periods in her personal life. She herself is a portrait of courage and hope. In 1979, she suffered a head-on automobile collision, which took the life of a close friend. Mankiller's face was crushed, her ribs and legs broken. She underwent seventeen operations and was bedridden for months. "I came very close to death, felt its presence and the alluring call to complete the circle of life," she says. Her recovery, as she describes it, was an awakening to "a very Cherokee approach to life—what our tribal elders call 'being of good mind.' "[2]

A year later, Mankiller was diagnosed with myasthenia gravis, a chronic neuromuscular disease. "The reality of how precious life is enabled me to begin projects I couldn't have otherwise tackled," she says of that time.[3] She spearheaded the Bell Community Revitalization Project, her tribe's most ambitious and heralded achievement. Residents of poverty-stricken Bell, Oklahoma, undertook a massive program to remodel dilapidated homes and build new ones and to lay a sixteen-mile pipeline bringing water to their homes for the first time. The project became a model for other tribes seeking self-sufficiency, and Mankiller's role in it paved the way for her election as tribal chief.

Initially, she was the target of harassment and even threats of death from those who resisted a female chief. But that changed quickly when her detractors saw her courage, competence, and commitment. Despite continuing struggles with her health, including a kidney transplant in 1990, she ran for reelection in 1991, feeling that much remained to be done. She won by a landslide. Under Mankiller's leadership, the Cherokees have experienced dramatic increases in services and businesses; launched many construction programs, including the building of new clinics and a Job Corps training center; and witnessed the birth of many self-empowerment projects for women.

Wilma Mankiller became an activist in 1969. That year, Native American students, including four of her siblings, occupied the abandoned prison on Alcatraz Island in San Francisco Bay. Centuries before, Native Americans of the Ohlone tribe had cared for the island, leaving it unspoiled as a refuge for ocean birds. European Americans had turned it into first a military fort, then a prison. In the 1800s, Native Americans who fought back against white enslavement were imprisoned and died there. The island was thus an appropriate place to take a stand, a symbol of the denial of Native American rights. The students claimed it as Indian land under an 1868 treaty. The Coast Guard removed the first occupiers, but others came in waves. The occupation, which drew the nation's attention to the plight of Native Americans, lasted nineteen months.

"When Alcatraz occurred," says Mankiller, "I became aware of what needed to be done to let the rest of the world know that Indians had rights too. . . . It was a benchmark."[4] From that moment on, she committed herself to helping her people assert their birthright to the land and to upholding the blessing of Native American culture.

"If I am to be remembered," says Wilma Mankiller, "I want it to be because I am fortunate enough to have become my tribe's first female chief. But I also want to be remembered for emphasizing the fact that we have indigenous solutions to our problems. Cherokee values, especially those of helping one another and of our interconnections with the land, can be used to address contemporary issues."[5]

NOTES

1. Wilma Mankiller and Michael Wallis, *Mankiller: A Chief and Her People* (New York: St. Martin's, 1993), 77.
2. Ibid., xxii.
3. Ibid.
4. Ibid., xxi.
5. Ibid., 250–51.

12 Tamar: Securing Her Rights

SCRIPTURE: Gen. 38:6–30

[Tamar] sent word to her father-in-law, "It was the owner of these who made me pregnant." And she said, "Take note, please, whose these are, the signet and the cord and the staff." (Gen. 38:25)

She was born in a remote village in the Philippines, in a bamboo hut. Heavy militarization and a feudal system of land ownership made a life of more than bare survival impossible. Her father left when she was four years old. He took her two-year-old sister with him; rumor in the village had it that her father had sold her sister. When she was in sixth grade, she had to quit school to help her mother around the house.

When she was thirteen, someone in her village offered to find her a job in Manila, as a babysitter or a waitress. She had nothing but a bleak future at home, and she knew that if she could make some money, she could send some back to help her mother and siblings. She went.

In Manila, she was taken to a strange, dark house. It didn't take her long to figure out that here there would be no children to watch or tables to serve. The first time a customer was brought to her, two women had to hold her down, one pinning her hands above her head and the other holding her feet while the man had sex on her.

For a year, she was kept in the house like a prisoner. Sometimes she had ten customers in one night, tourists from all over the world. Once she became pregnant. In her fifth month of pregnancy, she had an abortion by massage. One week after the abortion, she was with a customer again, crying in pain and pleading with him to stop.

On her fifteenth birthday, with the help of a customer, she managed to escape. She had the Philippine equivalent of $1.50 in her pocket and nowhere to go. She wandered around Manila, sleeping in the park at night, until she found a cousin who took her in. The cousin suggested that they go to Olongapo. She didn't know much about it, except that there were Americans there. She didn't know what else to do.

Olongapo, the city outside the U.S. Subic Bay Naval Base, has also been called "the R and R [rest and recreation] Capital of the World" and "Sin City." Thousands of sailors and marines have spent time on the city's infamous Magsaysay Street, which is lined with hundreds of sex bars. A recent estimate placed the number of "hospitality women" in Olongapo at eighteen thousand. Some were sold to sex entrepreneurs by their desperately poor parents. Many were lured by a vision of American dollars and the dream of marrying an American sailor who would take them away to a new life in the United States. Most, like this young woman, were deceived and left home thinking they were going to a better future, hoping to help lift their families out of grinding poverty. Once they got to Olongapo, they were trapped. Bar owners got most of the money that was exchanged, and they kept the young women perpetually in debt to them. Women who tried to resist or escape were beaten.

Brenda Stoltzfus, who worked for several years with hospitality women at Olongapo through the Mennonite Central Committee, began "buying" the time of the women, just as customers did—only she sat down with them and listened. She helped to establish a support center for the women.

Stoltzfus took this young woman to the center to talk one day. The young woman was eighteen then. Stoltzfus describes their first meeting:

> I remember her sad eyes. But there are many sad eyes in Olongapo. To me she was one of the many women in pain, the pain of Olongapo. I did not know how to reach into what I felt intuitively was a deep reservoir of pain. I did not know what to ask to draw it out or even if she wanted it drawn out. As so often happens in those situations, the facade of makeup and "hospitality" fell away and her vulnerability as an eighteen-year-old girl trying to survive a kind of hell few of us know anything about shone through.[1]

The young woman worked in three different bars in Olongapo. From 4:00 in the afternoon until 1:30 in the morning, she danced on a platform encircled by a bar, where servicemen sat and drank and leered. She was paid $2.50 for a night of dancing; more, if customers "bought" her. The last bar she worked in had fewer customers than the other two. When a ship came in to the base, sailors were told which bars had a high rate of venereal disease and which had women who had tested positive for the AIDS virus. This bar was one that carried a warning, keeping many sailors away.

She has an infant daughter to take care of now. At nineteen, she is both vulnerable and tough. She has been a slave of sexual abuse for all her teen years.

Subic Bay Naval Base recently closed after ninety years of U.S. colonial imposition in the Philippines. Thousands of hospitality women and their estimated twenty-three thousand Amerasian children are the legacy of U.S. exploitation. Most of the women have nowhere to go and no hope of dignified employment.

Unfortunately, the system that enslaved them still thrives. Sex tourism is big business in Asia. As a "morale booster," some Japanese companies reward their outstanding managers and salesmen with all-expenses-paid "sex holidays" to South Korea's brothels. Package tours carry men from all over the world to Bangkok, Thailand, known as the "biggest brothel in Asia." The package includes airfare, a hotel room, and a prearranged number of women "for the men to do with as they like," according to the promotional literature. Women are commonly paraded with numbers around their necks through hotel viewing rooms so that the patrons can choose the ones they want.

An information network includes magazines and books full of glossy pictures and details about women—as well as children—available for sex in various exotic locales. *Bangkok's Backstreets: A Guide to the Pleasures of the World's Open City* outlines where and how to meet prostitutes there. One paragraph states, "Every individual is unique, and that's perhaps even more true of the mind-boggling array of beauties Bangkok has to offer, just because the competition is so keen. But it's really rather silly to go ga-ga over one when, by conservative estimates, there are at least 499,999 others you haven't even met."[2]

Half a million women in this one city alone make a living by selling themselves, because they believe they have no other means of survival. They are making a choice of utter desperation. In a world that too often denies their humanity and devalues their labor, they have one commodity for which they know men are willing to pay. They grow up learning that as women they are worth little, mere property. That "truth" gets branded deeply in the soul.

Tamar was a victim of a patriarchal system that told her she was worth something only if she bore sons. God had struck her wicked husband dead. According to the law of levirate marriage, his brothers were obligated to marry her so that she would conceive.

Onan did not care for this arrangement, fathering children that would belong by law to his dead brother. Tricky and deceitful, he had sex with Tamar, but he withdrew before ejaculating so that he wouldn't impregnate her. God was displeased and struck him dead, too. The only brother left was still a child. But Judah, Tamar's father-in-law, promised that when he grew up, Shelah would fulfill the obligation to her.

Years passed, and Tamar was still wearing widow's clothes. Judah did not honor his pledge. Placing blame for the deaths of his first two sons on Tamar, he feared that Shelah too would die. Then one day, when Tamar heard that Judah was coming nearby to shear his sheep, she threw off her widow's garments and disguised herself. The rest is history.

She did it for survival. Even Judah knew that she was in the right. It was her duty, according to Hebrew law, to provide a son to carry on her dead husband's name and lineage. Judah had failed in his obligation to her. He had refused to give her his last son or to release her from the obligations of levirate marriage.

She caught him in his own double standard. A man who, soon after the death of his wife, had sexually used a woman he believed to be a prostitute had the audacity to pronounce death at the stake for Tamar's "playing the whore." His mouth likely dropped open when he saw his signet, cord, and staff in Tamar's grasp. "Take note, please, whose these are," she said simply. And Judah knew that he had been snared.

Tamar was clever. As a woman, she was powerless to change the system that bound her. But like Ruth, she took her well-being into her own hands. She is mentioned at the end of the book of Ruth in a blessing that was bestowed on Boaz from the people: "Through the children that the Lord will give you by this young woman [Ruth], may your house be like the house of Perez, whom Tamar bore to Judah" (Ruth 4:12). Perez was an ancestor of Boaz and King David, ancestors of Jesus. Tamar's deception is part of the genealogical history of the faith.

By traditional moral standards, Tamar's behavior may seem shameful. But she did what she believed she had to do. Similarly, the young women of Olongapo may be targets of judgment. But they too feel trapped, without options. The real issue is not how desperate women choose to secure their survival. The critical question is: What is being done to dismantle the savage structures of patriarchy that push them to such desperation?

NOTES

1. Mennonite Central Committee, *MCC Women's Concerns Report* (October-November 1989): 5.
2. Quoted in Ibid., 2.

13 Lot's Daughters: Violation Begets Violation

SCRIPTURE: Genesis 19

And the firstborn said to the younger, " . . . Come, let us make our father drink wine, and we will lie with him, so that we may preserve offspring through our father." (Gen. 19:31–32)

This is a disturbing story. It is one of the harshest reminders of the status of women in Old Testament times. A father was willing to hand over his young daughters to be gang-raped in order to save his male houseguests from the same humiliation. When the men of the city surrounded his house, Lot's response was to choose his obligation to the laws of hospitality, which mandated the protection of guests, over the dignity and safety of his female children.

As in the story of the Levite's concubine, the scene implies that homosexual rape was a "wicked" act while heterosexual rape was not. It is told as if no real harm would have been done had the young women spent the night being abused by a violent mob. Equally troubling is the way in which the story unfolds. Lot was allowed to argue and bargain with God. When Lot lingered, the angels took him by the hand and whisked him and his family away; when he protested about fleeing to the hills, they let him stop in the small city of Zoar. But when his unnamed wife looked back—likely in longing for all that was left behind—she was turned into a pillar of salt, according to the account.

Only Lot and his two daughters were left to fend for their survival. The two young women, who were to have been married soon, had lost their hope of a future when their husbands-to-be thought Lot was joking about the destruction to come. Their husbands had perished in the consuming fire, their mother in flight. Life as they knew it was shattered. The city in which they had grown up and all that was familiar were gone. They were doomed to live out their days in a cave with a father who had shown little regard for their humanity. Existence must have been grim in the cave that became their new home.

Their plan was desperate. They believed that no other man was alive on earth except their father. Like Tamar, they felt pushed to secure their own future. It was a devious and degrading scheme, but it worked.

I wonder what might appear if these two sisters could be subjects of a modern-day psychological examination. They could not have been unaffected by the fact that their father was willing to sacrifice them to sexual abuse and violence in order to protect strangers. I suspect that their profile would be something like this: dysfunctional family, controlling father, severe emotional trauma and loss, low self-esteem, tendency toward self-destruction.

In that sense, the daughters of Lot are everywhere. I have met them in jail, in shelters for battered women, on the streets. They are women confined by their devastating pasts or wandering, lost and aimless, to try to escape them. Most know that the world is willing to discard them. Yet still they struggle for their future, often making desperate choices.

I met Celia at the federal women's prison in Alderson, West Virginia. She had stayed for thirteen years with a husband who beat her. When he started to abuse her five children, she took them and fled to a friend's home. Enraged, her husband threatened to hurt each of the children, beginning with Nicole, the oldest, unless Celia came back. On a Sunday morning, while Nicole was walking to church, her father and two of his buddies waited for her on a street corner. They gang-raped her. Nicole was fourteen.

Celia went to plead with her husband not to hurt the other children. While she was with him, one of Nicole's other attackers arrived. A cousin of Nicole's, who was outraged by the rape and had followed the man, shot and killed him. When the police arrived, both Celia and the cousin were arrested. Circumstancial evidence convicted Celia, and she was sentenced to four years in prison in connection with the murder. She served it at a women's prison three hundred miles away from her children.

Nicole spent several weeks alone in the hospital, recovering from the rape. Hospital personnel feared that telling her that her mother was in prison would only add trauma to trauma. So for weeks she bore the devastation and isolation of knowing that her father had raped her and believing that her mother had rejected and abandoned her. Her father was later acquitted of the rape.

I met Nicole months later, on a Good Friday. Tears streamed down her cheeks like the rain that poured outside as she told me, "I don't have any money for food and I'm going to have a baby." She explained that the baby wasn't a result of "what my father did to me." The baby's father was Charlie, a twenty-eight-year-old man into whose arms she had run when she got out of the hospital looking for someone to love her. Charlie, a Vietnam War veteran and alcoholic who was unable to keep a job, had invited Nicole to live with him and his extended family—his parents, two brothers, and a sister with three small children. These ten people shared a two-bedroom house.

Nicole made the best of a desperate situation. She gave birth to a beautiful baby girl on Thanksgiving Day. She named the baby, my goddaughter, LaCelia.

During the years that followed, I was often amazed at the amount of devastation and crisis in Celia's and Nicole's lives—and in the lives of those around them. Shortly after Celia went to prison, her husband initiated legal action to get custody of the children, not because he was fit to have them but because he didn't want Celia to have them when she got out of jail. Many women in prison, I learned, lose their children this way, by reason of "abandonment." With the exception of Nicole, the children went instead to foster homes.

Celia was most concerned about her youngest daughter, Lisa, who was nine when Celia went to jail. Lisa had been separated from her sisters and put in a lonely and difficult foster situation. I met her when I picked her up to take her to Nicole's fifteenth birthday party. Dressed in her best Sunday dress and black patent-leather shoes, with a smile as broad and sweet as I had ever seen on a child, Lisa walked shyly toward me and extended her hand. Then she threw her arms around me, and her eyes filled with tears. Of all the children, she most resembled her mother. That afternoon of Nicole's party was the only time that Lisa's foster mother allowed her to be with her family.

Eventually, Nicole was able to talk about the rape and the war within her between love and hatred for her father. She asked me if I would help her find him. She wanted him to have the chance to meet his granddaughter, and she wanted to talk to him and tell him she was trying to love him in her heart. I was amazed at her courage. When our effort to find him was unsuccessful, Nicole was both disappointed and relieved.

There was never enough money. Once, after asking for money for food, she came back the next day asking for more. When I questioned her, she confessed, "Charlie and I used it to go dancing." Before I could react, she pleaded with the innocent smile of a fifteen-year-old, "Isn't it OK to dance when you're hungry?"

I will never forget a cold winter night when Nicole called to tell me that the heat had been cut off at the house because of an unpaid bill. I drove over to the house, expecting to find the family huddled together around the open oven for warmth. Instead, as I approached the house, I heard music blaring from the top floor. Inside, the family was dancing. The youngest child was giggling as she tried to show her bent-over grandmother how to pirouette and boogie at the same time. Pillows were flying and everyone was laughing, and Nicole shouted to me over the din, "We're trying to keep warm!"

Celia, after serving three years of her sentence, was released from prison on early parole just before Christmas. Her children had all gathered at Charlie's house, presents in hand, with great anticipation of their first Christmas together in three years. But Celia never arrived.

After years of confinement, she was finding freedom hard to deal with. So battered was her self-esteem, so wounded her spirit, that she could not find the confidence to carry on. Her children had suffered and now needed her, but she had little to give them. She did not know where to start to reestablish their life together as a family. She was afraid of disappointing them again and decided it would be better simply to stay away.

Despite secretarial skills that she had gained in prison, no one wanted to hire a woman with a criminal record. After months of searching and rejection, she finally took a cleaning job in a downtown government building. I met her one afternoon on her lunch hour in a dingy basement locker room. She looked thin and tired and sick. Dressed in a faded blue cleaning uniform, she coughed constantly. To look at her was to see a pile of broken dreams and crushed hopes. She had joined the underside of life in the capital city. Her work was dirty and degrading. With a small space heater as the only source of warmth, she cleaned the dark and cavelike cement-block basement of a building where, a few floors above, power was manipulated and traded every day.

She had started drinking and began to stay close to men who she thought could protect her from her violent and vengeful husband. They not only drank heavily but also dealt on a small scale in illegal drugs. The men preyed on her failure and despair. Several times she decided to get them out of her life, but she was never successful. Finally, she resigned herself to their presence in her life and her dependence on their attention and protection.

Celia shivered in the thin uniform as she talked. The cold aggravated a problem she had with her back and her joints, so she worked in constant pain. An infection left unattended had worsened and spread, so that her doctor said she needed a hysterectomy, but she didn't know when there would be enough money for it.

I was determined not to let this tragedy repeat itself in Nicole. When LaCelia turned two, Nicole started talking about wanting to go back to school to become a nurse's aide. She had finished only the eighth grade. I had seen her compassion and sense of responsibility toward her sisters take over when she realized that Celia wasn't going to get them back together, and I believed in her. We tackled a multitude of obstacles—day care for LaCelia, money for books and a uniform, a quiet place for her to study, the need to convince Charlie that her education was important.

Nicole began classes, but one disaster after another threatened to derail her hopes. Her September welfare check got stolen from her mailbox and with it the funds she was planning to spend on day care for LaCelia. In October a fire started in the mattress in the children's room and swept through the top of the house; all of Nicole's new school clothes were burned in the flames. During those two months, Charlie got and lost three jobs. With each job lost, he intensified his dependence on alcohol and became more abusive.

Through it all, Nicole kept going to school, realizing that her only ticket out of despair was a good job. She excitedly shared with me all that she was learning. She regularly drafted Charlie's family members into service as she practiced and gained proficiency in taking temperatures and pulses.

Graduation from her six-month course was scheduled for late February. But that day never came for Nicole. Early one January evening, she called and said there was a "family crisis" that she could not explain over the phone. I had long since stopped trying to guess what sort of crisis might strike next.

It was bitterly cold that week. *The Washington Post* was calling it the worst cold spell to hit the city in a century. At night, the windchill factor dipped the temperature to forty below zero. The house had been without heat and hot water for two months. Meals for ten were being cooked on an old hot plate. LaCelia had contracted bronchitis.

But it wasn't the cold or LaCelia's health that was the overriding crisis. It was Lisa. Lisa was the one daughter whom Celia had taken back into her home with her. But Nicole explained that her mother had dropped Lisa off with her a week before and had not come back for her.

In the time since I had last seen her, Lisa had grown into a beautiful young woman. When I asked her if she would like me to take her back to her mother, she burst into tears. Through her sobs, she explained that some men had been drinking at her mother's apartment and one of them had "touched" her. Lisa was fourteen now. The pattern was beginning all over again. In fact, during the week that Lisa had been with Nicole, Charlie's older brother Tyrone had paid Junior, a mentally retarded brother, to try to force Lisa to have sex with him. It was only a joke, Tyrone explained later when Lisa ran crying into Nicole's arms.

The innocence and magic were dead in Lisa. Sitting there on broken-down crates, wearing layers of clothing to keep out the cold, she wept and I shuddered in anger at the combination of bad luck and abuse that had set the course of Nicole's and Lisa's young lives.

The incident with Lisa turned out to be Nicole's undoing. As with her mother, the pressure had built until one day something snapped, and it just didn't seem worth trying anymore to keep everything together. The triple jeopardy of being poor, black, and female in America was too much to bear. Despite my pleas to her to finish school, three weeks before she was to graduate Nicole dropped out. She decided that she needed to pay more attention to her sisters' needs than to her own.

Nicole walked into my life on a Good Friday, and we never really got past it. If there is any resurrection at all in her life, I suppose it is that she has learned to dance when she is cold and hungry. Perhaps that is a legacy she will pass on to my goddaughter.

As for Lisa, I took her to supper that evening. She tried to sort through her feelings of fear, confusion, and shame. I wished that she had had a mother the last few years to answer her questions and help her come to grips with her budding womanhood. After dinner, I took Lisa home with me. She talked about how painful it had felt to have her mother go away to prison and now to have been left at Nicole's. Her voice broke as she said, "I guess my mother just doesn't want me."

It grew late, and Lisa and I made a bed on my floor for her out of sofa cushions and a sleeping bag. Before going to sleep, she gave me a kiss on the cheek. As I was about to drift off to sleep, she sat up and said suddenly, "Once I wanted somebody to love me, so I tried to have a baby. It died. . . . I didn't kill it. I would never have killed it." She put her head back on the pillow, and then she asked, "Did you say your prayers?" There was silence for a moment. Then she whispered, "God bless Nicole and my mother and you and my baby."

About an hour later, Lisa sat up again suddenly and started crying. "I can't sleep. I'm thinking about my baby," she sobbed. "I think I killed it. . . . The doctor said so." She blurted out the story through her tears: "I was staying with Nicole and I was at the phone booth, and I had to run home quick to go to the bathroom. I think I ran too hard. I started to bleed."

The story continued to spill out. It had taken an hour for an ambulance to come as Lisa lay frightened and bleeding. As she finished telling me the story, she lay down again and then smiled softly. "But it was OK. Nicole took real good care of me. She held my hand. And she just kept taking my temperature and my pulse to make sure I was going to be OK."

14 Potiphar's Wife and Delilah: Lies and Seduction

SCRIPTURE: Genesis 39; Judges 16

Now Joseph was handsome and good-looking. And after a time his master's wife cast her eyes on Joseph and said, "Lie with me." (Gen. 39:6–7)

Then the lords of the Philistines came up to [Delilah], and brought the money in their hands. She let [Samson] fall asleep on her lap; and she called a man, and had him shave off the seven locks of his head. He began to weaken, and his strength left him. (Judg. 16:18–19)

It is important for us to face Potiphar's wife and Delilah. They remind us that women can be villains as well as victims, motivated by lust or greed or ambition.

Potiphar's wife was likely a bored, lonely, rich woman whose husband spent much of his time away from home in the line of duty. She probably felt neglected, with little responsibility and few concerns.

Despite a series of cruel and traumatic events that had landed him in Egypt, Joseph remained a man of principle. The son of Rachel and Jacob, he was his father's favorite; he possessed a colorful coat to prove it. He had dreams that infuriated his brothers, who turned on him and threw him into a pit to die. But when a caravan of Ishmaelites came by on their way to Egypt, Joseph's brothers sold him into slavery. They kept his coat, killed a goat, and dipped the coat in its blood as evidence for the story they would tell when they got back home, that Joseph had been killed by a wild beast (Genesis 37).

So Joseph was acquainted with betrayal. He responded to it by holding more tightly to his own integrity. He was obviously admired and trusted by his master, Potiphar. He probably got more attention from Potiphar than Potiphar's wife did. Joseph was a handsome, young man. Potiphar's wife was a lonely, older woman. She was certainly determined. She tried in vain to seduce him. Finally, she seized him, and poor Joseph was forced to flee, leaving his clothes behind.

Her wicked lie put him behind bars. Some combination of jealousy, neglect, self-centeredness, and lust corrupted her, and Joseph paid the price. The story had a happy ending for him, however. He was given care of the other prisoners. He became an interpreter of dreams, including pharaoh's, and eventually, a leader in Egypt.

Potiphar's wife, by contrast, simply disappears from scripture, leaving a legacy of infamy. She hurt not only one man but also all of womankind. Whenever a woman lies, especially about sexual crimes, she jeopardizes the word of all women who have been victims.

Delilah is considered the femme fatale of the Bible. Her story picks up where Samson's wife's story left off. The Philistines were still angry at Samson and seeking revenge. Once again, they recruited a woman to help them in their efforts to outwit and subdue him. This time they offered her money.

The price was right for Delilah. She set out to discover the source of Samson's strength. She wasn't too bright about it; she asked him directly. And of course, he lied—three times. She kept falling for his tricks.

Now, Samson wasn't terribly bright either. You have to believe there was more brawn than brains there, because he finally told her the truth. She "nagged him" (that derogatory expression about women again), just as his wife had, so he gave in. He let out the secret to a woman who was clearly out to do him in—which she did, while he was sleeping in her lap, no less.

Samson's story didn't have a happy ending, for him or for the Philistines. They dragged him out of prison one day so that he could perform for the people, showing off some muscle and entertaining them. He literally "brought down the house." He and everybody around him died when he pulled down the supporting pillars (Judg. 16:23–30).

Like Potiphar's wife, Delilah was never heard from again. She likely headed to the coast with all the money she got from the Philistines. She was paid well for her betrayal.

Both of these stories reveal a rare picture of women disempowering men, a reversal of the way things usually unfold. Unfortunately, these two women used seductive power and accusation to get their way. Their behavior besmirches all womankind, strengthening the position of those who would stereotype women as temptresses, manipulators, and deceivers.

15 Jezebel and Herodias: In the Grip of Evil

Scripture: 1 Kings 16:29–33; 19:1–3; 21:1–16; 2 Kings 9:1–3, 30–37; Mark 6:14–29

So [Jezebel] wrote letters in Ahab's name and sealed them with his seal; . . . "Proclaim a fast, and seat Naboth at the head of the assembly; seat two scoundrels opposite him, and have them bring a charge against him. . . . Then take him out, and stone him to death." (1 Kings 21:8–10)

[The daughter of Herodias] went out and said to her mother, "What should I ask for?" She replied, "The head of John the baptizer." (Mark 6:24)

As with the stories of Potiphar's wife and Delilah, it is painful to read about Jezebel and Herodias. Both were women in the grip of evil.

Jezebel's name is synonymous with wickedness. She launched a pogrom against all the prophets of God. Only a hundred survived, and those by hiding out in caves (1 Kings 18:4, 13). The prophet Elijah became Jezebel's most zealous enemy. She threatened him with death, sending him fleeing into the wilderness, where in his despair he asked God to take his life (19:4).

She was married to arguably the most evil king in the history of Israel, Ahab. Their marriage was a conspiracy of power and greed. The pathetic scene of Ahab pining on his bed, refusing to eat, shows that Jezebel was the real power behind the throne. She abused that power and manipulated events to get her way. Like Potiphar's wife, she manufactured a lie that led to the persecution of an innocent man. But in this story, the victim died.

Jezebel certainly instigated and carried out some nefarious deeds. But because of the particular time and place in which she lived, her infamy swelled to archetypal proportions. She was a worshiper of the nature god Baal and of Asherah, the Canaanite fertility goddess. Eight hundred and fifty of their prophets ate at Jezebel's table (18:19). Their cult was perceived as one of the greatest threats to the faith of Israel.

Elijah arranged a showdown on Mount Carmel between Baal and

the God of Israel. The prophets of Baal prepared a bull and called on their god to set it on fire. They cried out, danced around the altar, even cut themselves with swords and lances until they bled, but nothing happened. Then Elijah built an altar, prepared the bull, and even doused it with water three times. He called out to the God of Israel. The fire not only consumed the bull and the altar but also licked up the water that had fallen into a trench around it (18:20–40). After this, the people returned to their God. Elijah killed all the prophets of Baal. Jezebel's death threat against him was her response.

The contest on Carmel culminated a longstanding and uncompromising war between the Israelites and the nature religion of the tribes around them. The Canaanite religion included powerful goddesses, female-dominated ceremonies of worship, and fertility cults. The Old Testament rejection of female symbols for God was likely rooted in the struggle against this influence. In the process of distancing Israel's faith from the nature religions, femaleness was deemed carnal and inferior. Women, whose bodily rhythms were seen as connected to the cycles of the moon, were pronounced "nature." Men were viewed as "spirit" and therefore possessors of superior faith and intellect. Women were considered suspect as leaders, in both religion and government.

Jezebel was easily cast as the foreign seductress who corrupted a king of Israel. She was the perfect target for patriarchal biblical religion. Her sensuality was seen as a threat to the purity of the religion of Israel. Like Potiphar's wife and Delilah, Jezebel fueled the negative stereotypes of women.

Herodias is Jezebel's New Testament counterpart. She was a woman who left one husband in order to marry his brother. John the Baptist had denounced this adulterous marriage, and Herodias held a grudge. Like Jezebel, she was likely a sensual woman, who encouraged her daughter to be the same. Historians have named the daughter Salome. Richard Strauss's opera *Salomé* depicts a young woman covered with veils, moving erotically and tossing them off one by one under the lustful gaze of Herod.

Whatever the actual form of Salome's dance was, so pleased was Herod by her performance that he promised his stepdaughter whatever she wanted, even up to half of his kingdom. Under her mother's influence, she made a ghastly request. John the Baptist, a prophet of God, was beheaded at Herodias's whim, his head brought in on a platter. We hear no more of Herodias in scripture, although legend has it that she died in exile and disgrace with her husband in Spain.

Jezebel's end, on the other hand, is unforgettable. She looked death in the face with her painted eyes, flamboyant to the finish. Jehu, the new king, was determined to rid the kingdom of Jezebel and all her family. Ahab and her two sons had already died. Jezebel fell to a most ignominious end.

Unfortunately, what she represented did not die with her. The word *jezebel* appears in the dictionary, defined as a scheming, wicked woman. This complicated queen's legacy lives on, three thousand years after her gruesome death. And the stereotypes of women as temptresses and manipulators endure as well.

Part 3. Questions for Reflection

1. How did the biblical women in this section make you feel?

2. Do you have any sympathy for the choices that any of the women in the biblical stories made? Why?

3. Are there instances in your own life when you acted out of your woundedness to hurt or manipulate others?

4. Which biblical woman in this section do you believe did the most to reinforce negative stereotypes about women? Why do you think she acted as she did?

5. Do you believe women are vulnerable to being unfairly accused of treachery, guile, or manipulation when, in fact, they act from personal strength or faith?

PART 4
Women in Relation to Men of Power

This section shows an array of responses to men who rule. Bathsheba could not escape a king's lust, but Vashti boldly refused to be exploited in the palace. Esther saved her people, the queen of Sheba made a daring and extravagant journey, and Claudia took her disturbing dream to the high court.

Each story highlights the difference in power between these women and the men around them who made decisions that shaped history. But each woman used the power available to her in an effort to make a difference for herself or her people. In the fascinating world of thrones and scepters, of opulent palaces and kingly caravans, the humble voices of women speak of compassion and justice.

16 Bathsheba: Used by a King

SCRIPTURE: 2 Sam. 11:1–15, 26–27; 12:15–18; 1 Kings 1:1–4, 11–21, 29–31

It happened, late one afternoon, when David rose from his couch and was walking about on the roof of the king's house, that he saw from the roof a woman bathing; the woman was very beautiful. . . . So David sent messengers to get her, and she came to him, and he lay with her. (2 Sam. 11:2, 4)

An intricate and astounding drama was set into motion by a king's lust. Having slept with and impregnated Bathsheba, a married woman, King David found himself in a desperate situation. He tried to extricate himself by arranging an unexpected furlough for Bathsheba's husband, Uriah.

It was likely an awkward scene when Uriah arrived. The king made small talk about the war and then encouraged Uriah to go to his wife, hoping his problem would be solved and no one would ever suspect that David was the father of Bathsheba's baby. But Uriah, a man of integrity, refused to revel in the comforts of home while the other soldiers were suffering the discomforts of war. David was forced to come up with plan B. He invited Uriah to stay with him in Jerusalem, filled him with wine, and tried again to convince him to go home to his wife. But still Uriah refused.

Backed into a corner of his own making, David arranged the soldier's death, even forcing Uriah unknowingly to carry the message of his own demise. Then, in what seems to be a bit of divine understatement, the scripture tells us, "The thing that David had done displeased the Lord" (2 Sam. 11:27).

The incident has gone down in faith history as "David's great sin." It apparently has never occurred to the biblical historians to call the incident "Bathsheba's great loss." With the exception of a brief notation that Bathsheba mourned the deaths of her husband and son, the thoughts and feelings, dreams and hopes, fears and strengths of Bathsheba appear nowhere in the story. And for nothing more than following the custom of purification after her period, she has been labeled by many biblical commentators "temptress," "adultress," and "seductress."

Set within a scenario of military intrigue and victory is this very

personal tragedy of a woman who is powerless to affect her own situation. Scripture gives her no identity apart from being the daughter of a
particular man and the wife of another. The only attribute assigned to
her is a physical attractiveness that arouses the lust of the king, who
uses his power to violate her and her marriage vow and then arranges
the death of her husband.

We can never know what resistance or willingness Bathsheba offered
to the king's demand. What we do know is that a woman of her time had
no right to say no to a king. She was a personal victim of the passions,
power, and prowess of a man infected with a foretaste of military victory
and a desire to conquer. Could she ever really love the king who had
taken her? Surely, at first she must have been plagued with ambivalence
about her situation, loving the child that she bore as part of her own
flesh and despising it for the sign that it was of her shame and pain. Did
she not wish that this baby were the child of her poor, fallen soldier
instead of a king? Did a day ever come when she whispered to herself, "I
want it to be a son; I want this child to have a life full of choices and not
a life full of pain"? Perhaps, as the child grew within her, the new life
became a sign of hope. Perhaps it even made the other sorrows bearable.
Perhaps, as old dreams died, she found room for joy.

But then tragedy struck. While the king fasted for the life of his son
and the elders rushed to his side, what quiet sorrow did Bathsheba feel
in her soul? What hatred for the sinner? Did she not cradle that dying
child and cry out to God for his life? In the frenzy of mourning, did
she not feel utterly alone with her grief?

I picture a heart torn in two. I picture a woman reflecting in that
broken heart, "No one can touch the pain of a woman who never even
had herself and now has lost everything."

After so much tragedy, Bathsheba's life appears to have taken a more
positive turn. She gave birth to Solomon and then to three other sons
fathered by David. She appears in the genealogy of Jesus (though
nameless as "the wife of Uriah" in Matt. 1:6) and was considered David's most favored wife. He clearly respected her, as is evidenced by her
intervention to guarantee Solomon the kingship after David's death
(1 Kings 1:17–18).

Interestingly, when Bathsheba went to David to make her request
on Solomon's behalf, the king was being attended by Abishag. This
young woman's presence is summed up in one paragraph:

> King David was old and advanced in years; and although they covered
> him with clothes, he could not get warm. So his servants said to him,
> "Let a young virgin be sought for my lord the king, . . . let her lie in

your bosom, so that my lord the king may be warm." So they searched for a beautiful girl throughout all the territory of Israel, and found Abishag the Shunammite, and brought her to the king. The girl was very beautiful. (1 Kings 1:1–4)

Scripture makes clear that Abishag and David did not have a sexual relationship; David was too old and infirm at that point. She was simply an attendant and an object to lie in his bed at night to keep him warm. She fulfilled the requirements for such a job: she was young, a virgin, and beautiful.

David's life ended much as this story began. From his palace roof, he spotted Bathsheba and made her an object, ignoring her feelings, her wishes, her humanity. And even as an old man, well past his sexual prime, he objectified another young woman, in a most literal way. She was nothing to him but a warm body in his bed.

Objectification underlies the current war against women in the United States. Rape and battery are its weapons, and pornography is its propaganda. Pornography is conservatively estimated as a booming $8 billion-a-year business in this country, with more than 165 pornographic magazines on the market and 13.8 million pornography readers. Of the ten most profitable magazines, six are "men's entertainment" magazines, with *Playboy* and *Penthouse* outselling *Time* and *Newsweek*.

Escalating brutality toward women has accompanied escalating profits in the pornography industry. From the Playboy "bunny" image to the depictions of macho acts of sadistic torture and bondage that are rampant in pornography, the message is the same: women must be made nonthreatening, either placated as pets or violently whipped into submission. In a recent study, researchers determined that 66 percent of the thousands of men interviewed had a "conquest mentality" toward women. As David S. Wells, editor and publisher of five men's magazines, put it, "Men don't want to be equal; it's as simple as that." [1]

Fortunately, Bathsheba moved beyond being only a victim of kingly abuse. Within the limits that bound her, she claimed her dignity and power, proving herself to be a woman and not an object. She modeled a way for every woman to turn tragedy into strength.

NOTES

1. Interviewed in *Not a Love Story*. Directed by Bonnie Klein. Produced by the National Film Board of Canada and Dorothy Todd Henault. Released by Esma Films, 1982.

17   Vashti: Refusing to Be Exploited

SCRIPTURE: Esther 1

> Queen Vashti refused to come at the king's command conveyed by the eunuchs. (Esth. 1:12)

Her husband was the most powerful monarch in the world at the time, ruler over 127 provinces. His wealth was legendary—as were his parties. For half a year, the soldiers and nobles and governors reveled in "the splendor and pomp of his majesty." Then he threw a weeklong banquet for the people, during which the drink flowed without end in a palace most exotic and ornate: gold everywhere—couches and goblets—and marble and gems to feast the eyes. It seems that people rarely said no to the king. He had expensive tastes, and he clearly enjoyed flaunting them. He also had the power and the wealth, as well as the people in his service, to get his way in all matters.

But then there was this woman. Her name was Vashti. She was his queen. She held her own party for the women, presumably a modest one since only fleeting mention is made of it.

After a week of nonstop eating and drinking, when the king and all the men in the palace were quite drunk, the king commanded his eunuchs to go fetch the queen. He wanted to parade her before the men, to show off her beauty. But something quite unprecedented and unexpected happened. The queen refused. She decided it was not in her best interest to parade before a hall of lustful, raucous, drunken men just to satisfy the command of one—even if he was the king, and her husband. She refused to be exploited.

This threw the palace into an uproar. The king was outraged. He had boasted about her to all of his friends, and she had disobeyed him. His honor and pride were at stake; and surely all of the women gathered at the palace were watching Vashti. He feared subversion throughout the kingdom. What if other women got the same idea, that they could defy their husbands? What if noble ladies began snickering behind the backs of the king's officials? What if men were no longer in control? Well, indeed, there would be "no end of contempt and wrath!" Something had to be done. Call the sages.

Now, perhaps there was already a little trouble in the kingdom. This issue of female insubordination must already have surfaced, or there would not have been such fear. The sparks had to be snuffed out before they became a forest fire. And so there went out a royal decree. Men are in charge, just in case you women forgot, just in case you have any silly notions and start to get a little out of hand. A woman's place is in the home—but the man is master there. And watch out for what happens if you ever step out of line. Vashti was never heard from again.

Meanwhile, King Ahasuerus wasted no time in lining up all of the beautiful young virgins in the kingdom to find himself a new wife. But that is a story to be told in the next chapter, when we get to Esther.

I love Vashti. I consider her the real heroine of the book of Esther. She was a woman who had her dignity and knew her convictions, rather than her place. And she was courageous enough not to compromise. Despite Memucan's declaration, there was none "better than she." And perhaps, there at her party, a young woman or two saw her example, decided to live by her convictions in her own way, then passed the courage on. Perhaps one was even named Esther.

On first glance, it would be difficult to find a woman more unlike Vashti than Sojourner Truth. One was a queen who lived in a luxurious palace; the other, a slave who never had a home of her own. One refused to stand before a gathering of men; the other refused to keep her seat.

In 1852, while she was lecturing against slavery around the country, Sojourner Truth stopped in at a women's rights convention in Akron, Ohio. Dressed in a plain, gray dress and a sunbonnet, this tall, gaunt woman made a stir as she marched up the aisle of the church where the meeting was held and took a seat on the pulpit steps. She remained still as various ministers spoke vehemently against the rights of women, declaring that Jesus Christ was a man and that Eve had brought sin into the world. But after a few hours, she could stay silent no longer. A hissing rush of disapproval greeted her as she stepped to the pulpit.

Sojourner Truth wheeled around to face one of the earlier speakers. "That man over there says that women need to be helped into carriages, and lifted over ditches, and to have the best place everywhere. Nobody ever helped *me* into carriages, or over mud puddles, or gave *me* any best place. And ain't *I* a woman?" Her voice grew more fervent. "Look at me. Look at my arm. I have plowed and planted and gathered into barns and no man could head me—and ain't *I* a woman?"

A murmur surged through the crowd, and Sojourner's voice thundered on. "I have borne five children and seen them most all sold off into slavery, and when I cried out with mother's grief, none but Jesus heard—and ain't *I* a woman?"

The crowd began to rock the church with applause and cheers, pointing scornful fingers at the ministers they had applauded just moments before. Sojourner straightened tall and continued.

"Then that little man in black there, he says women can't have as much rights as man, 'cause Christ wasn't a woman. Where did your Christ come from?" She repeated the question, her words thundering once more. "*Where did your Christ come from?*" She paused a moment, then gathered all the force of her voice. "From God and a woman! Man had nothing to do with him!" Glorious pandemonium broke loose in the church. But Sojourner was still not through.

She turned to the man who had mentioned Eve. "If the first woman God ever made was strong enough to turn the world upside down, all alone—these together ought to be able to turn it back and get it rightside up again. And now that they are asking to do it, the men better let 'em." She took her seat amid deafening cheers.[1]

And so we cheer women who refuse to let men—whether husbands or ministers or kings—"head" them. Ain't they some women?

NOTES

1. Arthur Huff Fauset, *Sojourner Truth: God's Faithful Pilgrim* (Chapel Hill: University of North Carolina Press, 1938).

18   Esther: A Queen
Saves Her People

Scripture: Esther 2—10

Then Esther said, " . . . I will go to the king, though it is
against the law; and if I perish, I perish." (Esth. 4:15–16)

Esther is one of only two women with books of the Bible
named after them, the other being Ruth. Her name appears fifty-five
times in scripture, more than any other woman's. She is considered a
heroine of legendary proportion.

Esther—"Hadassah" in Hebrew—was young and innocent when
her guardian cousin handed her over to the palace. No more than
fourteen or fifteen years old, she was not quite a girl but barely a
woman. She was brought in with all the other fair virgins and subjected
to a year of intensive cosmetic treatment with oils and perfumes. That
year and the days following must have been much like a protracted
modern-day beauty pageant with intense rivalry in the evening gown
and swimsuit competitions. But this time, the final test was not poise
and articulation during a brief interview; the "winner" was the girl who
satisfied and "delighted" the king in bed.

It is hard to imagine the damage done to the self-esteem of all those
vulnerable teenaged girls, waiting to see if they had performed well
enough in their first sexual experience to be recalled by the king. Hundreds of young women from all over the kingdom had been rounded
up for this degrading ritual of picking the next queen. How many
prayed to be chosen? And how many prayed to be set free?

Esther won the crown. But after a big banquet, the royal treatment
for her was limited. She had no real power. She shared her husband
with hundreds of other women, and she could go to him only when he
summoned her. Sometimes a month went by without her seeing him.

Esther grew up quickly, her innocence transformed into courage
when the lives of her people came under threat. She offered one of the
bravest declarations in all of scripture: "I will go to the king, though it
is against the law; and if I perish, I perish."

She was deeply spiritual for one so young. She knew that she alone
was able to bargain for the lives of her people, accepting Mordecai's

words, "Perhaps you have come to royal dignity for just such a time as this" (Esth. 4:14). She also knew that she needed the support of her people and her God, and she called for a three-day fast among all of the Jews in Susa. She herself kept the fast as spiritual preparation for her approach to the king.

Esther was also shrewd. She paved the way for her petition by gaining the confidence of Ahasuerus and Haman at her banquets. She let Haman believe that he was one of her "chosen" ones. In Haman, she had an enemy with an ego the size of Persia. He had a hobby of bragging about his riches, his sons, his promotions, his connections. One Jew's refusal to bow to him—one man who "neither rose nor trembled before him" (5:9)—triggered his death threat against all the Jews in the kingdom.

It is hard not to take pleasure in the picture of Haman, trapped by his own words, leading his mortal enemy Mordecai around the square on the back of a horse—or throwing himself on the couch and blithering away to Esther, pleading for his pathetic life. The greatest irony of all was his death on the gallows that he himself had built for the hanging of Mordecai.

Haman was no match for Esther. The courage of a strong woman conquered the power of a wicked man. The Jews lived to tell about it. And for two days every March, Jews still celebrate the Feast of Purim, twenty-four centuries after the woman whose name means "star" saved the lives of her people by risking her own.

We cannot leave this story without pausing for a moment to mourn the seventy-five thousand people who were massacred by the Jews on the day that they themselves had been destined for annihilation. As often happens, an endangered people turned their fear into vengeance.

From the annals of our own nation comes an example of a threatened people who held steadfastly to the principles of nonviolence and upheld the dignity of all humanity. In the late summer of 1993, I was sitting next to eighty-four-year-old Flora Smith in Sixteenth Street Baptist Church in Birmingham, Alabama. Thirty years before, a bomb had been planted by the Ku Klux Klan below a staircase along the outside wall of this church.

It was September 15, 1963, Youth Sunday, 10:22 A.M. The Sunday school hour was just finishing. Denise McNair, Addie Mae Collins, Cynthia Wesley, and Carole Robertson were in the ladies' lounge, getting ready to serve in the choir and as ushers for the church service. When the bomb exploded, the four girls were killed instantly.

Just a few months before, the church had been at the center of the struggle for desegregation in Birmingham, which had suffered so many racist bombings that the city had been nicknamed "Bombingham." The attention of the world became riveted on Birmingham when Police Commissioner Bull Connor unleashed vicious dogs and water cannons on the city's children as they peacefully marched for freedom. Birmingham's courageous children made history; public pressure forced city officials to reform harsh segregation laws.

Flora Smith decided in her own way to make history as well. She handed me a copy of a newspaper article from 1963. It explained that a conviction against her had been overturned. She told me the story.

The day before Mother's Day in 1963, she woke up and told herself, "I'm going to go to jail today and be somebody's mother tomorrow." She packed her bag with a toothbrush and her white dress and headed downtown. During the freedom march from the church, she broke away and went to the steps of City Hall. "Since I had a Bible, they didn't stop me," she said. "I just bowed down and started praying."

Flora Smith was eventually arrested for blocking the sidewalk and spent eight days in jail. She coordinated devotions and Bible studies for the two hundred other women there, many of whom had been swept off the streets by the police without warning and separated from their children. I asked her if she had been afraid. She smiled and said, "I didn't know what my husband would say—he was out of town." He was a pastor who was uninvolved in the civil rights movement.

Flora Smith told me that it was the story of Esther that inspired her to act. She knew her role in the jail was one of providing comfort and courage. "God had a reason for me being there," she said, just as God had had a mission for Esther. Five months later, her conviction was overturned when the court redefined "sidewalk" so that it did not include the City Hall steps.

Flora Smith's grandfather had been a slave. She was orphaned at age nine and finished only the seventh grade in school. But in 1983, when she was seventy-four years old, she enrolled in Miles College in Birmingham. Five years later, she became the college's oldest graduate. "I was so proud," she said, "I went to my room and wept."

We were in Sixteenth Street Baptist Church together at a service that included members of the church and of the Baptist Peace Fellowship of North America. Toward the end of the service, I looked over at her as the strains of "Oh Freedom" filled the sanctuary. Flora Smith's hands were folded, and her eyes were looking toward heaven. Her face looked transcendent, with a glow of dignity and pride. She was the first person to stand when the congregation began singing "We Shall Overcome." Arms crossed and hands clasped around the sanctuary.

When the singing was over, I asked her if in 1963 she had ever thought that thirty years later, blacks and whites would be sitting in that church together, singing freedom songs. Tears welled in her eyes as she said, "Praise the good Lord, I never thought I'd see this day."

19 The Queen of Sheba: An Adventurous and Audacious Ruler

SCRIPTURE: 1 Kings 10:1–13 (2 Chron. 9:1–12); Matt. 12:42 (Luke 11:31)

[The queen of Sheba] came to Jerusalem with a very great retinue, with camels bearing spices, and very much gold, and precious stones; and when she came to Solomon, she told him all that was on her mind. (1 Kings 10:2)

The story of the queen of Sheba's visit to King Solomon is an exotic tale—many would say erotic as well. Legends abound about the great affair these two had during her stay in Jerusalem. Ethiopian kings traced their lineage to a union between the two. Given Solomon's sexual appetite (legend has it that he had 1,005 wives and concubines), his attraction to foreign women, and both the queen's charisma and the awe in which she held him, it is not difficult to believe that they exchanged more than gifts and clever words. He did, after all, fulfill "every desire that she expressed" (1 Kings 10:13).

She likely resembled the "queenly maiden" so sensuously described in the Song of Solomon: "black and beautiful," "stately as a palm tree"; her neck encircled with strings of jewels and her skin fragrant with oil; her hair with "flowing locks . . . like purple; a king is held captive in the tresses" (S. of Sol. 1:5, 10; 4:10; 7:1, 5, 7). Perhaps this bearer of fragrant seasonings even said to the king words like those that close the Song of Solomon: "Make haste, my beloved, and be like a gazelle or a young stag upon the mountains of spices!" (8:14).

The story of her bold visit is recorded twice in scripture, as is Jesus' gospel affirmation that, even as a nonbeliever, the queen of Sheba recognized the wisdom of Solomon and the power of God. She traveled from western Arabia, an arduous journey of some twelve hundred miles over mostly desert terrain, with a caravan laden with treasures. Known as a clever woman, she went all that way to test the king's wisdom and to see if the stories she had heard about him were true.

She spoke her mind. And she posed riddles to him. An example from a Jewish legend says, "The Queen said, 'Seven depart. Nine

83

enter. Two pour. One drinks.' Solomon replied, 'Seven days represents the period of a woman's menstruation; nine months the period of her pregnancy; two pouring is a reference to her breasts; and one drinking, a reference to her baby.' "[1]

The queen of Sheba had enough poise and aplomb to visit a faraway king, to match wits and wealth with him. Before long, scripture says, "there was no more spirit in her" (1 Kings 10:5)—she was breathless with amazement. A proud woman, she was also humble enough to concede that Solomon's glory was even greater than she had imagined and that his God was worthy to be praised.

She was a premier diplomat. Solomon's expansion in trade and commerce followed her visit. She gave him glorious gifts out of her own wealth: gold (equivalent to almost $4 million by current U.S. standards, according to biblical scholars), precious stones, and more spices than the kingdom had ever seen in one place. But more important, she is an example of womanhood that is daring, self-confident, and sensual. The queen of Sheba was a woman at ease with herself and with her world.

In other ages also, women have confronted male authority with creativity and daring. Walking boldly into corridors of power to match wits and wisdom, women have changed the world. And most of them have done so without the queen of Sheba's wealth, status, or physical attributes.

Gay Martin lives in Dante, a small town in the coalfields of southwest Virginia. It was named by coal company operators years ago, who said it looked like their image of Dante's inferno. The townspeople say the coal companies made the town look that way, and as a sign of their rebellion, they pronounce their town's name "Daint."

As a young girl, Gay peddled milk and butter. Later she cleaned houses and worked as a janitor at a high school. She frequently nursed people who were ill, applying mustard plasters and onion poultices in the Appalachian tradition. "There's not much I haven't done," she told me. "And had it not been for the union," she added, "our patches would have been patched, and that patch would have been patched."

Gay's family has been connected to the United Mine Workers of America (UMWA) for four generations. Her father was injured in the coal mines and died at the age of forty-eight. Her brother survived the invasion of southern France during World War II, only to come home and die in the mines less than a year later.

Gay's husband, Gilmer, worked as a miner for thirty-nine-and-a-half years. In 1962, two of his fingers were cut off in a mine accident. Fifteen years later, he crippled his back. He also developed pneumoconiosis, or "black lung," a common ailment among miners. Coal dust coats the lungs of a victim, making breathing extremely labored; the heart enlarges to compensate for lack of oxygen, eventually giving out from the stress. In the spring of 1987, Gilmer had a stroke.

In February 1988, fifteen hundred widows, pensioners, and disabled miners received word from the Pittston Coal Company that the medical benefits promised to them for life under a 1974 agreement were terminated. Gilmer Martin was among those who were left stranded by the company's action. Gay joined other miners and their families in a UMWA strike that rocked southwest Virginia.

On April 25, 1989, she sat down in the middle of a road and blocked a coal truck. She and several other women were arrested and loaded onto a van. "It was eighty-two degrees outside," she said, "and the van had been closed up all day. They put us in there—stuck us in like sardines—shut the doors, and turned the heat on us. It was cruel—very cruel."

Gay had a heart condition, and she asked the state troopers in the van to let in some air. They ignored her. Then she asked if they could stop at a custard stand for a little refreshment. The troopers were not amused, she reported. "So I told the women, 'Let's sing some songs and maybe that will sort of soften their hearts.' And I started 'Amazing Grace.'

"I've always been a law-abiding citizen," Gay continued. "I haven't even received a ticket for driving. But I don't feel like this was breaking the law. This was a new experience for me, being hauled off to jail, but I was proud to go."

Gay said of the state trooper who arrested her, "I asked him did he mind telling me what I was charged with, and he said 'Misdemeanor.' I said, 'That's right. I am a miss, and tomorrow I'll be de meaner.' " When he asked for her name, Gay told him, "The thirty-sixth daughter of Mother Jones." The women had named themselves after Mary Harris "Mother" Jones, who was first arrested for her union activities at the age of seventy-two and was once called "the most dangerous woman in America." At the turn of the century, Mother Jones organized "mop and broom brigades" of women who kept watch at the mines to protect their husbands' jobs during strikes, brooms in one hand and babies in the other. She offered immortal words on which to build the union movement: "Pray for the dead, and fight like hell for the living!"[2]

Probably the most daring action of Gay and the other Daughters of Mother Jones was their sit-in at the Pittston offices. Pittston officials "claimed that they had all this security and that nobody could get in,"

Gay said. "Those security guards were pure thugs. They wore these bulletproof vests and these big leather gloves up to their elbows."

Thirty-nine women broke through Pittston's tight security one morning at ten o'clock. "We were there in the lobby," said Gay, "and we were all sitting down. We wore camouflage scarves, a white carnation, and a little miniature flag in our hand. And here comes this prissy lady out of one of the offices. She says, 'May I help you?' So we all started waving our flags and singing. And then the little prissy lady ran and told one of the men that was there, and he came out and his mouth flew open about that large. They put up their little privacy screen there to keep from seeing us, and we just sang."

The Daughters of Mother Jones spent the night singing in the Pittston office. The next morning at seven o'clock, Gay had to leave. She had promised to distribute garden seeds to low-income families that day through the We Care Food Bank, which she founded and ran. One of the reporters outside asked her, "Are you giving up?"

She replied, "No way! I'll be back. . . . There's a need for me on the other side of the mountain."

The reporter told her, "They won't let you back in."

Gay replied, "You don't know how many wigs I've got." She explained, "I was gonna come home after I got through and put on a dark wig and all kinds of change in makeup and a pair of sunglasses, and go back in and ask for a job." But as soon as Gay got home, her "crisis phone" rang, a line she has for whenever anyone in the community has an emergency food need or a problem to talk over. Gay was needed back at the Pittston office immediately; a woman who was seven-and-a-half months pregnant and had spent the night there with the other women had become ill. Gay went back, and she and a couple of other women looked up the hill at a special security guard. "And I told 'em," said Gay, " 'Now when we get there, we'll eyeball him.' And we joined hands and went back up the hill and got our sisters out of the 'Pittston Hotel.' "

A few weeks later, a busload of miners and their families were on a fifteen-hour trek from southwest Virginia to Greenwich, Connecticut, the "corporate capital of America." They were headed to the annual shareholders' meeting of the Pittston Coal Company to plead for a reinstatement of their health benefits and a new contract for the miners.

Paul Douglas—chairman, president, and chief executive officer of the Pittston corporation, salaried at $625,000 annually—brought the meeting to order. More than four hundred picketers from coal mining towns in four states kept a vigil outside in the pouring rain. The discussion inside was heated, with Paul Douglas pleading for reason and moderation from the miners.

Gay Martin had been trying to get the chairman's attention for almost an hour. Finally, he recognized her. With her voice quaking, she stood and spoke about Gilmer, about his years of backbreaking service in the mines and his current difficulty simply walking. In a passionate plea, she said, "We are humans, and we have human needs. I appeal to you to be human and return our rights." Paul Douglas responded glibly by talking about the competitiveness of the coal market. Gay interrupted him and said, "Don't you think men who have given their lives should have medical benefits?"

Douglas replied defensively, "This is the kind of rhetoric that doesn't represent the facts."

Back on the bus, a union organizer walked to the front and picked up the bus's microphone. "If I were running the world," he said, "I'd put Gay Martin in charge. And if Paul Douglas is making $625,000, I'd double that for her!"

A cheer went up from the crowded bus. Gay took over the microphone and said gently, "I think they have lost their ears—and I wonder how they live without hearts."

Later, speaking of the long struggle for justice, Gay said to me, "We're poor people, but we're proud people. The good Lord gives us the knowledge to stand up for what is right. If you don't stand up for your true convictions, you'll fall for anything. And I'm not gonna fall. I'm standing for my husband, 'cause he can't stand long."

Several months later, the Pittston Coal Company signed a contract with the United Mine Workers. Hampered by the strike and the adverse publicity surrounding it, the company was forced to the negotiating table. The boldness of Gay Martin and the other Daughters of Mother Jones played a part in making labor history. They had no wealth to offer—no spices, no gold or precious stones, as the queen of Sheba did, to pave their way to the powerful. But like that famous queen, they were clever, creative, and audacious. They walked into the corridors of power uninvited and took a stand. They carried the only gifts they had: heart, soul, and conscience. And the powerful had to take notice.

NOTES

1. Miriam Therese Winter, *WomanWitness*, (New York: Crossroad, 1992), 73.
2. Mary Field Parton, *The Autobiography of Mother Jones* (Chicago: Charles H. Kerr, 1974), 41.

20   Claudia: Intrepid Intervener

Scripture: Matt. 27:11–26

While [Pilate] was sitting on the judgment seat, his wife sent word to him, "Have nothing to do with that innocent man, for today I have suffered a great deal because of a dream about him." (Matt. 27:19)

She appears in only one verse in the Bible, and there she remains unnamed. But Greek Orthodox believers have canonized her as Saint Claudia and mark October 27 as her feast day. She says only twenty-two words in the scripture, but those words make her unique among all the people on the scene in Jesus' last hours. She was the only person to advocate his innocence.

In the hours preceding Jesus' appearance before Pilate, a conspiracy of male power and fear was propelling history toward the cross. Judas collaborated with the chief priests and betrayed Jesus with a kiss; Peter denied him three times; the high priest proclaimed him a blasphemer; the armed chief priests and elders bound him and delivered him to the governor for final judgment.

And there, into the highest court, Claudia sent word. She was a woman who trusted her dreams. She had been spoken to in imagery which told her that Jesus was righteous, and she had suffered with the knowledge. So, in the only way she could, she penetrated the bastion of male power—right to the judgment seat with her own judgment.

We can imagine her back in the governor's mansion, wringing her hands, fearful that things have gone too far but determined to do what she can to save an innocent man's life. Her husband had talked with Jesus, had witnessed the calm demeanor and unthreatening dignity with which he faced a barrage of accusations and the inevitability of his own death. Only Pilate could save him now; only the governor had the power to release a prisoner during the feast. She had to get through to him.

But Pilate left the choice up to the people. Would it be the notorious criminal Barabbas, or Jesus, the one who claimed to be the Messiah? The people, under the influence of jealous religious authorities who vigorously worked the crowd, shouted out their answer, demanding the crucifixion of Jesus. But Pilate had his doubts; those words from Claudia were still echoing in his mind. "But what evil has he done?" he asked the people. Still they clamored, more loudly, and Pilate feared a riot. With great drama and a bit of water, he washed his hands of the affair and declared that he was innocent of Jesus' blood.

If only, like his wife, he had wrung his hands rather than washed them. He took the cowardly option. Pilate refused to condemn Jesus, but he was not courageous enough to use his power to quell the escalating evil. The conspiracy rolled on; one woman's word was not enough to stop the march toward death.

From another era, across time and the globe, comes the story of women who sent word to their husbands in places of power—with a different result. Told to me by members of a Christian base community in Mexico, the story begins with a group of peasants in rural Brazil. They are being threatened with eviction from their small plot of land, so that the government can take the land and use it for a government project. This has happened before, and the outcome is always the same: the parliament declares the land government property; the people are forced out; and when they try to resist, some of them are killed by government soldiers. Fear is running high among the peasants. Their resistance has failed before. But if they leave, they abandon yet another harvest, and their hungry children will die.

The women offer a courageous solution. They gather up their children and journey into the city. Each mother finds the home of a member of parliament and sits on the front lawn. They are an odd sight, these ragged women and their hungry children, out of place in the city's wealthy districts, on its luxuriant lawns.

Soon the wives of the parliament members, whose husbands are off at work, send the servants out with bread. "We have not come here for bread," the poor mothers say, sending the servants away. Then the wives send the servants back out with money. "We do not want your money," they reply. After a while, overcome with curiosity or irritation, the wives themselves come out and ask the mothers why they are there. "We are going to die," the mothers tell them. "And this is such a nice place, we thought we would die here."

This personal encounter with tragedy raises concern in the wives. They ask questions of the mothers and soon learn of the government's theft of their land. Before long, the phones are ringing off the hook at the parliament, as husbands are barraged with the pleas of modern-day Claudias.

These men listened. No law passed in parliament to take away the peasants' land that day. The power of women transformed a sentence of death into an affirmation of life, born out of courage and compassion.

Part 4. Questions for Reflection

1. Which biblical woman in this section do you find the most interesting? Why?

2. What emotional conflicts do you think Bathsheba, Esther, and Claudia felt? What opinion did you form of the queen of Sheba as you read her story?

3. How did kingly power affect the men in the biblical stories? How did the power of women impact them?

4. How do you feel about power? Do you desire it, fear it, pursue it, avoid it? Do you believe that power can be used for good?

5. Do you know of any instances of backlash against women claiming their power, as in the case of the male officials' response to Vashti?

PART 5

Clever and
Courageous Heroines

In times of war and political upheaval, heroes and heroines always emerge. From among the crowd of those who would cower at oppressive power come courageous voices defending justice and advocating defiance.

Two humble midwives took on the mighty pharaoh. A prostitute provided safe haven. Wives of a king averted bloodshed. And three shrewd women stepped forward to vanquish powerful foes. Undeterred by fear, threats, or patriarchal assumptions about their place, biblical women changed the course of history. And their modern-day sisters, in all corners of the world, are doing the same.

21   Puah and Shiphrah: Defying Pharaoh

SCRIPTURE: Ex. 1:8–22

The midwives feared God; they did not do as the king of Egypt commanded them, but they let the boys live. (Ex. 1:17)

I have often thought that if I ever had a daughter (and if I didn't think she would spend her whole life explaining and spelling it), I would name her Puah or Shiphrah. I love these women! They are competent, courageous, and quick-witted.

I picture them as close friends, bound by their commitment to bringing forth life during a difficult time, when the life of the people of God was "bitter with hard service" (Ex. 1:14). Theirs is a vocation of hope, of possibility and promise for the future. The two were probably the principal midwives, under whom many others served, to a nation of almost two million people. How many women had they personally comforted and encouraged in childbirth? How many squalling babies did they bring into the world? We can never know, but I imagine them moving among the tents, a gentle and strong presence, an anchor for women whose time had come to deliver.

The Egyptians, once slaves of the Israelites (as in the case of Hagar), had become their enslavers. Pharaoh, fearful at the growth and strength of the Israelites, devised an abhorrent plan to resolve his dilemma. He ordered Puah and Shiphrah to destroy all the male children born to the Hebrew women. The female children were considered of such little consequence as to be no threat—a striking irony, since his plan was ultimately thwarted by two Hebrew women.

Certainly, pharaoh's edict was meant to instill fear and to force compliance, for his oppressive authority was legendary. Who are two simple midwives in the face of such power? But Puah and Shiphrah, fearing God but not the Egyptian king, chose life for those around them. Perhaps they discussed it together at length, weighing the cost, for certainly they were risking their own lives by their disobedience. Or maybe their strength of conscience led each to know right away that there was no choice but to refuse pharaoh's order. At any rate, they tenderly caught all the male children along with the female as they came into the world.

They must have rehearsed their story, knowing that they would be called to the palace for their defiance. When the king confronted them, they had the audacity to say (perhaps with a suppressed smile, even as they faced this ruthless ruler), "These Hebrew women are not like the weak, pampered Egyptian women; they are vigorous—they have their children before we can even get to them!" I picture pharaoh's face flushing red, put in his place by two shrewd women. But he did not take vengeance; the scripture tells us that, for their faith, God preserved Puah and Shiphrah and blessed them with many children of their own.

I met a descendant of Puah and Shiphrah in the spring of 1988. She lives in Soweto, the sprawling black township in South Africa, where the brutal repression of modern-day pharaohs also has been legendary. Here, children of life, who joined the struggle for their freedom, have faced arrest, torture, and death.

Albertina Sisulu lives next to a school, and her door has always been open to the children fleeing when police would storm the schoolyard. The children would jump the fence and fill up her house, knowing that she would not open the door to the police, even when they arrived with guns drawn. Sisulu has known many of the children from birth, for she serves her people as a nurse and midwife. For years, she has gone among the shacks in the townships and squatter camps—the corrugated-iron and cardboard homes built on dust and ashes—to usher new life into a frightening world.

"It's terrible, especially in places like the shacks," she said. "There's only one room. The mother has, say, five children. And she is going to have a baby in that room. It's perhaps midnight; the children can't be taken out of the shack. All you can do is get a blanket, and somebody must hold the blanket at the ends to shield the woman. . . . There is no water. There is nothing. This poor woman is cold. And soon you just hear the baby crying."

Albertina Sisulu has been midwife to a movement, as more and more of these children who took their first breath under apartheid have grown up to join the struggle for freedom. She herself has known that struggle intimately. As early as 1952, during a nationwide Defiance Campaign, she became involved in resistance to apartheid. In 1956, she was a leader of a massive women's protest. That was the year that the South African government made the mistake of trying to force women to carry passes, the dreaded form of racial control and discrimination. Twenty thousand women from all over South Africa converged on the prime minister's office in Pretoria. There they sang the defiant chant that for four decades has been the rallying cry of South Africa's women's movement: *Wathint' Abafazi, Wathint' Imbokotho*—"You have struck the women, you have struck the rock."

For Albertina Sisulu, government persecution has been the normal fare of life. For seventeen years she was "banned," prohibited from writing or speaking publicly and restricted in whom she could see and what meetings she could attend. She spent ten years under house arrest and has been tried for treason and imprisoned repeatedly, once with her son. So threatening was she to the defenders of apartheid that when the South African government banned seventeen anti-apartheid organizations just days before I met her, it singled her out and gave her individual restrictions.

In 1964, her husband, Walter Sisulu, was sentenced to life imprisonment in the same trial that put Nelson Mandela behind bars; he was released with Mandela in 1990, after spending twenty-six years in jail. Of the Sisulus' eight children, two have been imprisoned and three have lived in exile outside of South Africa. Speaking of her youngest daughter, Albertina Sisulu said, "It was worst when they arrested her, the little one. We couldn't see her for almost a year. We didn't know where she was. And when she came out of jail, she was mentally affected because they were torturing her. She has long hair, and she told me, 'Mama, they would pull me by my hair and knock me against the wall. And I would pass out, Mama.'

"That makes you feel you must work harder to see the end of apartheid. . . . That is why I'll never bow down to any orders from the government. That is why I'm prepared to go on with the struggle until the last day of my life."

That promise, echoed by many other voices, has put fear into the hearts of the pharaohs of this age. They feel threatened, Sisulu said, because "they are a minority ruling a majority." Like the pharaoh of Egypt, they tremble at the strength of a people rising up to claim their freedom.

Albertina Sisulu is a woman who has experienced overwhelming losses. Yet her eyes sparkle with life, and her heart overflows with radiant hope. "I wouldn't be alive if I weren't staying with God," she told me. "If you believe in him, you're never disappointed." She stated her steadfast belief that, one day soon, South Africa would be "a democratic, nonracial, peaceful country." She explained, "My hope is based on the world's history; there's nothing without an end. I pray to God that one day I will see my people free." She added with conviction, "In the Bible there is no black and white. God calls us his children—all of us."

Six years later, Albertina Sisulu's dream came true in a most poignant way. History was made as black South Africans went to the polls for the first time. Some of the elderly were carried on the backs of family members and friends, and most voters had to wait in long lines for hours to cast their ballots. Dignity and patient determination were written on their faces.

On May 10, 1994, Nelson Mandela was inaugurated as the first black president of South Africa. In the light of a glorious sun, President Mandela took the oath of office. He was sworn in by a woman who had earned the right to bestow on him the power of the people. Albertina Sisulu beamed with pride as all the world watched. And today, the once-persecuted midwife of a movement takes her place in the South African parliament.

Six years ago, such change seemed impossible to imagine. But the proud hope and brave sacrifice of many South Africans transformed history. Confronted with such courage and faith, the pharaohs of this age had to listen.

22 Rahab: Hiding the Enemy

SCRIPTURE: Joshua 2; 6:1–5, 15–25; Heb. 11:30–31; James 2:24–25

Then the king of Jericho sent orders to Rahab, "Bring out the men who have come to you, who entered your house. . . . " But the woman took the two men and hid them. (Josh. 2:3–4)

It was not a crimson cord like the one tied by Rahab—a symbol of life preserved—that appeared on the door of a parish house in El Salvador in November 1980. It was quite the opposite: a message of death. The crude sign depicted a bloody human head with a knife embedded in it and the words "This is what will happen to anyone who comes to this house because the priests and nuns are communists."

One of the nuns who lived there was Ita Ford, a Maryknoll sister who had spent eight years in Chile before responding to an urgent call for U.S. missionaries to come to El Salvador. The tiny Central American country whose name means "the Savior" was engulfed in violence after the assassination of Archbishop Oscar Romero in March 1980.

It was said by a friend of Ita that "her twinkling eyes and elfin grin would surface irrepressibly even in the midst of poverty and sorrow."[1] Ita was soon joined by Maura Clarke, also a Maryknoll sister, who was known in Nicaragua as "the angel of our land" during the years that she served there. Upon her arrival in El Salvador, Ita described Maura to her family as "very Irish," with a "huge, loving, warm heart. For all these people who come in who are traumatized, or who have been hiding, scared for their lives—I just think Maura's going to be God's gift to them."[2]

On the evening of December 2, 1980, Ita and Maura were returning to El Salvador from a Maryknoll regional conference in Nicaragua. They were met at the airport by Dorothy Kazel, an Ursuline sister, and Jean Donovan, a lay church worker. Together, these latter two were widely known as "The Rescue Squad" by other U.S. missionaries in El Salvador. From their base in La Libertad, the energetic and dauntless pair traveled the countryside in a white Toyota van, picking up supplies, transporting refugees, and accompanying grief-stricken families in search of disappeared loved ones. Jean, who serenaded her friends with Irish folk ballads on her guitar and gave children frequent rides on her motorcycle, had been dubbed "Saint Jean the Playful." Dorothy, quoting Augustine, had said she wanted to live as "an alleluia head to foot."[3]

On the morning of December 3, when the four women were unaccounted for, members of their mission team began a search. Two sisters found the remains of the white van, a stripped and burned-out shell, abandoned at the side of the road to the airport. The bodies of the four women were found by a milkman in a shallow grave in a cow pasture. At least two of the women had been raped before being killed.

When U.S. Ambassador Robert White asked the local justice of the peace why the deaths had not been reported, he answered simply, "This happens all the time." Indeed, in the decade after the deaths of Ita, Maura, Dorothy, and Jean, seventy-five thousand Salvadorans lost their lives in the violence, most at the hands of the military and right-wing death squads.

The four women had come to El Salvador fully aware of the risks. Ita had written to her younger sister, "You say you don't want anything to happen to me. I'd prefer it that way myself—but I don't see that we have control over the forces of madness. And if you choose to enter into other people's suffering, to love others, you at least have to consent in some way to the possible consequences."[4]

The work of the four women had nothing to do with communism, as their detractors accused; that was only the convenient pretext of the time. Ultimately, it was Matthew 25 that got these four women killed. It was that simple mandate to love the poor: to feed the hungry, clothe the naked, visit the sick and imprisoned, take in the homeless refugees. And in El Salvador, more and more loving the poor meant comforting the tortured and burying the dead. At the U.S. Embassy, the night before she was murdered, Jean Donovan asked Robert White, "What do you do when even to help the poor, to take care of the orphans, is considered an act of subversion by the government?" Without words, she answered her own question. What you do is continue—even in the face of death.

It wasn't easy. Jean wrote to a friend, "Several times I have decided to leave El Salvador. I almost could except for the children, the poor, bruised victims of this insanity. Who would care for them? Whose heart could be so staunch as to favor the reasonable thing in a sea of their tears and helplessness? Not mine, dear friend, not mine."[5]

Like Rahab, Ita, Maura, Dorothy, and Jean offered shelter and saved lives. They refused to accept that the military which enforced brutal injustice—and which did away with those who found a challenge to its power in the Bible's promises of justice for the poor—had the last word. Instead, final word was faith. These four women incarnated the truth that faith without works is dead. They paid for that truth with their lives. But they went to their deaths knowing, with all the fervor with which Rahab had proclaimed it, that "God is indeed God in heaven above and on earth below" (Josh. 2:11).

Rahab is a complicated character. In the worst view, she was a traitor. Her actions led to the downfall of her city and the massacre of her own people. Yet from the biblical writers' perspective that the Israelites were empowered by God to conquer and destroy their enemies, she emerges as a hero. She risked her own life to hide and save the lives of the Jewish spies. Above all, she is known as someone who, even from outside the community of faith, understood and proclaimed the power of God.

Rahab appears in the genealogy listed in the first chapter of Matthew. She was an ancestor of Jesus, a woman who passed on her courage, resourcefulness, and belief. Ita, Jean, Dorothy, and Maura are daughters of Jesus and therefore descendants of this remarkable woman and recipients of her gifts.

In the closing words of her last book, Penny Lernoux, who spent many years in Latin America, quoted a young Guatemalan peasant woman. The words were a reflection on the gospel mandate to lay down one's life, offered a few months before this woman was killed by the Guatemalan military. "What good is life," she said, "unless you give it away?—unless you can give it for a better world, even if you never see that world but have only carried your grain of sand to the building site. Then you're fulfilled as a person."

The four women in El Salvador certainly carried their grain of sand to the building site, even when threatened with death. Maura wrote, shortly before her murder:

My fear of death is being challenged constantly as children, lovely young girls, old people, are being shot, and some cut up with machetes, and bodies thrown by the road and people prohibited from burying them. A loving Father must have a new life of unimaginable joy and peace prepared for these precious, unknown, uncelebrated martyrs. One cries out, "Lord, how long?" And then too what creeps into my mind is the little fear or big, that when it touches me very personally, will I be faithful?[6]

Indeed, Maura Clarke, Ita Ford, Jean Donovan, and Dorothy Kazel were faithful to the end. They have found that place of unimaginable joy and peace. They join Rahab in the roll call of the faithful, part of that "cloud of witnesses" that is still being gathered together. By their courage, they inspire us to live by love and risk for faith.

NOTES

1. Information provided by Lee Miller and Margaret Swedish, Religious Task Force on Central America (1747 Connecticut Ave. NW, Washington, DC 20009).
2. Ibid.
3. Ibid.
4. Ibid.
5. Ibid.
6. Ibid.

23 Jael, the Woman of Thebez, and the Woman of Abel of Beth-macaah: War Heroines

SCRIPTURE: Judg. 4:1–24; 5:24–30; 9:42–57; 2 Sam. 20:1–2, 6–7, 14–22

> Jael wife of Heber took a tent peg, and took a hammer in her hand, and went softly to him and drove the peg into his temple. (Judg. 4:21)

> A certain woman threw an upper millstone on Abimelech's head, and crushed his skull. (Judg. 9:53)

> Then the woman went to all the people with her wise plan. And they cut off the head of Sheba son of Bichri, and threw it out to Joab. (2 Sam. 20:22)

These three women have in common that they are celebrated as heroines of Israel. But though their stories are full of bravery, intrigue, and ingenuity, they are not told and retold as the stories of their male counterparts are; we know much more about Samson's strength, David's triumph over Goliath, Daniel's courage in the lions' den, and the persistent faith of Shadrach, Meshach, and Abednego in the fiery furnace. The names of these three women are likely not even familiar to many followers of the faith.

Jael was a crafty woman. Sisera, who had brutally oppressed the Israelites for two decades, considered her an ally. He fled to her tent after the destruction of his army. She welcomed and nourished him, gaining his trust. Then she killed him.

The unnamed woman of Thebez acted similarly against a cruel king. Had she been a man, we probably would have a name credited to this deed. Her weapon was a millstone. So embarrassed was Abimelech to have been done in by a woman that, with his last breath, he ordered his armor bearer to run a sword through him. Because of this woman's strength and bravery, her people were delivered from a man whose claim to fame was that he had killed his seventy brothers to become king. Had she not acted, the people of Thebez likely would have shared the fate of the thousand men and women who burned to death in the Tower of Shechem.

The wise woman of Abel of Beth-maacah, like her two courageous predecessors, delivered her people from a massacre. In the midst of a siege, she negotiated their way out of doom. While troops battered the wall on which she stood, she bravely stepped forward, calling to the powerful Joab, King David's commander in chief. Reminding him that her town carried a long tradition of wisdom and peace, she appealed to Joab's sense of heritage. She convinced him that it would be pointless to destroy the whole town because of one scoundrel who had sought refuge among them. Off with his head!

While we can applaud the valor of each of these women, the violence with which they acted gives pause. Each must have felt that she was achieving a greater good by sacrificing one person to save many. But the ending of the song praising Jael (Judg. 5:24–30) provides a rare and poignant glimpse at the escalating effect of violence. We see a grieving mother, peering out the window for her son, asking herself what has delayed his chariot. Even a cruel commander is somebody's son. Sisera is already defeated and dead, but his mother pictures him dividing the spoils of victory, which includes capturing young women and taking them as sexual slaves. One violent act leads to another. There is more than enough grief to go around.

In more recent centuries, followers of the faith have changed the course of history not by violence but by trying to take Jesus' difficult command to "love your enemies" to heart. They have seen in Jesus' sacrifice on the cross a model of nonviolence, a willingness to die rather than kill.

Perhaps strongest within the pacifist tradition has been the witness of the Quakers. Their convictions about nonviolence and the equality of all people are rooted in the belief that each person, regardless of race, class, or gender, bears the mark of God. Despite their witness to dignity, humanity, and peace, many Quakers were treated violently and inhumanely, some even martyred, including several Quaker women.

The first Quaker convert, Elizabeth Hooten, was born in England in 1598. She was imprisoned within three years of her conversion for exhorting people to repentance and peaceful living. Years later, when she was an elderly woman, she went to Boston; there she was tied to a cart and dragged eight miles through eleven towns because she refused to change her message. In each town she was beaten; then she was abandoned in the New England wilderness, in the middle of winter.

Another English Quaker, Mary Fisher, spent sixteen months in prison for "speaking to a priest."[1] Undaunted, on her release she preached pacifism to college students, for which a local mayor had her stripped to the waist and beaten. In 1655, she also traveled to Boston, where her books were burned and she was stripped and searched for marks of witchcraft, thrown in prison once more, and eventually sent back to England.

In 1657, Fisher heard a call to take the gospel to the sultan of Turkey. One writer, referring to her treatment at the hands of the Boston Puritans, commented, "Her experience with the tender mercies of the righteous may have made the infidel Turkish terror seem rather faded."[2] On her arrival in Turkey, the British consul put her on a ship headed back to England, but she talked the captain into letting her off at the next port. Alone in a foreign country where she didn't speak the language, she walked six hundred miles to find the sultan, who was encamped with his army of twenty thousand. When she announced that she had a message from God, she was received like an ambassador. All the army officers and government leaders gathered, and she spoke through a translator. She spoke what the Holy Spirit had put in her heart, and the sultan proclaimed it truth.

Yet that same year, the colony of Massachusetts passed stiff laws against "the cursed sect of Quakers." People caught teaching Quaker doctrines were to be whipped, have their ears cut off, and have their tongues bored with a hot iron. If they persisted, they were to be banished. Return from banishment earned them death.

Mary Barrett Dyer was imprisoned in Boston for her beliefs. Her husband secured her release by promising that she would leave Massachusetts. A year later, she returned to visit imprisoned Quaker friends and was sentenced to hang, along with two Quaker men. They walked to the scaffold hand in hand, praising God, while a drummer drowned out their testimonies.

Dyer was given a reprieve because of her husband's pleas. Refusing to abandon preaching her faith, she was condemned again six months later. As she mounted the platform, her former pastor urged her to repent of her errors. She went to her death saying, "Nay, I cannot, for in obedience to the will of the Lord God I came, and in his will I abide faithful to the death."[3]

Mary Barrett Dyer died on June 1, 1660, in a land that was

allegedly founded on freedom by people fleeing religious persecution. She and her Quaker sisters never wavered in their commitment to nonviolence, believing that the light of God shines in every human being. They have gone down in history as courageous women who waged peace.

NOTES

1. Nancy A. Hardesty, *Great Women of Faith* (Grand Rapids: Baker Book House, 1980), 58.
2. Ibid.
3. Ibid., 60.

24 Michal: Daring and Disguises

Scripture: 1 Sam. 18:20–29; 19:9–17

So Michal let David down through the window; he fled away and escaped. Michal took an idol and laid it on the bed; she put a net of goats' hair on its head, and covered it with clothes. When Saul sent messengers to take David, she said, "He is sick." (1 Sam. 19:12–14)

It was April 27, 1860, in Troy, New York. A small crowd had gathered in front of the courthouse, trying to get a glimpse of a runaway slave named Charles Nalle, who was being taken inside. A small woman elbowed her way up the steps. A fury rose inside her at the thought that this strong man was about to be forced back into slavery. She believed with all her heart that God intended human beings to be free.

She found a young boy in the crowd and told him to run into the streets yelling, "Fire, fire!" as loud as he could. She smiled as the crowd swelled in response to the false alarm. She needed a lot of people on those steps and in the street.

She bent over, drooping her shoulders, taking the posture of an old woman. Pulling her sunbonnet over her face, she slowly moved next to one of Nalle's police guards. He tried to urge her out of the way. But she did not move. Then, without warning, she knocked the guard down and grabbed Nalle by the arm. She pulled him along with her through the now-huge crowd. When they reached the street, they fell to the ground. The woman snatched the sunbonnet off her head and hastily tied it around Nalle's head. When they stood up again, it was impossible to pick him out of the crowd.

They ran while sympathizers blocked the street to hold back the police. On a narrow side street, a man driving a horse and wagon asked her what was going on. Out of breath, she quickly explained. The man turned over his wagon to her, declaring that he didn't care if he ever saw it again as long as Charles Nalle made it to safety.

For Harriet Tubman, the rescue of Charles Nalle was a minor adventure. This daring woman had crossed swamps and rivers, hidden in haycocks and attics, followed the North Star on clear nights and damp moss on the north side of trees on rainy ones—all the time outwitting masters and outrunning pursuers to guide slaves to freedom. She had first made the trip to freedom from a plantation on Maryland's Eastern Shore alone. She described what happened when she crossed into Pennsylvania: "I looked at my hands to see if I was the same person now I was free. There was such a glory over everything, the sun came like gold through the trees, and over the fields, and I felt like I was in heaven."[1]

But Tubman was never content to live in safety with her own hard-won freedom. She returned to Maryland to conduct first her sisters and brothers, then an array of strangers, and eventually her elderly parents to Pennsylvania. The passengers on her "underground railroad" spanned all ages, including babies who were given a few drops of paregoric to keep them quiet or a touch of opium to put them to sleep.

Her fame spread as stories of her achievements passed among the slave cabins along the Eastern Shore. Her incredible strength, fearlessness, and religious fervor earned her the name Moses. She often announced her arrival outside the door of a slave cabin by softly singing "Go Down, Moses," late at night. Then the whispers would spread: "Moses is back." Slavemasters, who never saw evidence of her except the sudden disappearance of their slaves, assumed this "Moses" was a man.

Indeed, she was like the biblical leader who ushered the Israelites to freedom; she even referred to Maryland as "the land of Egypt." But if she had ever been told the story of Michal, Harriet Tubman might also have found a sense of kinship with this sister who let her husband down to safety and masterminded a disguise to trick her father's messengers. Charles Nalle was saved by Tubman's bonnet. Others were hidden in wagons under blankets or bricks. Tubman herself once walked undetected right by her former master on her way to get slaves. Dressed as an old woman in a sunbonnet, she carried two chickens under her arm. As her master approached, she let the chickens go. Screeching as she went, she chased the squawking chickens down the road and heard her master laugh and shout, "Go to it, Granny!"

Michal and Harriet shared a unique strength and courage. For Tubman, it came early. She attempted her first escape from slavery as a child, spending five days hiding in a pigsty. Also while still very young, she defied the demand of an overseer to hold another slave for a whipping after he had attempted an escape. When he ran again, Tubman moved in front of the doorway to block the overseer from chasing the man. The overseer picked up a two-pound weight and hurled it at the fleeing slave. The weight hit Tubman in the forehead, opening a huge gash. She was thrown backward by the blow and fell, unconscious and bleeding. For weeks, her family feared that she would die. And for the rest of her life, she suffered violent headaches and occasionally lapsed into a comalike sleep. But these episodes never stopped this dauntless

MICHAL   107

woman from taking dangerous steps toward freedom for herself and others. Michal's strength allowed David to escape death. Unlike most women of her time, Michal declared her love for a man she desired for a husband. She needed her father's approval, of course—and her father happened to be the king. Saul gave his approval, not out of respect for her wishes but because he saw his right to demand a present in exchange for her as an opportunity to do away with David, of whom he had become quite jealous. So he demanded the foreskins of a hundred Philistines, as proof that David had killed them. But Saul never expected David to return with this rather bizarre prize. David surprised him, bringing back twice as many as required. And poor Michal went down in history as likely the only woman ever handed over in marriage in exchange for a couple hundred foreskins!

But she loved David. In the process of saving his life, she both risked her own and defied her powerful father. Cleverly, she put the idol in the bed to trick the messengers. And when questioned by her father, she told him that David had threatened to kill her if she didn't help him escape. Her quick wits ensured that David would live to be king.

Michal paid dearly for her courage. Saul handed her over to another husband, Palti (1 Sam. 25:44). Apparently, David quickly forgot the risk she took for him. Years later, David demanded her back, not out of love for her but in an effort to strengthen his political alliances; for by this time he had taken two other wives and many concubines. Her return was marked by the tragic weeping of Palti, who pitifully followed her until he was ordered away by David's messenger (2 Sam. 3:14–16).

By then, Michal likely carried a deep resentment toward David. She had risked everything, but David hadn't been willing to oppose her father to keep their marriage together. Palti's grief indicates that Michal and her second husband shared a deep bond, which David mercilessly wrenched apart. And Michal was forced back into a life with now King David, as part of a considerable harem.

The last we hear of Michal is an interchange between her and David. From a window, she saw him "leaping and dancing" before the ark of the Lord, wearing nothing but a linen ephod, an apronlike ceremonial garment that covered only the front of his body (2 Sam. 6:12–23). She was scandalized at his shameless display in front of the women of the palace and "despised him in her heart." David arrogantly reminded her that he had been chosen king "in place of your father and all his household." Their last recorded exchange sounds typical of feuding partners in a marriage gone sour. Michal again paid the price, it seems. The final words written about her declare, "And Michal the daughter of Saul had no child to the day of her death" (2 Sam. 23)—likely an indication that David never took her to his bed again.

Harriet Tubman didn't have much better luck with men. She dearly loved her husband, but he refused to escape with her to freedom and even threatened to betray her to the master if she left. She snuck away one night when he was sound asleep, after the light of the fire had died down.

She returned for him once. She was disguised that night in a felt hat and man's suit, torn and covered with burrs after an arduous journey back to Maryland from Pennsylvania. She crept past the other cabins on the plantation and knocked at the door of the one she had shared with her husband. When he answered, he looked at her with scorn. A woman got up from a stool by the fireplace and came and stood beside him. She was young, slender, and beautiful—quite a contrast from the strong and indomitable Harriet, standing there in a tattered man's suit. The couple laughed at her when she said, "I came back for you, John"; and there was a great emptiness in her.

But Harriet Tubman decided not to be defeated by her losses. She gathered up a group of other slaves to take with her back north to freedom. So fearless was she—and so hated by slavemasters—that by 1860, rewards for her capture totaled sixty thousand dollars.

Believing in a God of mercy and gentleness, Harriet Tubman refused to join slave uprisings, though she did help lead a daring rescue of 750 slaves on a South Carolina river. She served as a scout, spy, and nurse for Union troops during the Civil War and made pies and home-brewed root beer for the army camps. Though she never learned to read or write, she recited often from the King James Bible and was a renowned storyteller.

In 1903, she turned her home over to the African Methodist Episcopal Zion Church as a home for the sick, poor, and homeless; she lived there until her death. In her lifetime, she had conducted more than three hundred slaves to freedom. On her gravestone are etched her immortal words: "On my underground railroad I never run my train off the track and I never lost a passenger."[2]

NOTES

1. Ann Petry, *Harriet Tubman: Conductor on the Underground Railroad* (New York: Pocket Books, 1955), 92.
2. Ibid., 221.

25 Abigail: Bold Maker of Peace

SCRIPTURE: 1 Sam. 25:2–42

Then David received from her hand what she had brought him; he said to her, "Go up to your house in peace; see, I have heeded your voice, and I have granted your petition." (1 Sam. 25:35)

I cringe a little when I read the story of Abigail. She was trapped for a time in a marriage to a hard-drinking, surly, uncaring man, whose name even meant "fool." She appears accustomed to covering for his excesses and meanness and all of the ways he embarrassed himself, her, and others around him.

Some modern psychologists might rush to call this a codependent marriage. Abigail's personality seems to fit. It is hard to imagine that she could have stayed in her marriage without some serious blows to her self-esteem. She seems rather obsequious, falling down on her face in the story more than once, claiming the blame for her husband's selfish actions, calling David "my lord" thirteen times in eight verses (not to mention answering his marriage proposal by calling herself a slave, willing to wash his servants' feet).

But fortunately, there is more to Abigail. Like so many other women in similarly undermining marriages, she chose to use her pain for strength. Her humility and reconciling nature, which in some circumstances can be unhealthy self-effacement, became a transforming power that saved a people from destruction. Abigail stepped forward and acted boldly.

If it were not the case that blood was about to be spilled, this tale would almost have a comic feel to it: David shouting, "Every man strap on his sword!" then charging off and leaving two hundred behind to protect the baggage; Abigail arriving on the back of a donkey with five sheep carcasses, two hundred loaves of bread, and a major cache of raisins, then "my lord"-ing David to humiliating excess; her cruel and drunk husband turning stonelike; and then, Abigail marrying a king whose idea of wooing was apparently to send his servants after her.

Clearly, the character with the most sense in this story is Abigail. Nabal is selfish. David is rash, deciding to punish Nabal's stinginess with a bloodletting. Abigail is obviously trusted for her integrity and ingenuity, because the young man in the group sent by David came to her to ask her what to do. One wonders how David would have gotten by without the astute women in his life.

While the men were strapping on their swords, Abigail used the only power she had: the gifts of generosity and peace. She refused to be caught between her husband's stupidity and David's anger. Single-handedly, she prepared a feast, slipped out without her husband finding out, and pleaded with David to spare her household. She could be considered, as author Edith Deen put it, "the earliest woman pacifist on record."[1] Her integrity put David to shame. He reconsidered and put away his sword. But she still had to face one more confrontation—with her husband. She did not back off, and she was rewarded with her freedom from his cruelty and control.

Abigail was a wise woman. She knew that David would one day be king. She saved him from an unwise massacre and a bad conscience. And David recognized her wisdom and blessed her for her good sense. When, once again, the men rattled their swords—when the Amalekites made a raid and captured her along with the other women—we can believe that she clung to her dignity and strength. She was likely a calming influence on the other women until their rescue and an advocate for them before her enemies (1 Sam. 30:1–5).

Women throughout history have been peacemakers and reconcilers in seemingly hopeless situations. Unwilling to be driven by either fear or revenge, they have advocated peaceful resolution of conflict.

Clare of Assisi was such a courageous peacemaker. In 1234, the Italian city of Assisi was under attack by the Saracens, a brutal band of Muslim mercenaries. Some had scaled the walls of the San Damiano monastery and climbed down into the cloister where Clare and her sisters lived. Clare, who was seriously ill and bedridden at the time, called the sisters together. She prayed that God would deliver them and then exhorted them not to be afraid. Offering to be their ransom, she told the sisters she wanted to be put out before them. She took a small box containing the elements of the Eucharist and asked the sisters to carry her to where the Saracens had intruded. So surprised were the invaders by the presence of this woman that they fled not only the monastery but the city as well.

Around the world, images of women holding steadfastly to prayerful, nonviolent resistance abound. Philippine nuns placed flowers in the barrels of approaching soldiers' guns during the revolution to overthrow the brutal dictator Ferdinand Marcos. Russian mothers faced advancing tanks with bouquets and bread during the coup of 1991.

Women in England established a women's peace camp at Greenham
Common, a nuclear weapons site, decorating the fence around it with
symbols of life. By the power of prayer and peace, women are slowly
chipping away at political systems entangled in violence and driven by
war. They are changing hearts of stone into hearts of flesh.

One of the most dramatic examples comes from a remote village in
a South American jungle. Sarah Corson, a founder of Servants in Faith
and Technology (SIFAT) in Alabama, was on a mission to set up an
agricultural project in a village where she and her husband had earlier
started a church and built a fish hatchery. She was with seventeen
young people, including two of her sons. One Thursday night, around
midnight, thirty soldiers rushed toward the house where they were all
staying. Sarah was paralyzed with shock as the soldiers stormed over
the clearing leading to the house. She remembered with fear that,
earlier that day, a neighbor had overheard a conversation near the
military camp in which soldiers had blamed Americans for recent resistance to a military takeover of the country. The soldiers had vowed to
exterminate all Americans in the region.

Sarah Corson prepared to die. But as the soldiers approached, she
found herself offering them warm words of welcome. The commander
shoved his rifle against her stomach and pushed her into the house.
The soldiers began pulling everything off the shelves and out of draw-
ers. Sarah calmly explained that she and the others were there only to
set up projects and teach the Bible. The commander, stating that he
had never read the Bible, said, "Maybe it is a communist book, for all I
know." Sarah asked him to let her talk about it.

While he kept his gun pointed at her and the other soldiers continued ransacking the house, Sarah opened a Spanish Bible to the Sermon
on the Mount. She read about Jesus' command to love one's enemies.

"That's humanly impossible!" the commander shouted.

"That's true, sir," she answered. "It isn't humanly possible, but with
God's help it is possible." She challenged him to let her prove it by
killing her slowly: "Cut me to pieces little by little, and you will see you
cannot make me hate you. I will die praying for you because God loves
you."

The commander lowered his gun and stepped back. Then he ordered everyone in the house to march to a truck. But before they
reached the truck, he turned around and led the women back to the
house. He told Sarah that the women would be raped repeatedly in the
jungle camp, so he could not take them there. He also told her that this
was the first time he had disobeyed an order from a superior officer—

and that he would pay with his life if he were found out. He said as he left, "I could have fought any amount of guns you might have had, but there is something here I cannot understand. I cannot fight it."

The village waited in agony for word of the men who had been taken. The local people insisted that the church service not be held on Sunday, because soldiers considered any gathering a source of political agitation. But on Saturday night, a messenger arrived with word from the commander of the attack that he would be in church on Sunday. He wanted Sarah to come and get him; if she did not, he would walk the ten miles. It sounded to Sarah like a threat. She sent a message throughout the town that night. "We will have the service after all," she said, "but you are not obligated to come. In fact you may lose your life by coming. No one knows what this soldier will do. Do not come when the church bell rings unless you are sure God wants you to come."

Sarah picked up the commander and his bodyguard at the military camp. Holding their rifles, they marched coldly into the church and sat down. The church was packed before the first hymn was over. The people came in fear and trembling, but they came.

It was church custom to welcome visitors by inviting them to the platform, singing a welcome song, and waving to them. Then the congregation would line up to shake the visitors' hands, embrace them, and offer a personal greeting. Sarah decided only to offer the commander and his bodyguard the song. Stunned to be invited up front, the two soldiers stood with their guns across their backs. The people sang weakly and waved timidly. But then, the first man on the front seat came forward and put out his hand. As he bent over to hug the soldier, Sarah overheard him saying, "Brother, we don't like what you did to our village, but this is the house of God, and God loves you, so you are welcome here." Every person in the church followed his example, even the women whose eyes were red from weeping for their loved ones whom the commander had taken prisoner.

The commander was incredulous. He marched to the pulpit and said, "Never have I dreamed that I could raid a town, come back, and have that town welcome me as a brother." Pointing to Sarah, he said, "That sister told me Thursday night that Christians love their enemies, but I did not believe her then. You have proven it to me this morning. . . . I never believed there was a God before, but what I have just felt is so strong that I will never doubt the existence of God as long as I live."

The commander stayed for lunch with the congregation and offered money from his own pocket to parishioners who had had loved ones taken away. Two weeks later, all of the men who had been taken were released from the basement cell where they had been imprisoned and some had been tortured.

Sarah Corson was overcome with gratitude to God for putting divine love in her heart for a person she could not love on her own. She remembers the last words the commander said to her: "I have fought many battles and killed many people. It was nothing to me. It was just my job to exterminate them. But I never knew them personally. This is the first time I ever knew my enemy face to face. And I believe that if we knew each other, our guns would not be necessary."[2]

NOTES

1. Edith Deen, *All of the Women of the Bible* (New York: Harper & Row, 1955), 101.
2. Sarah Corson, "Welcoming the Enemy," *Sojourners* 12, no. 4 (April 1983): 29–31.

Part 5. Questions for Reflection

1. Which biblical woman in this section do you think was the most courageous? Why?

2. What did you feel toward Rahab as you read about the destruction of Jericho? What did you feel reading the stories of Jael, the woman of Thebez, and the woman of Abel of Beth-macaah?

3. Do you believe that women, more than men, have a particular capacity for and calling to peacemaking? Why or why not?

4. Do you know of any instances, either personal or historical, of women intervening to avert conflict and bring peace?

5. How can you build your own courage to respond, despite fear, in situations requiring response?

PART 6
Devoted Mothers

This section is a tribute to all of the women through the ages who have patiently and courageously raised children in the way of faith. Prayer, surrender, guidance, and love mark the lives of such mothers.

Jochebed preserved her son's life, while Rizpah mourned the murder of her children. Hannah pleaded with God, and an unnamed mother appealed to Solomon. Eunice and Lois brought up Timothy to devote his life to serving God, as they had devoted theirs in faith.

Today, the power of maternal love continues to move the world toward compassion and peace. Around the globe, in situations of war and upheaval—from South Africa to Northern Ireland to El Salvador—mothers pray, plead, march, and keep vigil, demanding a better future for their children.

26 Jochebed: Shrewd and Determined Love

SCRIPTURE: Exodus 2:1–10

When [Jochebed] could hide him no longer she got a papyrus basket for him, and plastered it with bitumen and pitch; she put the child in it and placed it among the reeds on the bank of the river. (Ex. 2:3)

Neither the mother nor the sister in this story is mentioned by name. But we learn in Ex. 6:20 that the mother is Jochebed. And the sister, Miriam, emerges later with her own prominence.

We know that Jochebed's son, like all Hebrew male infants of the time, was born under pharaoh's death sentence. After Puah and Shiphrah and the other Hebrew midwives refused to kill the male newborns, pharaoh ordered that the babies be thrown into the Nile River.

Jochebed must have been resourceful and clever indeed to have kept her son hidden for three months. What a mixture of terror and joy must have permeated her days, as she celebrated a new life but struggled to keep it secret. Every cry must have sent a shudder through her. And what care she took when she realized that she might have to give her son up to save him, weaving a small basket from long stalks of marsh grass, carefully waterproofing the miniature ark as she smeared it with bitumen and pitch. It was a labor of love and loss. Jochebed set the basket afloat amid the tall reeds near the bank of the Nile, with Miriam perched to watch from a safe distance. Other baby boys had lost their lives in this river, but Jochebed claimed it as a river of life for her son.

The daughter of the pharaoh came to bathe and discovered the infant. Recognizing him as a Hebrew child, she "took pity on him." Miriam sprang into action. "Shall I go and get a Hebrew woman to nurse him?" she asked. And of course, she went and brought back her own mother.

Did Miriam and Jochebed hope for this outcome all along? Had they carefully plotted it? Or did God's providence direct the action of this drama? Whatever the case, the resourcefulness and faith of two

Hebrew women—as well as the mercy of a king's daughter (who herself was acting against her father's edict)—launched a blessed life; for that baby was Moses. He owed his life to three daring women.

It is no coincidence that the children of Jochebed played major roles in faith history. Aaron the priest, Miriam the prophet, Moses the liberator—the heroes of the exodus all stepped forward into greatness, grounded in the love of a faithful, courageous mother.

The death sentence in South Africa has been only a little more subtle than in pharaoh's Egypt. At the edge of Cape Town, beyond a "Not Open to the General Public" sign, I visited an isolated island of misery built on dust. The maze of pieced-together shanties and shacks is a squatter camp called Crossroads. Here a four-year-old girl had swathed her head with a discarded plastic bag, tying it in a knot and pulling out the ends to fashion a hair bow for herself; government control and destitution made it impossible for little girls to dream of silk or satin bows in Crossroads. A group of young boys had pieced together bits of paper and plastic and string to make a kite, while another had created a crude push-toy out of fragments of wire stuck through a tin can.

In Crossroads, children were fortunate to reach the age of four. Diarrhea, dehydration, and the severe malnutrition called "kwashiorkor" claimed many of them as infants. At the medical clinic, intake forms for children read, "Siblings: alive _____, dead _____." At the edge of the camp, rows of tiny empty graves wait in ominous expectation.

Childhood ended almost before it began in South Africa. Razor wire and rifles, petrol bombs and armored personnel carriers called *casspirs*, and the whips known as *sjamboks*—all have been part of the landscape for the children of apartheid. These children raised fists in defiant determination as soon as they were old enough to understand the struggle, an understanding that came early. Their energy threatened South Africa's ruling powers, who targeted them in massive numbers for detention and torture.

June Mlangeni described the plight of many South African mothers at the launching of the "Unlock Apartheid's Jails" campaign in December 1987:

> We constantly wait for the knock on the door at ungodly hours, that knock which will take away yet another child. We sit in our homes day after day wondering what is happening to our children who are in prison and those who live as moles underground because they must continue with our struggle. The effect of this type of worry causes the worst

heartbreak any person can endure. . . . This government has robbed us
of everything we hold dear. . . . We are being robbed of watching our
children grow, and they are locked away from us.

These mothers launched their own resistance on behalf of their children. In Soweto, row upon row of small, starkly identical houses cover
endless dusty hillsides. Each home has a large, crude, hand-painted
number on the outside front wall. These numbers were the work of the
South African police, who got tired of mothers rubbing out less visible
numbers to protect their children from police searches. The police
painted numbers to help them distinguish the houses, the mothers
rubbed them away, and the police painted again.

The mothers never rested. They wandered from police station to
prison in search of children snatched from them in the dark, thousands
since the South African government imposed a state of emergency in
1986. They were conductors of an underground railroad, leading their
sons and daughters to protection in exile in South Africa's neighboring
states. These mothers have known what it means to give their children
up in order to save them.

Virginia Kekane's fourteen-year-old son was badly beaten with
sjamboks by a riot squad. Police broke down her door in the middle of
the night searching for her eighteen-year-old. Both of her sons went
over the border. That was fifteen years ago. They have not made contact with their mother since then, for fear of endangering her life.
"Sometimes we sit around the table, my other four children and I, and
talk about them growing up," Kekane told me. "I wonder how they are
behaving now. I keep telling myself that if they're out of the country,
they're away from those people, and safe. But I feel very bad about it."
She began to weep softly. "They were very close to me."

Like so many women in South Africa, Virginia Kekane does not
dwell on her own pain but thinks of those mothers whose burden is
greater. She has said that women joining together "encourages us,
gives us strength—especially the mothers whose children were shot
dead or are still in detention. We help each other; we give each other
courage." She told me that she has conquered her fears: "I'm not afraid
at all. Going back would be a waste of time. Let's go on and on,
because there must be an ending [to apartheid]. If we can't realize it,
our children in exile—we will never see them anymore. We are the
mothers. We are concerned about our children. Something must be
done."

Elizabeth Nhalpo, who spent five years in prison for her part in starting the underground railroad, said of the risks she has taken, "I don't do this for me. I do it for my children—and my grandchildren. I want them to enjoy the fruits of freedom."

These women said that they are mothers of the *Imfuduso*, the exodus. This distinction they share with Jochebed. They wandered for forty years in the brutal wilderness of apartheid. But always, they were determined to see that their children reached the promised land. For their courage, the mothers can now bask in the light of the new day that has dawned in South Africa. Hand in hand with their children, they are beginning to build a new world.

27 Hannah: Pleading with God

SCRIPTURE: 1 Sam. 1:1–2:8; 2:18–21

[Hannah] made this vow: "O Lord of hosts, if only you will . . . give to your servant a male child, then I will set him before you as a nazirite until the day of his death." (1 Sam. 1:11)

We first see Hannah as a despondent woman, afflicted by barrenness and tormented by the woman with whom she must share her husband. Each passing year, the time of sacrifice at the Temple brought a humiliating reminder of her sorrow and a crescendo of desolation. As her husband, Elkanah, handed out portions to his other wife, Peninnah, and "all her sons and daughters," Hannah was reminded of her failure to conceive.

Her husband appears to have been doing his best to be sensitive to her, openly declaring his love for her. But he did not quite understand the depth of her pain, asking, "Am I not more to you than ten sons?" (1 Sam. 1:8). If only he had thought to say "Are you not more to me than ten sons?" he might have offered a bit of consolation; for surely, a large part of Hannah's grief was her inability to provide him with male heirs.

Hannah is the last in a line of well-known women in the Old Testament who lamented their lack of children. Sarah gave her slave Hagar to Abraham so that he might have a son and laughed in doubt when told she would conceive in old age; Isaac prayed to God for Rebekah to conceive; Rachel was envious of her sister, Leah, and said in despair and bitterness to Jacob, "Give me children or I shall die!" (Gen. 30:1)—then handed over her maid. Only Hannah took her case directly to God.

Hannah went herself to the Temple one day. In deep distress, she cried out to God. She vowed that if God would grant her a son, she would dedicate him to God's service as a nazirite, one consecrated through special vows, including a vow never to cut one's hair.

Hannah sought God humbly (referring to herself three times as God's "servant," as Mary the mother of Jesus would refer to herself later) yet confidently, sure of her faithfulness and God's promises. She was a passionate woman, in both her distress and her joy. Her plea was filled with urgency and emotion, and she literally poured herself out in

121

both anguish and hope, unafraid and unashamed of the fervor within her. Like the observers of the first Day of Pentecost, the priest Eli mistook spiritual ardor for drunkenness. Watching her lips move and hearing no words, Eli chastised her. But when she explained, he gave her a blessing that God might grant her request.

In time, Hannah conceived and gave birth to Samuel, whose name means "asked of the Lord." When he was weaned, Hannah took her young son to the Temple to turn him over to the priest. What a bitter-sweet moment, after years of waiting and pleading for a child, when Hannah had to let go. But she never wavered from her vow. She "lent" her son to the Lord, counting God's gain as greater than her loss.

Hannah sang a song of thanksgiving as she released her son into God's care and service. She glorified God for bringing justice, and the echoes of that song eventually reached the lips of Mary. Hannah praised the God who "raises up the poor from the dust" and "lifts the needy from the ash heap, to make them sit with princes and inherit a seat of honor" (1 Sam. 2:8).

She is a marvelous model of how personal suffering can be the entry point to understanding the pain of the poor. Her own cry did not stifle the cries of other women to her ears but enabled her to hear those cries all the more clearly. In heartfelt prayer, she claimed her liberation and then claimed it for all who suffer. She understood the vulnerability of women and their children. Thirty-two centuries later, the majority of the poor are still women and children, giving her hymn of justice and liberation a relevance that spans all time. Her song ended on a prophetic note, foreshadowing the coming of a king, an "anointed" one.

As the days unfolded, Samuel grew up in the Temple and Hannah was blessed with three more sons and two daughters. As was said later of the boy Jesus, Samuel grew "both in stature and in favor with the Lord and with the people" (2:26). Hannah visited him every year when her husband went up to make the sacrifice, a formerly devastating annual ritual that now was a joyful event. We can imagine her trying to picture her son's growth each year, choosing just the right cloth, lovingly making a special robe for him to cherish through the year, a reminder of a mother's special and tender love.

In contrast to Samuel, the priest Eli's sons were "scoundrels" who stole the sacrificial meat and slept with women at the Temple. A man of God came to Eli and prophesied their destruction, conveying God's declaration "I will raise up for myself a faithful priest, who shall do according to what is in my heart and in my mind" (2:35).

That priest, of course, was Samuel. As an adult, he took on the role appointed for him from the beginning, and God "was with him and let none of his words fall to the ground" (3:19)—just as his mother's words did not meet with emptiness when she pleaded for a son. He became a renowned prophet and the last judge of Israel. Peace prevailed during his reign, until the people began to demand a king. Taking a vial of oil, Samuel anointed Saul the first king of Israel (10:1). Thus the vow of a faithful mother affected the history of an entire nation.

The song begun by Hannah and picked up by Mary has wafted through several more centuries to Detroit, Michigan. Thousands of crack houses, where illegal drugs can be purchased, dot the city landscape. The dropout rate in Detroit's schools is 60 percent. It is estimated that there are a quarter of a million more legally owned firearms in Detroit than there are people. "Weapon checks" are a routine part of high school life.

In 1986, 365 children under the age of sixteen—one for each day of the year—were shot, 43 fatally. One who lost his life that year was Derick Barfield. He was sixteen years old when some schoolmates opened fire with a nine-millimeter automatic weapon on him and his brother as they sat in a car at a gas station. Derick was an athlete who wanted to be a minister.

"There was an emptiness in my heart," Clementine Barfield, Derick's mother, told me. "There was something inside of me that said, 'This should not be.' " With little more than the sheer determination to find a way to make sure others would never have to suffer what she had, Barfield began contacting other mothers whose children had been killed.

On January 4, 1987, six parents of murdered children and several concerned citizens met in a small Detroit church. News of the meeting spread quickly, and more than 350 people came to the second meeting. Four weeks later, on the coldest day of the year, fourteen hundred people turned out for a memorial service, filling the pews of a large cathedral and spilling over into the choir loft and aisles. Families of the slain children marched in a procession, carrying babies and Bibles, many of the family members with eyes wet with tears. At the close of the service, a candle was lit for each of the murdered children.

Thus was launched Save Our Sons and Daughters (SOSAD). Its first office was in the home of Vera Rucker, in the bedroom that had belonged to her sixteen-year-old daughter, Melody, who was murdered at a back-to-school party. Phone calls came in to the office twenty-four hours a day. Young people called for help, struggling with drug addictions or contemplating suicide; mothers who had just lost children called in the middle of the night and talked for hours; one teenager who had seen five friends killed in a few months called just to talk about the hurt and the anger and the fear.

Slowly, a support network for grieving families was built up. Direct action campaigns were launched, including courageously picketing crack houses. On a sweltering July day, two thousand people marched through Detroit to push for gun control. SOSAD began sponsoring projects to build up self-esteem in the city's youth and offer alternatives to the violence of the streets—everything from making furniture to workshops on nonviolent conflict resolution in local high schools. One Detroit resident told me the creation of SOSAD was the "turning point in Detroit from powerlessness and hopelessness."

It all began with one mother, who has a vision for a movement that will spread across the country and around the world. "We made people aware," explained Clementine Barfield. "Now the work really begins. People ought to be marching, and sitting in, and dying, if need be. . . . We have to create a whole consciousness movement—not just here in Detroit, I'm talking about all over the United States, all over the world if need be. We have to raise children of peace.

"We're talking about young people not being concerned about growing up and planning what they're going to do with the rest of their lives, because they don't see a 'rest of their lives.' You hear them in the streets, and they're screaming loud. They're not screaming to each other; they're really screaming to us. They're screaming to people to help them, to change this whole madness, to make things better for them. And if we don't do it, and do it soon, we can just write off our future."

When Clementine Barfield first began contacting other mothers in 1986, her ultimate goal was to work for gun control. "But the more I see and learn, I know the guns are not the problem," she said. "The guns are just a symptom of a far, far greater problem. The greatest problem that we have today as human beings is a lack of spirituality.

"We're losing our children younger and younger. And if we don't do something about it soon, we're going to lose all of them. . . . It's going to take some strong spirituality to bring them back into the fold."

Clementine Barfield's passionate faith pushes her to keep pouring out her life for the sake of the children. "If I didn't have a strong belief in God, I think I would just give up," she said. "I have to rely on a strength that's greater than me." She spoke sadly of the things that Derick missed by having his life cut short. "If I dedicated my whole life, which I have, to trying to make things better," she said, "it still would not equal what I have lost. I feel as though my son had unlimited capabilities. He would have done a fantastic job as a minister. But even now I feel as though Derick is ministering; he's doing it through me."

Like modern-day Hannahs, mothers still plead with God for the lives of their children. In tragedy, they learn to let go. And in faith, they carry on.

28 Rizpah: Raw Courage

Scripture: 2 Sam. 3:6–10; 21:1–14

> Then Rizpah the daughter of Aiah took sackcloth, and spread
> it on a rock for herself, from the beginning of harvest until
> rain fell on them from the heavens; she did not allow the birds
> of the air to come on the bodies by day, or the wild animals by
> night. (2 Sam. 21:10)

It rends the heart to read the story of Rizpah. She is one of
the most tragic figures in the Bible. To begin with, she was a concubine, meaning she was a slave. The one who laid claim to her was King
Saul, a man of great power.

First Samuel 31 tells of the gruesome death of Saul. Badly wounded
by Philistine archers, Saul fell on his own sword to save himself from
further pain and humiliation. The next day, the Philistines decapitated
his corpse and fastened it to a public wall.

His death placed Rizpah in jeopardy. She would have been joined to
the harem of Ishbaal, Saul's son; but Ishbaal leveled a charge against
Abner, the commander of Saul's army, that he had raped Rizpah. For
Abner to have slept with her was seen as treason, aspiring to the kingship. Furious at the charge, Abner transferred his loyalties from the
house of Saul to the house of David. Rizpah remained in the role of
helpless concubine as the argument over her escalated. The charge of
violation had nothing to do with her humanity or dignity but with a
violation of the king's property.

The war between the two houses was protracted and bitter. In
bloody times, vengeance and countervengeance prevail. A three-year
famine in the land during the reign of David pushed him to take action. Believing that the famine was punishment for Saul's massacre of
the Gibeonites, David asked the surviving Gibeonites what they
needed for expiation. They demanded seven of Saul's sons. David gave
them five of Saul's grandsons and his two sons by Rizpah, Armoni and
Mephibosheth. Some translations say that the young men were
hanged, others that they were impaled, on a mountain at the beginning
of the barley harvest. We can believe that their deaths were horrible.
Rizpah was once again consigned to be a helpless onlooker in the

vengeance games of men, triply jeopardized as a concubine, widow, and mother without sons.

But Rizpah did something amazing. Moved to action by her profound grief, she refused to remain merely a victim and spectator. Alone, in an act of defiance, the woman whose name means "glowing coal" went to the mountain, to the distorted, sun-scorched bodies of her beloved sons. She spread sackcloth on a rock, making herself a place that would be her home for five long months. She was a victim of the sins of others, but still she made a vigil with sackcloth, the symbol of penitence.

What a vision she must have been, spread on that rock for week after week, weary from grief and the task of protecting the sacred bodies that had been so dishonored. When vultures hovered near, she flailed her arms to scatter them. When wild beasts came with an appetite for decaying flesh, she drove them away with rocks and shouts. In the stifling heat of the day and the chilling air of night, she remained, quivering with fatigue and perhaps fear. Some people probably applauded the courage of this devoted mother. Others must have thought she was mad. They praised or pitied or mocked her. But she never gave up.

One morning, she awoke to gentle drops of rain mingling with her tears. From the beginning of spring to the first rain of autumn, she had kept her solitary vigil. King David was so moved by her perseverance that he gathered up the bones of Saul, his son Jonathan, and those over whom Rizpah had kept watch. Left in a state of dishonor for so long, the bones of David's rival and his kin were finally buried with honor.

Rizpah, the pawn in the games of vengeance and division between the houses of Saul and David, becomes the reconciler. She who is victim of their sins offers the sacrifice that moves God to open the heavens and return abundance to the land.

Rizpah is every mother who has grieved, every mother who has suffered the loss of a child, every mother who has learned to forgive. She is the mother in Nicaragua who plants a cross in memory of her fallen son, demanding that he not be forgotten. She is the mother in South Africa who compiles affidavits of torture and murder and delivers them to the office of the minister of law and order in Pretoria, demanding justice. She is the Palestinian mother rocking a refugee camp with resistance on behalf of her murdered child.

In El Salvador, she fasts at the tomb of the late archbishop Oscar Romero and occupies the cathedral in San Salvador, demanding an end to the repression. She has journeyed to the volcano outside the city, now a dump, where human corpses are strewn among the garbage. A modern-day Rizpah, she waves away the vultures as she searches for a body she hopes not to find.

She walks a path in Guatemala more traveled than any other—from prison to hospital to morgue. It is a path worn bare by the constant steps of weary but determined feet in search of the truth. Each mother who walks it carries the faint hope of finding a disappeared loved one alive. But each knows that finding a body is better than living one more day with the haunting uncertainty that obsesses the soul when there is no trace.

In Argentina, her name is Hebe Pastori Bonafini. She marches through the Plaza de Mayo with a picture of her disappeared son, his name embroidered on her white kerchief, demanding that the government account for him. She is a dressmaker. She and the other mothers who march weekly in their silent circle have been beaten and dragged away by their hair. Forty were once imprisoned in a cell that they shared with a dead young man who had been tortured beyond recognition. "On seeing him," Hebe says, "the pain came back. We didn't know if he was one of our sons. The police do these kinds of things to put pressure on us, to show us how powerful they are, how regrettably powerful they are."[1]

Government officials say that the mothers are barren women hallucinating that the military has stolen the children of their dreams. Authorities dismiss them as *las locas*—"the crazy ones." Hebe's hands turn into fists when she speaks of her sons, both university students in their twenties when they disappeared. "Every morning when I wake up, I think only about my sons and what I can do to take them from where they are. It is as if lions grew inside of me, and I am not afraid."[2]

In Northern Ireland, Maura Kiely is a modern-day Rizpah. Her son Gerard was killed as he attended Mass in Belfast, one of a multitude of victims claimed in the violence between Protestants and Catholics. "People say that time heals," says Kiely. "Time itself does not heal. It is what we do with time that can heal."[3]

Time moves on, and days come and go, but the sun never sets on repression and war. From Belfast to Beirut, Kabul to Krakow to Kigali; from Sarajevo to Santiago and San Salvador to Saigon; in Gaza and Guatemala City; in Managua and Manila, Moscow and Mogadishu; in Phnom Penh and Pretoria and Port-au-Prince, the war machine cranks around the clock and through the ages, its shots heard 'round the world.

But in a world where too many hands grasp rifles and too many fists beat bodies, other hands are reaching out to clasp one another in an act of comfort. The healing truth that one mother found in Northern Ireland is being discovered, day in and day out, in other corners all across the globe. They call themselves Mothers of Heroes and Martyrs (Nicaragua); Detainees' Parents Support Group (South Africa); Committee of Mothers and Relatives of Political Prisoners, Disappeared, and Assassinated (El Salvador); Mutual Support Group for the Appearance Alive of Our Loved Ones (Guatemala); Mothers of the Plaza de Mayo (Argentina); the Cross Group (Northern Ireland); Save Our Sons and Daughters (United States).

In every language, and by their lives, they reflect the truth about their own suffering that Maura Kiely learned: "I believed that life for Gerard was not taken away, just changed, and that we had still to struggle to live the faith for which he died. There are, I believe, no accidents in this life as far as God is concerned. Out of evil, it is said, comes good. I committed myself to work for reconciliation among bereaved families."[4]

Thanks to one mother's courage and capacity to forgive, Protestant and Catholic families in Northern Ireland are sharing their grief together. In South Africa, white women of the Black Sash have protested apartheid's oppression of black women. In Israel, Jewish Women in Black have held weekly vigils to demonstrate their opposition to their nation's continued occupation of Palestinian lands. Despite government declarations that these women are enemies to one another, they have claimed a bond as sisters.

On every continent, mothers of grief are becoming mothers of hope as they transform their sorrow into a force for change. These mothers are finding that what they do with their time can indeed heal—not only themselves and one another but also the nations. One of the strongest forces on earth is in their possession: the power of mother love. They have set loose on the globe a hope that is shaking the very foundations of the world. And as they meet and pray and weep and strategize, they offer a precious gift: a promise to the world's children that they will not be lost or forgotten.

NOTES

1. Elizabeth Hanly, "A Seventh Year of Unknowing," *Sojourners* 12, no. 4 (April 1983): 22.
2. Ibid.
3. From a taped interview with mothers of the Cross Group, Belfast, Northern Ireland, 1987.
4. Ibid.

29 A Compassionate Mother: Sacrificial Love

SCRIPTURE: 1 Kings 3:16–27

The woman whose son was alive said to the king . . . "Please, my lord, give her the living boy; certainly do not kill him!" (1 Kings 3:26)

The sun was just cresting the eastern horizon as I walked into the cemetery at the entrance to the tiny Nicaraguan town of Jalapa. The faint light of dawn made visible row upon row of crude, homemade crosses; simple wreaths of faded plastic flowers; and a sign bearing tribute to Jalapa's martyrs. Some had died in the freedom struggle against forty years of domination by the brutal U.S.-backed Somoza dynasty; others had given up their lives during recent raids by U.S.-funded contra forces, most of whom had been members of former dictator Anastasio Somoza Debayle's ruthless national guard.

The contras found Jalapa an easy target: isolated, surrounded by jungle, and just six kilometers from the Honduran border. They lived covertly in the border area until March 1982, when they made their presence known by beheading several of Jalapa's citizens.

It was now December 1983. I was ending a week in Jalapa with a dozen other North Americans as part of Witness for Peace. We were the first of a decadelong wave of people of faith from the United States who came to pray, to document contra atrocities, and to try to offer some protection to the Nicaraguan people from our government's undeclared war against them. We had been told that to understand Nicaragua, we must talk with the mothers.

During our stay, we met two-week-old Martita, whose mother had fled on foot from her home in the mountains just days before giving birth. Like six hundred other families in the area, Martita and her mother were refugees who had been temporarily resettled in old tobacco barns. Her father was fighting with the militia and had not yet seen his beautiful, young daughter.

We spoke with a mother in nearby Teotecacinte, who had been cooking when she got word of a contra attack. She sent her young daughter, Rosita, to the deep ravine that the family had dug for shelter, while she put out the fire in her clay oven. Before running to the shelter, Rosita chased after her puppy to keep it safe with her and got caught in the assault. Her mother ran out and scooped up her daughter's dead body. It wasn't until she got inside the shelter that she realized Rosita had been decapitated by a mortar. "It is incomparable suffering for a mother to lose a child," she told us through her tears. "We feel the loss of a child in our own flesh."

The night we had arrived in Jalapa, as the sun set behind the mountains where young men kept watch on the border, singing drifted out of the small church at the heart of the town. Voices of children were giving praise to the mother of God. We had arrived during La Purisima, the festival of Mary, which is marked with processions and hymns and is considered as important in Nicaragua as Christmas. It is a celebration but also a remembrance that Mary bore Jesus and gave him up to death, a Passion with which too many mothers of Nicaragua readily identify.

Now, a week later, we were preparing to leave Jalapa and head home. Our last day began like every other. A bright green parrot outside our window gave new meaning to the phrase "rudely awakened." Hanging upside down from the branch of a dead tree, it argued in Spanish with a crackling radio for dominance of the dawn.

Before long, the borrowed church bus that was taking us back to Managua came into view. The road from Jalapa was narrow, rutted, and steep. Shallow streams across our path slowed progress, as did the cows that occasionally wandered in our way. Stooped women pounded laundry against rocks in the water by small homes with orange clay-tile roofs. Crosses at the side of the road marked the sites where martyrs had fallen.

Transportation was infrequent on the desolate stretch. We stopped to pick up a young mother walking by the road with an infant in her arms. She needed a ride to a hospital in the next town. After an hour of driving, we were flagged to a stop at a makeshift military checkpoint. We were informed by a militia member that there was contra mortar fire on the road ahead. It was too late to turn back, and he instructed us to drive as fast as we could over the treacherous road to safety. We left in a cloud of dust.

We heard rounds of mortar fire in the distance as we bumped along. The young mother cradling her baby began to grow ill. She looked at her son lovingly, then handed him to one of the women in our group. And then she asked us if we would take Ricardo back to the United States with us.

"But wouldn't it be hard for you to be separated from him?" the American woman asked.

"Yes, but I will follow," the mother replied. "I will come as soon as I can."

"But there are problems in the United States, too."

Ricardo's mother began to weep softly. "But at least there isn't a war. Please take him to safety. I don't want him to grow up in a war."

She was a poor woman, struggling just to stay alive. She understood powerlessness as well as the mothers of King Solomon's time, who were likely members of his harem whose lives were out of their own control. But above all else, she loved her son.

Ricardo's mother felt the pain of the mother in the scripture: a love so great that she was willing to suffer separation to save the life of her child. When Solomon suggested dividing the living infant in half with a sword, "because compassion for her son burned within her," the biblical mother was willing to give him up—to give up his joyful laughter in the morning, his playful loving throughout the day, and the comforting feel of him nursing at her breast as he dropped off to sleep at night. It was her deep and sacrificial love that showed Solomon the truth of her claim to be the boy's mother.

Ricardo stayed with his mother in Nicaragua. I think of him often, and of Martita and Rosita. It is perhaps the greatest scandal of our age that every day, forty thousand children on our globe die; fifteen million every year. Some die from war, others from neglect, most from starvation and hunger-related diseases. The estimated $2.5 billion a year needed from the world's nations to ensure the survival of most of the world's children is equal to what the world now spends on wars and weapons in *one day*.

All of these deaths are preventable, as senseless today as it would have been in Solomon's time to take a sword to a living infant. Often only mothers stand in the way, the last defense against the ravages of famine, greed, and violence. It does not take the wisdom of Solomon to know that sacrificing our children means only that we all die a little.

30 Eunice and Lois: Mentors of Faith

SCRIPTURE: 2 Tim. 1:5; 3:14–15

I am reminded of your sincere faith, a faith that lived first in your grandmother Lois and your mother Eunice and now, I am sure, lives in you. (2 Tim. 1:5)

"Think you could help me walk some chickens back from the market, chop their heads off, and pluck them?" Valearia Latham wanted to know. This was New Haven, Connecticut, in the late 1970s. I had never before received such a request as the chaplain of a low-income housing tenement for the elderly.

Valearia Latham was a rotund woman in her eighties. She had a round, caramel-colored face dotted with freckles and wreathed by wiry, salt-and-pepper hair that stood out in all directions. That face bore a perpetual smile. She was planning to eat the chickens and save the feathers in an old pillowcase for making into a pillow one day. The task was not exactly in my job description, but she clearly needed some assistance and I thought that I might learn a few things. I had never herded chickens before.

But on the morning of the big venture, she called to tell me there would be no trip to the market that day. Word had gotten out to the neighbors. The toothless and rather crotchety man next door had said, "We have enough problems around here without having a bunch of birds running around like chickens with their heads cut off!" He didn't mean it to be funny, of course. But Valearia Latham laughed until tears came down her cheeks at that one. She had an infectious sense of joy.

She was a mother of 13 children and a grandmother of 104. She spent many hours reading her family Bible, and we always prayed together on my visits. Despite her severe rheumatism, backaches, and hearing problems, she never engaged in self-pity and was always eager to talk about her love of God. She was fond of exhorting me to keep deepening my faith, reminding me that "standing in the Lord isn't the same as *standing still* in the Lord!" One afternoon, deeply absorbed in the large Bible open on her lap, she suddenly looked up into my eyes and said, "I know I'm gonna see the Lord face to face real soon. But until that day, I'm gonna keep looking for him in here."

Sitting beside her was like being transported down south to the home she had left in North Carolina. She told me tales of legendary courage and faith from the early days of the civil rights struggle. Her home had been a resting place for freedom riders and others who had come to join the fight for equality in the South of the 1950s and '60s. Her children were raised on the stories of their heritage that were told around her large dinner table—and on the stories of the Bible. And they, in turn, passed these stories on to their children. Each member of the family was grounded in the love of a God who stood beside sons and daughters who stood up for justice.

Valearia Latham still offered hospitality in large portions. Her pantry was always overflowing with collard greens and sweet potatoes. She gave me my first—and last—meal of pigs' feet, tails, and ears. Hers was the best southern fried chicken I have ever tasted. She served it at Christmas when my seminary friends and I came caroling, explaining, with a wink in my direction, "Because they probably eat pigs' feet with the same lack of relish you do."

She never had many of the world's goods. But Valearia Latham knew the gifts of the Spirit intimately: faith, courage, generosity, compassion. She passed them on to all her progeny—and to a few fortunate ones like me who were privileged to sit at her feet for a time. I suppose that she and Eunice and Lois get together from time to time up in heaven and talk about the grandchildren. Maybe she makes them fried chicken with sweet potatoes and collard greens. They probably laugh a lot.

Eunice and Lois appear by name in only one verse in the Bible. But from these twenty-eight words and a few others addressed to Timothy, we can assume a great deal about the two women. Lois, Timothy's grandmother, must have played an important role in his upbringing, along with his mother, Eunice. This reference to Lois is the only instance in the Bible in which the word "grandmother" appears.

Both women were Jewish Christians. Timothy's father was a Greek. They lived in the area around Derbe and Lystra, where Timothy, at the age of fifteen, heard Paul preach. Timothy was highly respected by his elders. Paul immediately recognized the outstanding qualities of this young man of faith and invited Timothy to join him on his missionary journeys (Acts 16:1–5).

It was probably Eunice's duty to intervene on Timothy's behalf and convince his nonbelieving father that his son had been called by God to spread a faith that the father didn't share. Surely, it must have been difficult for all of Timothy's family to let go of him at such a tender age, releasing him to the risks of travel and persecution. But he had been well prepared to receive this special calling.

It is not difficult to imagine Eunice and Lois rocking the infant Timothy to sleep in their arms, singing hymns of triumph, such as those that had come from the lips of Miriam, Deborah, and Mary, for lullabies. We can picture them vividly recounting tales of legendary strength and courage, introducing the young boy Timothy to the heroes of the faith, and teaching him to read and understand the scriptures. And when it came time for them to let go, they must have done so with pride and a flood of tears and prayers for his well-being.

The strong grounding in the faith that was passed on from grandmother to mother to son laid the seeds for Timothy's character as a man. He was loyal, compassionate, generous, and devoted to serving Christ. Two women were the vessels of teaching and example that prepared the way for a fruition of faithfulness.

Paul's respect and love for Timothy grew quickly and deeply as they traveled together, spreading the gospel. Paul began to consider his young companion "my loyal child in the faith" (1 Tim. 1:2) and "my beloved child" (2 Tim. 1:2). But the two who truly claimed such a bond were Eunice and Lois. They stand as stellar examples of devoted motherhood.

Part 6. Questions for Reflection

1. By which story in this section do you feel the most engaged? Why?

2. In many places around the globe, love for one's children is the driving force behind social change. If you are a parent, do you feel any conflict between choices or risks you would like to take and your children's needs?

3. If you are not a parent, do you feel that you are missing out on a crucial part of life?

4. Do you believe that the role of being a mother is valued in our society?

5. How could our society be changed to be a better place for families as well as single people?

PART 7
Leaders and Prophets

When asked to name female leaders in the Bible, most people can come up with Miriam, Deborah, and Priscilla. A prophet, a judge, and an early church leader, these three women left their mark on faith history. Less well known are Huldah and Phoebe, an interpreter of the law and a missionary of the gospel, respectively.

Today, some pockets within the church prohibit women from offering leadership, and others restrict the fullness of women's gifts. But these five women and the contemporary witnesses who have been paired with them invite us all to serve freely wherever God calls us.

31 Miriam: Freedom Leader

SCRIPTURE: Ex. 15:19–21; Numbers 12

Then the prophet Miriam, Aaron's sister, took a tambourine in her hand; and all the women went out after her with tambourines and with dancing. And Miriam sang to them: "Sing to the Lord, for he has triumphed gloriously; horse and rider he has thrown into the sea." (Ex. 15:20–21)

Miriam is the only woman in the Bible whose recorded story spans childhood to death. We first meet her as a girl on the bank of the Nile River, watching over the infant Moses as he floats in a basket. It was young Miriam who negotiated her brother's survival, at the cost of her own relationship with her mother, Jochebed. We hear nothing more of Miriam until she is an adult; but it is likely that while her mother tended her brother in the luxury of the pharaoh's palace, Miriam grew up apart from them in the slave quarters reserved for Israelites.

This shrewd and courageous child matured into a shrewd and courageous leader of her people. She is mentioned alongside her brothers Moses and Aaron as one who was raised up by God to deliver her people from bondage (Micah 6:3–4).

The slavery of the Israelites under the Egyptian pharaoh was brutal and oppressive. The people were forced to gather straw and make bricks, the taskmasters beaten when quotas were not filled. As the people's suffering increased, Moses and Aaron pleaded with pharaoh to set the Israelites free. But the pharaoh's "heart was hardened." Despite a barrage of grotesque plagues sent by God against Egypt—including the Nile turning to blood, the country swarming with frogs and flies and gnats and locusts, the land taking volleys of hail and rain and fire, and the people being struck with boils—pharaoh was unrelenting.

Not until the plague of death did pharaoh change his mind. All of the Israelites were ordered by God to kill a lamb and put its blood on the lintel and doorposts of their homes. These homes God chose to "pass over." But in every Egyptian home, at midnight, the firstborn was slain. So great was the grief of the Egyptians that the pharaoh ordered Moses and Aaron to gather up all of the Israelites and their herds and go. The people left hastily, before their bread had time to rise. And thus was initiated the Jewish festival of Passover, with its ritual of unleavened bread, which has been observed for centuries.

After 430 years of slavery, "about six hundred thousand men on foot, besides [women and] children" (too unimportant to count), fled from Egypt, along with a multitude of sheep and cattle (Ex. 12:37–38). God led them with a pillar of cloud by day and a pillar of fire to light the way by night.

But after a time, having lost his source of cheap labor, the pharaoh changed his mind once again. He and his soldiers and horses and hundreds of chariots pursued the Israelites and caught up to them where they were encamped by the Sea of Reeds. The Israelites were fearful, cursing Moses for having brought them into the wilderness to die. But at God's command, Moses lifted his rod, stretched out his hand, and parted the waters of the sea. The pillar of cloud moved between the Israelites and their pursuers, and the people of God walked across the dry bed of the sea. As the Egyptians followed, Moses stretched his hand back over the sea and the waters rushed over the soldiers and horses and chariots.

What a gasp of collective relief must have arisen from the Israelites, safe on the other shore—and then a moment of stunned silence as they pondered what they had just witnessed. Then Miriam the prophet picked up a tambourine and sang a song of triumph; its echoes were to be picked up by Deborah, who sang a victory song, and then by Hannah and Mary the mother of God, whose praises of justice have reverberated through time. One of the oldest poetic couplets in the Old Testament, the Song of Miriam culminated the wondrous story of the exodus.

The other women, shaken from their quiet awe, joined Miriam, dancing and playing tambourines as they reveled in their freedom and the protection of their God. In creative, feminine harmony, they raised a chorus of deliverance, dancing a whirl of liberation by the sea. It was an incredible moment in faith history, captured in the poetry and movement of women.

This was Miriam's finest moment. Her story takes a tragic turn after she challenges Moses for having married a foreigner, a Cushite (Ethiopian) woman (Numbers 12). Behind this confrontation appears to be Miriam's desire for recognition of her gifts. The words spoken against Moses in this matter are credited to both Miriam and Aaron. They ask, "Has the Lord spoken only through Moses? Has he not spoken through us also?" (Num. 12:2). God is displeased with their complaint but strikes only Miriam with leprosy; Aaron, apparently, is untouched.

Despite her brothers' pleadings on her behalf, Miriam is put outside the camp for seven days. Certainly, that week of exile and disease must have been her most painful, especially since she alone bore the curse.

Could it be that the male writers who interpreted the story believed that only Miriam deserved to be banished? Did she step outside the bounds they had delineated for women? Was she punished for speaking her mind, for wanting a share of the recognition accorded to her brother? We can never know all of what motivated Miriam to level her challenge, whether pride, xenophobia, or simply a need to protect her younger brother, as she had from the day of his birth. But we do know that her sin was not unforgivable; the Israelites did not move ahead until she was welcomed back among them.

We can imagine Miriam in her last days, a strong woman, encouraging the other women during the difficult times in the wilderness as she had helped to usher them across the Sea of Reeds. She likely played a helpful role when the people began to murmur against her brothers, when quail and manna sustained them and the Promised Land seemed so far away.

Like Moses, Miriam never made it to that land flowing with milk and honey. She died and was buried in the wilderness (Num. 20:1). She remains a beloved prophet in history, a woman whose life from the beginning was marked by courage. Her Hebrew name, which shares the same root as the Greek name Mary, means "rebellion" or "hope of change."[1] Indeed, Miriam will always be remembered for helping to lead her people in a rebellion for freedom.

A similar rebellion swept the United States in the middle of this century. In the summer of 1962, a bus left rural Ruleville, Mississippi, for the Sunflower County Courthouse in Indianola. It was carrying black women and men from nearby plantations to register to vote. On the way back from Indianola, a police car flagged down the bus and carried the driver off to jail. Fear and panic swept the bus. But out of the crowd came a strong, clear voice, singing. It was the voice of Fannie Lou Hamer, singing the song that she made famous in the civil rights struggle, "This Little Light of Mine." Immediately, calm descended on the bus as others joined in.

The owner of the plantation where Hamer worked, hearing that she had tried to register to vote, evicted her when she refused to remove her name from the courthouse rolls. That same night, night riders came through and shot up the home where Hamer and her family were staying.

Fannie Lou Hamer, the youngest of twenty children, was born in

1917 to a family of sharecroppers in the Mississippi Delta, then the poorest region of the poorest state in the nation. Jim Crow laws were in effect: all public facilities were either segregated or reserved for whites. The sharecropping system, just one step removed from slavery, had been devised to keep blacks in grinding poverty and perpetual debt to plantation owners. Through the hard work of her parents and all of their children, Hamer's family was one of the very few to break out of the oppressive system. But their hopes and dreams were destroyed when a white man poisoned all their livestock.

For twenty years, Hamer worked on various plantations, saying one day as she was picking cotton, "Hard as we have to work for nothing, there must be some way we can change this."[2] A door opened in August 1962, when she was urged by a friend to attend a rally sponsored by the Southern Christian Leadership Conference (SCLC) and the Student Nonviolent Coordinating Committee (SNCC), which ended with a call for blacks to register to vote. At the age of forty-five, Fannie Lou Hamer decided to answer that call. When she went to register, she was confronted with the infamous and outlandishly complex Mississippi literacy test, which required blacks to copy and interpret an arcane section of the state constitution to the satisfaction of the county examiner. Hamer, like most blacks, failed the first time. But she told the clerk that he would see her every thirty days for the rest of her life until she passed. She was finally registered five months later, in January 1963.

Fannie Lou Hamer plunged full time into the freedom movement as a SNCC field secretary. She traveled cotton fields by day and spoke in churches at night, recruiting others to register to vote. She received death threats by phone and mail and was harassed by Mississippi authorities, the Ku Klux Klan, the White Citizens' Council, and the FBI.

Her worst confrontation with "law and order" came in June 1963, when she was returning from a voter education workshop in Charleston, South Carolina. At the bus station in Winona, Mississippi, she and others with her sat at a whites-only lunch counter. Police officers came and threw them in jail, where they were brutally beaten. Hamer heard the officers plotting to kill the protesters and throw their bodies in the river where they would not be found. She and the others refused to sign statements at gunpoint saying that their wounds were self-inflicted. Two days later, after intervention from civil rights workers and the U.S. Justice Department, they were released. Her wounds never left her: she suffered kidney damage and developed a blood clot in her left eye that permanently impaired her vision.

But Hamer never became bitter. She said after her ordeal, "It wouldn't solve any problem for me to hate whites just because they hate me. Oh, there's so much hate, only God has kept the Negro sane." She added, "I feel sorry for anybody that could let hate wrap them up. Ain't no such thing as I can hate anybody and hope to see God's face."[3] She kept her sense of humor, even in the midst of persecution. "They tried to brand me as a communist," she said once, "and I know as much about communism as a horse do about Christmas."[4]

Fannie Lou Hamer went on to become Mississippi's most beloved freedom fighter and a nationally recognized civil rights leader. As a founder of the alternative Mississippi Freedom Democratic Party (MFDP), in 1964 she led the challenge against the whites-only Mississippi Democratic Party at the national convention in Atlantic City, stirring the nation with her authority and courage. This was the first mountaintop from which she proclaimed, "Let my people go!"

As a prophet "speaking truth to power," Hamer took on the chief negotiator, Hubert Humphrey, who was in line for the vice presidency. She confronted his pleas for "reasonableness" with her testimony about people who had been threatened and fired from their jobs for registering to vote, urging him to listen to his conscience. When it became clear that that round of their challenge was lost, she ended a high-level negotiating session by saying simply, "Senator Humphrey, I'm gonna pray to Jesus for you."[5]

The MFDP carried its challenge all the way to the U.S. Congress. In January 1965, Hamer went to Washington along with other representatives elected from the MFDP. While Congress considered the merits of the MFDP case, the white congressmen from Mississippi had to step aside for a few minutes. Hamer and two other women from the MFDP took seats as the first black women in the U.S. House of Representatives. Soon enough, however, Congress voted to reseat the white men. Though the MFDP challenges failed, they were a major force in generating the pressure that led to the passage of the 1965 Voting Rights Act.

Fannie Lou Hamer was one of the first critics of the Vietnam War and an avid fighter for women's rights. She worked tirelessly for the poor people of Sunflower County. She led the battle to get the Head Start program in Mississippi and organized the Freedom Farm Cooperative to obtain land for farmers who had been left unemployed by farm mechanization. She helped raise money to build low-income housing, start a day-care center, and bring a garment factory to Ruleville to provide jobs. She was an organizer for Martin Luther King

Jr.'s final dream, the Poor People's Campaign. Above all, she led her people to freedom. The name Fannie Lou, too, shares a root with "rebellion."

A lifetime of hard physical labor, a decade of pouring herself out in the freedom struggle, and numerous health problems, including lingering effects from childhood polio and the Winona beating, finally took their toll. Fannie Lou Hamer died in March 1977. By her grave on Freedom Farm Cooperative land is a simple marble headstone. It bears the words that were her motto and rallying cry: "I am sick and tired of being sick and tired."

She had said before her death, "Sometimes it seems like today to tell the truth is to run the risk of being killed. But if I fall, I'll fall five feet four inches forward in the fight for freedom. I'm not backing off that and no one will have to cover the ground I walk as far as freedom is concerned."[6] She took us much farther along than she ever imagined.

As L. C. Dorsey, a sister in the civil rights movement, said of Hamer, "She really was the prophet feeding the people the truth."[7] This prophet revealed much about herself in a musical work she created by combining the freedom message of the exodus with the incarnation message of Christmas. Hamer joined Moses' words to pharaoh from the old slave spiritual—with its refrain "Let my people go!"—to the Christmas spiritual "Go Tell It on the Mountain." But she will be most remembered for her rendering of the song that everyone connects with her, the one that opened many a freedom rally and meeting; for she is indeed a shining light. "This little light of mine, I'm gonna let it shine. . . . Let it shine, let it shine, let it shine!"

NOTES

1. Ann Johnson, *Miryam of Nazareth* (Notre Dame, Ind.: Ave Maria Press, 1984), 13.
2. Danny Collum, "Stepping Out into Freedom," *Sojourners* 11, no. 10 (December 1982): 12.
3. Edwin King, "Go Tell It on the Mountain," *Sojourners* 11, no. 10 (December 1982): 18.
4. Ibid., 20.
5. Ibid., 19.
6. Collum, "Stepping Out," 16.
7. L. C. Dorsey, "A Prophet Who Believed," *Sojourners* 11, no. 10 (December, 1982): 21.

32   Deborah: An Inspired Judge

SCRIPTURE: Judg. 4:1–16; 5:1–23

At that time Deborah, a prophetess, wife of Lappidoth, was judging Israel. She used to sit under the palm of Deborah between Ramah and Bethel in the hill country of Ephraim; and the Israelites came up to her for judgment. (Judg. 4:4–5)

Deborah was a prophet and judge in Israel. The Hebrew phrase *'eshet lappidot* describing her has been translated as "wife of Lappidoth." We know nothing about this man Lappidoth; this is a unique instance in the Old Testament in which a woman was more well known than her husband, defined by her gifts rather than her relationships and earning respect in her own right. Scholars have pointed out that the same Hebrew phrase can also be translated "spirited woman" or "woman of fire."[1]

The period of the judges in the history of Israel is a fascinating and somewhat disturbing one. God raised up judges in response to cycles of unfaithfulness and repentance (Judg. 2:16–19). The Israelites would sin and turn from God, giving in to idolatry and immorality and suffering at the hands of their pagan enemies. Then, when the people cried out from their oppression and promised to return to faith, God raised up a judge.

Deborah was the fourth judge and the only one who is actually described serving a judicial function. The judges were in essence tribal heroes or deliverers, whose authority was acknowledged by the people to be from God. They helped to keep Israel from being destroyed or co-opted into the surrounding cultures. A voice for divine will, Deborah sat under a palm tree, where she dispensed the wisdom of her judgments to the Israelites who came to her with their difficulties and disputes. She was also known for her talents as a military strategist and a leader of songs—a very gifted woman. So loved was she that she was called a "mother in Israel."

She was the one who told Barak of God's plan for his life. She summoned him and told him of God's command to go to Mount Tabor for a military victory over Sisera, general of the enemy's army. Reluctant, Barak told Deborah that he would go off to war only if Deborah went with him; he needed her for courage, and he had complete confidence in her. Although facing nine hundred Canaanite chariots made of iron and a fleet of archers, Barak and his foot soldiers prevailed with swords. According to the story, God opened the heavens, sending pounding hail and rain that deflected the aim of the archers, panicked the horses, and mired the chariots in mud.

We know the end for Sisera from the story of Jael. And once again, we should bring to mind that grieving mother standing by the window—and all the mothers and brothers and daughters of the "enemy" troops. We might wish that Deborah had used some of her considerable power to confront the masculine warmongering that was in vogue in her day, that as a wise and respected woman, she might have tried to change the rules. Nevertheless, for her courage she deserves an honored place in history. Indeed, two women were the heroes of this story. Interestingly, neither of them appears in the list of heroes recounted in Hebrews—although Barak does (Heb. 11:32).

The recounting of the story ends with the Song of Deborah. Spanning the entire fifth chapter of Judges, Deborah's song is considered the oldest extant large segment of Hebrew literature. It is similar in style and spirit to Miriam's "Song of the Sea" in Exodus. Though it includes Barak and Jael as her partners in heroism, the song bears Deborah's name and is primarily a tribute to her. It points to the near-anarchy that existed before she arose as a judge, a time when "caravans ceased" and "travelers kept to the byways." It poetically recounts the military triumph, when "the stars fought from heaven" and "loud beat the horses' hoofs with the galloping, galloping of his steeds" in the face of the "onrushing torrent" that "swept them away."

The song praises Deborah for all time as a deliverer raised up by God, who empowered her people in a war of liberation. Forty years of peace endured during Deborah's reign as judge. Patriarchy was not strong enough to override God's choice of a wise, spirit-filled "woman of fire" to lead her people.

Centuries later, in the winter of 1147, Pope Eugenius III called for a synod to discuss a much talked-about German nun, Hildegard of Bingen. A bishop returned with his commission from their investigation of Hildegard to report, "I found her, Holy Father, as a flaming torch which our Lord has lighted in His Church." The pope replied: "Then we must not put it under a bushel."[2] Hildegard herself described her experience of God at the age of forty-two: "Heaven was opened and a fiery light of exceeding brilliance came and permeated my whole brain, and inflamed my whole heart."[3]

When she was eight, Hildegard's parents offered their tenth and last child as a "tithe to the Lord." They put her into the care of Jutta, the daughter of the local duke, whom Hildegard's father served as a knight. Jutta lived in a cell adjoining a Benedictine monastery, and at the age of fifteen, Hildegard took vows as a nun.

Hildegard was best known in her own time and in later ages as a prophet. Pilgrims came from all over Europe to consult her, as the Israelites had journeyed to Deborah's palm. In letters and direct encounters, Hildegard counseled the great leaders of her time, including popes, German emperors, and British kings. Although in frail health, in her fifties she traveled throughout Germany by horseback and in her seventies throughout France, delivering her prophetic words and denouncing corruption, decadence, and power struggles in the church.

It was a difficult time to be a prophet. In the early part of her century, heretics were burned at Cologne, and by the end of it, the Inquisition had visited its tortures on Europe. Thousands of warriors marched off in the Crusades to seize the Holy Land back from the Muslims, and confusion ravaged the church. During Hildegard's lifetime, thirteen popes and twelve antipopes claimed the holy throne.

Hildegard understood well what she called the "wretched" state of women in her day but never allowed her gender to hold her back. Even in the last year of her life, at the age of eighty, she refused to sway from acting with moral courage. The archbishop (whom she had reproved for living a life of luxury in Italy) went after Hildegard and her sisters because they had buried at the monastery a revolutionary youth who had been excommunicated from the church. Church officials ordered her to dig up and remove the body from sacred ground. When she refused, her convent was placed under interdict for a year, meaning that all Masses, sacraments, and music were prohibited. Never giving in, Hildegard went out to the cemetery and, with her walking stick, erased all the lines around the grave so that it could not be found.

Like Deborah, Hildegard's talents were many. She composed dozens of hymns and wrote the first known morality play, which is still performed today. She wrote nearly three hundred letters, dozens of poems, and nine books, three of which were considered major theological works. Her most celebrated book, *Scivias* (Know the Ways of the Lord), took her almost ten years to complete. Under her direction, her community of sisters "illuminated," or illustrated, manuscripts with an artistic flourish.

Among Hildegard's books was a rudimentary encyclopedia of natural and herbal medicines. Her interest in medicine stemmed from her own experience with chronic illness, and her monastery garden flowered with medicinal herbs. People came from all over for a touch of healing from this remarkable woman. She is credited with an early theory on the circulation of blood (and, on a more mundane level, with an early version of indoor plumbing).

Hildegard spoke of God as "true justice," which, along with wisdom, she understood as God's feminine self. She gave us a beautiful image of suckling justice from the breast of God, where we are refreshed and strengthened. She was in awe of the splendor and glory of creation. She believed that all that God created was interdependent, and she wrote with cosmic understanding about the earth as a sacred trust and the spirit that dwells in all its parts. God spoke these words to her in one of her many visions: "I am the supreme and fiery force who kindled every living spark. . . . I am the fiery life of the essence of God: I flame above the beauty of the fields; I shine in the waters; I burn in the sun, the moon, and the stars. And, with the airy wind, I quicken all things vitally by an unseen, all-sustaining life."[4]

Legend has it that when Hildegard died at the age of eighty-one, two streams of light appeared in the sky and crossed over her room as she left this world and went on to glory. Like her sister Deborah—and all of the female prophets before and since—she left her mark as a "woman of fire."

NOTES

1. Miriam Therese Winter, *WomanWitness* (New York: Crossroad, 1992), 33.
2. Joanne Turpin, *Women in Church History* (Cincinnati: St. Anthony Messenger Press, 1990), 92.
3. Gloria Durka, *Praying with Hildegard of Bingen* (Winona, Minn.: Saint Mary's Press, 1991), 28.
4. Ibid., 71–72.

33 Huldah: Consulted by the King

SCRIPTURE: 2 Chron. 34:1–2, 8, 14–33

Those whom the king had sent went to the prophet Huldah
. . . .She declared to them, " . . . Thus says the Lord: I will
indeed bring disaster upon this place and upon its inhabi-
tants." (2 Chron. 34: 22–24)

After a period dominated by paganism, the God-fearing king
Josiah was leading a campaign to restore the faith of the Israelites.
Under the direction of Hilkiah, the high priest, men were at work
repairing the Temple in 621 B.C.E. Amid the dust and rubble, Hilkiah
found a scroll. Believing the ancient scroll to be of great importance,
Hilkiah dusted it off and had it presented to the king. When Josiah
heard the words written there, he tore his clothes, knowing that if
these words were indeed from the Lord, much more sweeping reforms
were required than he had in mind.

But Josiah needed someone to authenticate the scroll. His high-
ranking delegation could have gone to one of the well-known
prophets, Jeremiah, Zephaniah, or Nahum, all of whom were helping
the king in his campaign to restore the faith. But the king's cabinet
chose a woman.

According to Jewish tradition, Huldah conducted an academy in
Jerusalem. To be chosen for this most auspicious task, she was surely a
woman of intellectual prowess and spiritual depth. Like Miriam and
Deborah, Huldah was a prophet. With the mandate "Go inquire of the
Lord," five personal messengers of the king, including the high priest,
visited her home with the sacred scroll. Clearly, Huldah was viewed as
someone with whom God spoke directly.

Huldah opened the scroll carefully and read intently. She confirmed
its authenticity. It was the long-lost Book of the Law, the heart of what
today is known as the book of Deuteronomy. It was one of the most
important books in the history of Israel.

The importance of this story is made clear by the fact that it is
recorded twice in scripture. An account that is identical—except for
some elaboration of the destruction of the idols after Huldah's prophecy—is found in 2 Kings 22:8–23:3. It is only the male bias of history

that has made Huldah less familiar to us than her male prophet counterparts.

Huldah made history that day. Until then, no writings had been named as Holy Scripture, designated as authoritative testimony to God's will. Huldah set in motion a canonization process that culminated eight centuries later with the gathering of dozens of manuscripts into what we today call the Bible. According to biblical commentator Arlene Swidler, Huldah was "the first Scripture authority, the founder of biblical studies."[1]

Huldah understood the full import of the scroll that had been placed in her hands. She prophesied the wrath of God toward the kingdom of Judah because of the people's unfaithfulness. Trusting her insight completely, the king immediately went into action, gathering all the people and their leaders and making a covenant before God.

The king took decisive and astounding measures in response to Huldah's interpretation of the law. He destroyed all the idols to Baal and deposed the idolatrous priests who made offerings to the sun, the moon, and the stars. He burned a false image, beat it to dust, and threw the dust on the graves of the people. He broke down the houses of the male cult prostitutes and the false altars. He removed the horses at the Temple entrance that had been dedicated to the sun, and he burned the pagan chariots. He broke the pillars of the false temples and covered the sites with human bones. He put away all the mediums and wizards. And then he commanded the people to keep the Passover (2 Kings 23:4–20).

After many years of unfaithfulness, the people returned to the rituals of their tradition and entered again into a covenant with God. The words of a woman, who opened herself to be used as a vessel for the word of God, sparked conversion throughout the kingdom.

We know little else about Huldah's life, except that she was married to a man who kept the king's wardrobe. But surely, she must have commanded respect far and wide throughout the kingdom of Judah for her prophetic courage. The words she uttered were not easy to speak. But she voiced the painful truth of the word of God, joining the ranks of the prophets who continually called the people away from the error of their ways and toward the way of God. The Mishnah, the first section of the Jewish Talmud, notes that the two southern gates to the Temple Mount were called the Huldah Gates in her honor.[2]

Two thousand years later, another woman was consulted by kings—and popes. Born in 1347, Catherine of Siena was the twenty-fifth and last child in a dyer's family. She developed a love of God early, and her parents gave her a small basement "cell" with a plank for a bed, a log pillow, a lamp, and a crucifix, where she prayed, fasted, and meditated.

Pressured by her parents during her teen years to marry, Catherine cut off her hair and declared herself married to Christ. At sixteen she took monastic vows, joining the Dominican Third Order. For three years she lived in seclusion, seeking spiritual union with God. She heard a call from Christ to go out into the world. She was uncertain at first, asking of God, "Who am I, a woman, to go into public service?" But God's answer was clear to her: "The word impossible belongs not to God; am not I he who created the human race, who formed both man and woman? I pour out the favor of My Spirit on whom I will. Go forth without fear, in spite of reproach. . . . I have a mission for you to fulfill."[3]

Catherine began by visiting prisons, comforting the accused and their families at executions, and feeding and clothing the destitute. When the plague swept through Siena for the second time in twenty-five years, claiming the lives of hundreds every day, she dedicated herself to nursing the sick. She became much in demand as a peacemaker, healing rifts within and between families. Though frail of health and small of stature, she never closed the door on a need that was presented to her. Her spirit and work were so notable that she soon had a following of disciples, both men and women. Called the Caterinati, this community of followers included a poet, an artist, and many people who had been rescued from lives of illness, idleness, or despair. Though she was younger than her faithful followers, they affectionately called her "Mama."

Catherine's empathy for the world's suffering led her to critique both the social system and the church of her time. A century and a half before Martin Luther launched his reformation, Catherine took on the Roman Catholic Church, criticizing the power of the pope's representatives and the luxury of the churches, accumulated at the expense of the poor. She lectured Pope Gregory XI, who was weak in character and lived in the papal court in opulent and decadent France. She urged him to escape the corrupting influence of the French monarchy and return to Rome to begin the business of cleansing and purifying the church, which she believed was in grave peril because of its unfaithfulness.

A medieval Huldah, Catherine minced no words about God's judgment on moral weakness and the idolatries of power, saying once to the pope's face, "To the glory of Almighty God I am bound to say that I smelled the stink of the sins which flourish in the papal court while I was still in my own town."[4] She suggested that if the pope was unwilling to exercise moral authority, he should resign. Catherine's persistence eventually convinced Gregory to return to Rome. His successor, Urban VI, actively sought her advice on reforming the church.

Although Catherine came from humble origins, had no formal training, learned to read only at age twenty, and never learned to write, she, like Huldah, had great success in bringing the people back to the ways of God. Her advice to heads of state was equally direct. She dictated letters to kings, queens, and princes, advocating fairness and peace. She became a well-known diplomat, taking her peacemaking abilities beyond families to settle the disputes of the various city-states of Italy, which were vying with one another for political and economic power. She helped draw up peace treaties and advised rulers. When she got caught between the violence of pro-papal and anti-papal forces, she offered herself up to an angry mob with drawn swords in order to save the people with her; her courage so stunned the mob that it fled.

Catherine spent the last months of her life in Rome, sending letters to European rulers and church officials, trying to save the papacy from disaster. She addressed the Sacred College of Cardinals, urging them to have faith. When she concluded, Pope Urban said to the gathering, "This poor little woman puts us to shame by her courage."[5]

As schism in the church began to look inevitable, Catherine, at the young age of thirty-three, suffered two strokes. She died believing that she had failed in her effort to unite the church. But she had single-handedly changed history by ending the church's seventy-year captivity to French corruption and domination, and many historians believe that if she had lived, the Great Schism that divided the church might have been averted.

In her time, Catherine was considered the most powerful woman in Europe. She served as the conscience of the church and the soul of the state. Before she died, she spent three months dictating her spiritual guide *Divine Dialogue*, keeping three secretaries busy with the task of recording it. For this gem of faith, she was granted the title "Doctor of the Church."

Catherine of Siena was a truly remarkable woman. She possessed the rare combination of mystical union with God, compassionate care for the suffering, and prophetic courage to confront the powerful. She will be remembered as a saint of exquisite faithfulness—and, like Huldah, as a prophet who never flagged from "speaking truth to power."

NOTES

1. William E. Phipps, "Huldah and the Presbyterians," *The Presbyterian Outlook*, March 2, 1987.
2. Miriam Therese Winter, *WomanWisdom* (New York: Crossroad, 1991), 336.
3. Nancy A. Hardesty, *Great Women of Faith* (Grand Rapids: Baker Book House, 1980), 42–43.
4. Joanne Turpin, *Women in Church History* (Cincinnati: St. Anthony Messenger Press, 1991), 112.
5. Ibid., 117.

34 Phoebe: Bearer of the Gospel

SCRIPTURE: Rom. 16:1–2

I commend to you our sister Phoebe, a deacon of the church at Cenchreae, so that you may welcome her in the Lord as is fitting for the saints, and help her in whatever she may require from you, for she has been a benefactor of many and of myself as well. (Rom. 16:1–2)

A fresco in a Roman catacomb, dating to the end of the first century C.E., portrays a group of seven women celebrating the Eucharist. Interestingly, a later mosaic copy of this fresco has altered the picture. Male clothing has been added to one of the figures, beards to some of the others. The women have been changed into men.

The Roman fresco is just one confirmation that women served as priests and bishops in the early church. Dorothy Irvin, an archaeologist, theologian, and photographer for the Biblical Archaeological Institute at Tübingen in Germany for several years, has uncovered a variety of telling evidence. Inscriptions on ancient tombstones bear names of women with titles such as "ruler of the synagogue," "mother of the synagogue," "presbyter," and "honorable woman bishop." An early mosaic portrays a woman and is inscribed "Bishop Theodora." A fourth-century catacomb fresco depicts a woman being ordained by a bishop, and many other frescoes are depictions of women dressed in vestments and assuming positions of liturgical leadership.[1]

Although biblical scholars disagree about Phoebe's precise role in the church at Cenchreae, a seaport next to Corinth, we can assume that she was among the prominent church leaders who both kept and spread the faith. Known as a benefactor of Paul and many others in the ministry of spreading the gospel, she was a woman of authority and influence who had earned great respect. It is likely that her home in Cenchreae was a meeting place for Christians, where she would have presided over the breaking of the bread.

Phoebe brought a multitude of talents and resources to the early church. Paul calls her "sister," just as he calls Timothy and other well-known church leaders and missionaries "brother." He compares Phoebe to the saints. His description of her as *diakonos* in Greek has often been mistranslated as "deaconess," consigning Phoebe to a subservient, helping role. But Paul uses the same word to refer to himself, Timothy, and others who had a central and unique position in building up the early church.

With the words of introduction recorded in Romans, Phoebe carried Paul's epistle to the Roman Christians. In choosing her as his messenger, Paul had conferred a rare honor on this woman, who must have exhibited the courage and strength necessary for making the arduous journey, as well as the faith and presence to be well received and regarded.

The thirteen verses following the commendation of Phoebe (Rom. 16:3–15) contain the names of more than two dozen Christians in Rome to whom Paul sent greetings. It is worth noting that nine of these are women. They are commended for their courage (Prisca) and their hard work (Mary) and are named "apostle" (Junia), "workers in the Lord" (Tryphaena and Tryphosa), and "beloved" (Persis). Junia (whose name some translators have mistakenly changed to the male Junias) was imprisoned for her faith and acknowledged by Paul as a believer before him. Nowhere does Paul imply that these women were second-class Christians or that their gifts were unwelcome in the church.

Other church women appear throughout the New Testament. Some are merely mentioned by name in greeting (Nympha in Col. 4:15; Claudia in 2 Tim. 4:21; Apphia in Philemon v. 2). Little is known about these women. Translators have been in disagreement over Nympha's gender. Some biblical historians believe that Apphia, from the church in Colossae, was martyred by stoning during the reign of Nero. Likely they all offered leadership in house churches, as did Chloe, whose representatives bore news of dissension in the church at Corinth to Paul (1 Cor. 1:10–11). Euodia and Syntyche, leaders of the church in Philippi, had a personal disagreement (Phil. 4:2–3). Paul, rather than silencing or reprimanding them, took their argument seriously, commending them as having "struggled beside me in the work of the gospel" and urging a friend to mediate between them.

Damaris, a woman of Athens, became a believer when she heard Paul preach against idolatry (Acts 17:34). Some historians believe that she was one of the *Hetairai*, an intellectual class of women associated with philosophers and statesmen. She must have been a woman of distinction to have been named, especially in the same reference with Dionysius, a judge.

The four daughters of Philip the evangelist were blessed with the gift of prophecy (Acts 21:8–9). Although they remain unnamed in the text, they were well known for their transmission of the apostolic tradition and their illumination of the word of God. That they are mentioned at all is likely due to their father's having been chosen as one of the seven men considered to have been the first deacons of the church (Acts 6:2–5). How many other women, without such a family connection, fulfilled the calling laid out by the prophet Joel, quoted by Peter at Pentecost: " 'In the last days it will be, God declares, that I will pour out my Spirit upon all flesh, and your sons and your daughters shall prophesy, and your young men shall see visions, and your old men shall dream dreams. Even upon my slaves, both men and women, in those days I will pour out my Spirit; and they shall prophesy' " (Acts 2:17–18)?

One who heard that call in more recent history was Antoinette Brown. Born in 1825, Brown believed that God was calling her to the ordained ministry. She was told, however, that her pursuit of the ministry would upset the very moral order of the universe; friends urged her not to combat the harmony that results from "established, ordained masculine headship."[2]

Antoinette Brown laid the groundwork for what has become a widely accepted feminist interpretation of 1 Cor. 14:34–35 and 1 Tim. 2:11–12, those thorny passages that admonish women to be submissive, keep silence in church, and hold no authority over men. Her paper on the subject argued that these verses, rather than prohibiting women from preaching, were intended to silence disruptive, idle speech so that women could learn and be *empowered* to preach. The paper created a major uproar at Oberlin College, where she was studying theology.

Antoinette Brown opened the door for an interpretation that returned women to the equality they experienced in the years closest to Jesus' days on earth. And with raw courage and determination, she took on the male church establishment and pursued her call to ministry.

Brown completed her theological studies in 1850. Oberlin College officials refused to allow her to preach and would not arrange for her ordination, withholding her master's degree until 1878, almost thirty years later. Despite the resistance of college officials, on September 15, 1853, Antoinette Brown became the first woman officially ordained by a recognized denomination in the United States. She began her ministry at a Congregational church in New York State. That same fall, she created a furor in New York City when she rose to speak at a temperance convention, where it was assumed that only men could be heard. Her rising to the platform was accompanied by so much stomping and pounding of canes that the air filled with dust and she was unable to speak.

Brown refused the request of a mother in her parish to preach hellfire and damnation to a dying son, instead offering him the love of God and a peaceful death. The same mother caused dissension when Brown refused to preach on the evils of fornication and infant damnation at the funeral of a baby born to an unmarried mother. Above all else, Brown preached the grace and mercy of God.

She left parish ministry for a time, going to work for a year in New York City's slums and prisons. In articles and a subsequent book, she protested the social system that led to oppressive circumstances for the poor. She declared, "I pity the man or woman who does not choose to be identified with the cause of the oppressed."[3] She was a popular lecturer at women's rights conventions, often called on to offer her exegesis of biblical passages on women. She also founded a Unitarian church in New Jersey. When she was more than eighty years old, she traveled to the Holy Land, bringing back water from the River Jordan to baptize her grandchildren.

Antoinette Brown was such a gifted pastor and preacher that Oberlin College eventually recognized her contribution. Perhaps in an effort to correct their earlier mistake, college officials conferred on her an honorary doctorate of divinity in 1908, when she was eighty-three years old. On November 2, 1920, at age ninety-five, she was the only one of the original advocates of women's rights to exercise the right to vote. She died a year later.

After Brown was silenced at the temperance convention, she was asked how she continued in the face of such powerful and organized opposition. Antoinette Brown answered with words that are the testimony of her life: "There came rushing over my soul the words of Christ, 'I came not to send peace, but a sword.' . . . Above me, and within me, and all around me, there was a Spirit stronger than them all."[4]

NOTES

1. Janice Nunnally-Cox, *Foremothers* (New York: Seabury, 1981), 128–29.
2. Nancy A. Hardesty, *Great Women of Faith* (Grand Rapids: Baker Book House, 1980), 97.
3. Ibid., 101.
4. Ibid., 100.

35 Priscilla: Leader of the Church

SCRIPTURE: Acts 18:1–3, 18–19, 24–26; Rom. 16:3–5a

Greet Prisca and Aquila, who work with me in Christ Jesus, and who risked their necks for my life, to whom not only I give thanks, but also all the churches of the Gentiles. (Rom. 16:3–4)

She was courage personified. Her saga of faith began in Rome, where the emperor Claudius expelled all of the Jews around 50 C.E. Uprooted from home and family and emotional moorings, Priscilla fled the land of her birth and journeyed with her husband, Aquila, into exile in the bustling port city of Corinth. She shed her aristocratic heritage and started a new life as a tentmaker, spending her days weaving goat's hair into shelters and selling her creations at the marketplace. She shared the trade with Aquila—and before long, with an itinerant preacher who arrived at the door one day and stayed for a year and a half.

When Paul left for Ephesus, Priscilla and Aquila accompanied him, sharing a call based on faith and friendship. Once again, Priscilla left the familiar to tread on new and risky ground, this time for the sake of spreading the gospel. In Ephesus, as in Corinth, the couple exercised a team ministry, co-leading a church in their home, providing an excellent example of leadership through an equal partnership of spouses. At least once a week, believers gathered to break bread, pray, and sing. They shared word from similar communities across the empire, news of joys and persecutions brought to them in letters from missionaries who traveled the expansive network of Roman roads.

Priscilla and Aquila taught the gospel in the shadow of the looming temple of Artemis, one of the "seven wonders of the world." A cult of prostitution surrounded Artemis, the pagan goddess of fertility, ensnaring many of the young women of Ephesus. Each spring, thousands of pilgrims converged on the city, providing a lucrative market for the local silversmiths, who made replicas of the temple and idols of the many-breasted Artemis. So invested were the profiteers in their idols that a riot broke out when Paul and his companions began preaching the gospel and turning people away from the cult (Acts 19:23–41). In such a heated and hostile environment, Priscilla kept preaching her faith.

Perhaps the most fascinating glimpse of Priscilla comes in her inter-action with Apollos, who, eloquent and fervent, had come to Ephesus to preach. After hearing him, Priscilla and Aquila gently took him aside to correct some theological inaccuracies in his presentation and to expand his vision of the way of God. Apollos's preaching was based on John's view of baptism and repentance. Priscilla and Aquila taught him about baptism by grace and the Holy Spirit, bringing him to an under-standing of conversion through Christ.

There is no hint here that Priscilla was out of bounds, that she had entered territory reserved for men. She was a learned woman and a capable teacher, whose spirit reflected the Spirit of God. How shocked she would have been to learn that centuries later, Christians would quote scripture to prohibit the pastoral leadership of women—includ-ing a passage addressed to the Christians in the city where she first established her ministry!

As noted earlier, two passages have presented particular challenges to women: 1 Cor. 14:34–35, which exhorts women to "be silent in the churches," and 1 Tim. 2:11–15, permitting "no woman to teach or to have authority over a man." Biblical scholars have determined the pas-toral letters (1 and 2 Timothy and Titus) to be pseudonymous, rather than the work of Paul. They were written after the early charismatic era of the church when gifts were offered freely at the nudging of the Spirit, at a time when the church began to establish itself as an institution.

A radical change in the status of women in the faith took place from the early apostolic period (around 50 c.e.) to the beginning of the second century. Women, who in the early stages—when they had faced no barriers to the roles they could play or the leadership they could offer—had exerted great influence, were increasingly restricted as the church moved from a house-based, communal structure that chal-lenged society's norms to a patriarchal institution that embraced those norms. The church's growing preoccupation with social acceptability led over time to an orientation that paralleled the patriarchal order of the dominant culture of the Roman Empire. What have been mistak-enly assumed to be theological assumptions about the position of women were most often reflections of the restrictions of the various cultures through which Christianity spread. As the church began to conform to the society around it, it lost much of its early social radical-ism, including its insistence on the equality of women.

The Corinthians passage has mystified scholars, particularly because it contradicts Paul's partnership with and affirmation of female leaders in the church and his words elsewhere in the scriptures. Some scholars believe that the particular chaos being experienced in Corinth called for unusual measures. Others are convinced that these words are not Paul's but insertions from another writer that reflect the attitude of the later church, when men sought to solidify their control over the institution and its teachings and to restrict the influence of women. Or perhaps the passage simply reflects Paul's humanity. As a patriarchal Pharisee in many aspects of his doctrine, Paul himself was being educated, enlightened, and liberated by the likes of Priscilla and her sisters in leadership in the churches. And he did not always get it right.

Perhaps when Priscilla spoke to Apollos about baptism, she recited a baptismal creed that was used by the early church: "As many of you as were baptized into Christ have clothed yourselves with Christ. There is no longer Jew or Greek, there is no longer slave or free, there is no longer male and female; for all of you are one in Christ Jesus" (Gal. 3:27–28). Even at initiation into the Christian faith, the equality of women was well established. The early converts were baptized into a new social order in which differences of race, class, and gender were irrelevant. They were called to a new form of relationship based on the equality they all shared as the children of God and as members of Christ's church. Priscilla and Aquila became models of the new order of things.

After the emperor Claudius died (rumored to have been poisoned by his fourth wife), Priscilla and Aquila returned home to Rome. They were not forgotten by Paul, as his greeting in the letter to the Romans attests. He—and all the Gentile churches, according to Paul—remained indebted to the couple, who apparently had risked their own lives to save his, perhaps by intervening during the Ephesus riot or while he was in prison. His greeting of Priscilla by the diminutive Prisca reflects the intimacy of their enduring friendship.

Four of the six times that the couple's names appear in scripture Priscilla's appears first, an indication of her prominence and the wide respect she was accorded. She was one of the most influential women in the early church. She was clearly considered an equal by both her husband and Paul and was granted the status of coworker by the famous missionary apostle.

It is believed by some historians that Priscilla and Aquila were martyred in Nero's persecution of Christians in 64 C.E. If so, I am sure they went to their deaths with the kind of courage that marked their lives.

Priscilla's legacy lives on. Many scholars believe that she was the author of the letter to the Hebrews. One of the oldest catacombs of

Rome, the Coemeterium Priscilla, was named in her honor, as was the Church of St. Prisca, believed to have been built over her family home. "Acts of Prisca" was a popular tenth-century legendary writing.

It is clear that throughout Judeo-Christian history, the Spirit has blown where it has wanted to. Despite attempts to imprison it by doctrine or law, it tapped Miriam and Deborah and Huldah, Phoebe and Priscilla, and a host of other women known and unknown to carry on its work. God has not been satisfied to carry on the work of faith with only half of the available servants. Writing in the mid-1850s, Salvation Army cofounder Catherine Booth declared:

> Oh, that the ministers of religion would search the original records of God's Word in order to discover whether the general notions of society are not wrong on this subject, and whether God really intended woman to bury her gifts and talents, as she does now, with reference to the interests of his Church. Oh, that the Church generally would inquire whether narrow prejudice and lordly usurpation has not something to do with the circumscribed sphere of woman's religious labours, and whether much of the non-success of the Gospel is not attributable to the restrictions imposed upon the operations of the Holy Ghost in this as well as other particulars."[1]

Catherine knew God's Word. By the time she was twelve, she had read through the Bible eight times. As a young woman, she heard William Booth preach at her church, and eventually they became engaged. When he made the mistake of writing to her that he thought woman had "a fibre more in her heart and a cell less in her brain,"[2] Catherine replied that she would not marry a man who did not consider and treat her as an equal. Thus began her lifelong commitment to women's rights—and William's as well.

Citing Deborah, Huldah, Miriam, and Anna, Catherine wrote a rebuttal to those who forbade women to preach and pray in public: "If the Word of God forbids female ministry, we would ask how it happens that so many of the most devoted handmaidens of the Lord have felt themselves constrained by the Holy Ghost to exercise it. Surely there must be some mistake somewhere, for the Word and the Spirit cannot contradict each other."[3]

Soon Catherine was preaching frequently, sharing the good news of salvation with millions. Both William and Catherine yearned for a team ministry as evangelists, but year after year the Methodist Church denied their request. Finally, at a yearly meeting, Catherine listened from the balcony as William preached. He caught her eye. She nodded. And together they walked out of the meeting—and the denomination.

Without a church or financial resources, their only possession was a vision from God. While conducting a mission in 1865 among prostitutes in London, Catherine realized that she and William had to leave behind respectable church trappings forever and take the gospel to the masses of suffering people in the cities. Their call became the simple command of Matthew 25: to feed, clothe, and shelter the poor. So began the Salvation Army.

Although Salvation Army letterheads and news stories still declare "William Booth, Founder," one biographer has noted of Catherine, "It was she, not William Booth, who laid the first stone of the Salvation Army."[4]

1. Nancy A. Hardesty, *Great Women of Faith* (Grand Rapids: Baker Book House, 1980), 105.
2. Ibid., 104.
3. Ibid., 106.
4. Ibid., 107.

Part 7. Questions for Reflection

1. Which biblical woman in this section do you admire the most? Why?

2. Why do you think women are still denied leadership in parts of the church?

3. Have you encountered any efforts within your church, family, or workplace to restrict the offering of your gifts? How have you responded?

4. Do you feel any internal resistance or lack of self-confidence in offering your gifts? Have you been surprised by the response of others to your offer of a gift?

5. How do you feel about living in a society in which the major institutions of religion and government are led almost exclusively by white men?

PART 8
Faithful Widows

Anna the prophet recognized Jesus as the Messiah when he was only eight days old. Women at the dawn of Christian faith, changed by their own recognition of God's gift in Jesus, were at the forefront of ministries of hospitality, service to the poor, and leadership in house churches.

Many of these women were widows, living beyond the constraints of patriarchal marriage arrangements, free to give themselves to the building up of the faith. Like the Old Testament widow of Zarephath, they opened their homes to the word of God and practiced sacrificial generosity. Their role was critical in the spreading of the faith. Their task has been taken up generations later by women who still offer their homes, gifts, and time in service to the gospel.

36 The Widow of Zarephath: Sacrificial Generosity

SCRIPTURE: 1 Kings 17:8–24

[The widow] went and did as Elijah said, so that she as well as he and her household ate for many days. The jar of meal was not emptied, neither did the jug of oil fail, according to the word of the Lord that he spoke by Elijah. (1 Kings 17:15–16)

The small town of Ocotal in northern Nicaragua was under alert; contra forces had been sighted in the area. Our North American delegation spent the night in the Baptist church, which we shared with refugees who had fled their scattered mountain homes during contra attacks. Gunshots in the distance punctuated the night.

We awoke before dawn and washed our faces in a rain barrel outside the church; the water had been turned off throughout the town because of a severe shortage. The refugee women had arisen even earlier. Firewood was already stacked in their dome-shaped clay oven, and they were slapping out tortillas as a glint of sunlight appeared on the eastern horizon. They had fled with their children and little more than the clothes on their backs, but they invited us to partake in their meager breakfast.

I was profoundly moved by this simple gesture. These women were sharing everything they had with us, affluent strangers from a country that was sponsoring a war against them. Our communion of tortillas and coffee at dawn was a sacrament of generosity and reconciliation. The refugee women did not know where they would spend the following night or where the next meal would come from. They simply lived for each day and shared all that they had, trusting that God would provide. They are daughters of the widow of Zarephath.

We meet this widow as she is out gathering sticks in a time of famine, probably a gaunt and stooped figure at the gate of the town. She is preparing to fire up the oven for her last meal. The prophet Elijah has just come from the wilderness, where ravens fed him with bread and meat in morning and evening. Now the widow will be God's instrument for the sustenance of the prophet.

Elijah called for water and bread. The widow replied that she had no bread, only a handful of meal in a jar and a little oil in a jug. She explained to Elijah that she and her son would eat what was left and die. But the prophet told her not to be afraid and asked her to make him a cake, declaring that God would replenish the meal and the oil.

We know that this woman was not one of the Israelites; she refers to Elijah's God as "the Lord *your* God." Much later, Jesus mentioned her after his inaugural sermon in the synagogue (Luke 4:25–26). Until Jesus spoke about prophets being rejected by their own people, the crowd was filled with awe. But when he reminded them that God could have chosen any of many widows of Israel to feed Elijah but chose a foreigner, the awe turned to rage. We find Jesus being driven out of town to the edge of a cliff.

God chose the widow of Zarephath for her compassion and generosity, not for any religious credentials. And she responded, at great sacrifice and risk. How difficult it must have been for this loving mother to deny her son food. How long had she saved this last crumb of sustenance until they could bear no longer not to eat? And how did she explain to her poor, hungry child that this stranger would eat before him?

Her fear must have been great. But she trusted that the promise of God would be fulfilled. She was not disappointed. The jar of meal never grew empty, and the oil never failed. Her trust enabled God to perform the miracle, and her entire household ate for days. Her circumstances went from desperate to abundant because of her faith in a God who was not even her own.

Later, the woman's son became ill and died. She responded as many of us might, demanding answers of God, unable to accept that this was her son's fate. She spoke ardently to Elijah: What do you have against me? Have I sinned to deserve this? Is this the reward for my sacrifice and trust? Touched by the woman's anguish, Elijah carried her son upstairs and laid him on the prophet's own bed. He cried out to God and, stretching himself over the boy three times, pleaded for his life.

God honored the plea of widow and prophet. The woman knew then, beyond a doubt, that Elijah's God is a God of truth. This relationship bound up in miracle began with a sacrament of bread and water and oil—a communion based on sustenance and trust.

Generations later, another poor widow crept up to the church treasury and inconspicuously dropped in two copper coins—a penny's worth, not even enough to buy a loaf of bread. She believed her paltry donation would go unnoticed among the big bills that the rich folk had placed in the plate. But a prophet noticed. Jesus had seen her generosity: "Truly I tell you, this poor widow has put in more than all those who are contributing to the treasury. For all of them have contributed out of their abundance; but she out of her poverty has put in everything she had, all that she had to live on" (Mark 12:43–44).

Still more generations later, poor widows slap out tortillas at dawn. It seems that no one pays attention to this common, daily ritual. But Jesus notices these women, too. Like the widow of Zarephath and the widow at the treasury—and like Jesus himself—these women invite us all to sacrificial generosity, trusting that God will provide.

37 Anna: Recognizing the Messiah

SCRIPTURE: Luke 2:21–40

At that moment [Anna] came, and began to praise God and to speak about the child to all who were looking for the redemption of Jerusalem. (Luke 2:38)

The birth of Jesus typically conjures colorful images of quaint shepherds, operatic angels, and star-struck, exotic kings bearing gifts. Often the nativity scene becomes a charming pastoral portrait with lowing cows, warm straw, and a haloed Mary so transcendent that the birth of Jesus is a virtual out-of-body experience.

What we usually forget is the door slammed shut at the inn; the crescendo of pain that grows worse by the minute—and nowhere to go; then, finally, a dank, dark stable. We forget the agony and the blood and the exhausting effort it took to bring the Messiah to birth.

The people of Israel longed for this Messiah, but they had a different image in mind. The Roman occupation of Jewish lands and lives was brutal, and most Jews looked for a warrior on a swift steed, whose might would send the Romans into flight and set the Jews free.

The priest Simeon was among those "looking forward to the consolation of Israel" (Luke 2:25); so was Anna. These two wonderful, wise, elderly prophets were models of faithfulness, and the story of their glimpse of the Messiah offers rich clues about the times and the revelation that was to come through Jesus.

The task before Mary and Joseph was clear, according to Hebrew law: "If a woman conceives, and bears a male child, she shall be ceremonially unclean seven days. . . . On the eighth day the flesh of his foreskin shall be circumcised. Her time of blood purification shall be thirty-three days; she shall not touch any holy thing, or come into the sanctuary until the days of her purification are completed" (Lev. 12:2–4). Interestingly, the next verse points out that the birth of a female child rendered the mother unclean for two weeks and required purifying for sixty-six days—twice as long as for the birth of a son.

When the days of purification were completed, the mother was required to go to the priest with "a lamb in its first year for a burnt offering, and a pigeon or a turtledove for a sin offering," which the priest offered to the Lord to "make atonement on her behalf; then she shall be clean from her flow of blood" (Lev. 12:6–7). The law elaborated that "if she cannot afford a sheep, she shall take two turtledoves or two pigeons" (12:8). Jesus was to be specially consecrated to God as "the first to open the womb" (Ex. 13:2, 12). The visit of Mary and Joseph to the Temple shows both how faithfully they followed the customs of their faith and their poverty: they offered two birds for sacrifice. The parents of the Son of God could not afford a lamb; he himself would become a lamb of sacrifice.

Simeon knew the latent power of this child. He knew the political uproar that was to come, the "falling and rising of many" that would divide Israel; he understood that Jesus would one day expose the hearts of both the compassionate and the wicked. Cradling Mary's baby, with tenderness draped across his weathered face Simeon turned to this young mother and told her that this child would bring dire consequences, that salvation would come at a price, that her own heart and soul would be pierced with grief.

Anna was also at the Temple. She lived there, fasting and praying day and night. For seven years in her young life she had been married. Then she lived out the rest of her eighty-four years as a widow and prophet in the Temple. She too recognized the Messiah; one glimpse and she knew. Her prayer and dedication had prepared her for this. She thanked God for revealing to her the incarnation of salvation and hope. Then she spent the rest of her days sharing that hope, speaking to all who sought the redemption of Israel.

The biblical authors chose not to record Anna's words, but there is a striking mutuality in the story of Simeon and Anna. Both had longed and waited; and both knew that salvation had political as well as personal consequences. They both knew immediately that they were in the presence of a rare blessing. In their old age, they were rewarded for years of devotion and faithfulness.

When I think of Anna, I picture Mary Glover. Mary left her home in North Carolina as a young woman and has lived out the many decades of her life in inner-city Washington, D.C. Her neighborhood is still referred to as the "Fourteenth Street riot corridor," twenty-six years after it went up in flames following the assassination of Martin Luther King Jr. It bears the scars of that time even today: vacant lots, dilapidated tenements, broken glass, and shattered hope. Its infant mortality rate is worse than that of several Third World nations. It has been invaded by an illegal drug trade that has strangled the dreams of its youth. For years, the neighborhood had the highest homicide rate in the city, making it, as one resident told me, "the most murderous neighborhood in the most murderous city in the most murderous nation in the world."

I first met Mary Glover about ten years ago, on a bitterly cold winter day. She came through the Saturday morning food line at Sojourners Neighborhood Center for a bag of groceries. Today, Mary is one of the people who runs the food line. Early every Saturday morning, before the line opens, all the volunteers gather around and Mary begins with a prayer. It is a prayer she offers to God every day of her life: "We thank you, Lord, for our lying down last night and our rising up this morning. We thank you that the walls of our room were not the walls of our grave, that our bed was not our cooling board nor our bedclothes our winding-sheet."

Mary Glover begins each day thanking God for another day to serve him. She lives a life marked by devotion and praise. She has little in the world's eyes; but she is thankful for so much.

I am most touched by the way Mary ends her prayer on Saturday mornings: "We thank you for the feet that are coming through this line for food today and the hands that are giving it out. We know, Lord, that you're coming through this line today, so help us to treat you right. Yes, Lord, help us to treat you right. We thank you, Lord."

Mary Glover recognizes the Messiah. She takes to heart the words of Jesus from Matt. 25:34: " 'Come, you that are blessed by my Father, inherit the kingdom prepared for you from the foundation of the world; for I was hungry and you gave me food, I was thirsty and you gave me something to drink, I was a stranger and you welcomed me, I was naked and you gave me clothing, I was sick and you took care of me, I was in prison and you visited me. . . . Truly I tell you, just as you did it to one of the least of these who are members of my family, you did it to me.' "

Mary Glover knows where Jesus can be found: in the guise of the stranger, the outcast, the forgotten one. Like Anna, she would not have prayed for salvation from a conquering hero; she would have recognized the Messiah the moment a tiny, vulnerable child was placed into her arms. She would have known that this was part of God's plan all along. She would have understood that incarnation meant God choosing to take on all the weakness and fear and need that mark humanity; that salvation would come through a cross; that Jesus had chosen to be right there with her in all her suffering.

And like Anna, Mary Glover has dedicated her days to sharing her glimpses of salvation. In a neighborhood where violence and fear often seem to rule, she is a true evangelist, a messenger of the good news of the gospel. In the food line, on the street corners, in her encounters with strangers and friends, Mary Glover misses no opportunity to praise God and pass along her hope.

38 Dorcas: Radical Service to the Poor

SCRIPTURE: Acts 9:36–42

Now in Joppa there was a disciple whose name was Tabitha, which in Greek is Dorcas. She was devoted to good works and acts of charity. (Acts 9:36)

We were just sitting there talking when lines of people began to form, saying, "We need bread." We could not say, "Go, be thou filled." If there were six small loaves and a few fishes, we had to divide them. There was always bread.

We were just sitting there talking and people moved in on us. Let those who can take it, take it. Some moved out and that made room for more. And somehow the walls expanded. . . .

I found myself, a barren woman, the joyful mother of children. It is not easy always to be joyful, to keep in mind the duty of delight.

The most significant thing about the Catholic Worker is poverty, some say. The most significant thing is community, others say. We are not alone anymore.

But the final word is love. At times it has been . . . a harsh and dreadful thing, and our very faith in love has been tried through fire.

We cannot love God unless we love each other, and to love we must know each other. We know Him in the breaking of the bread, and we know each other in the breaking of bread, and we are not alone anymore. Heaven is a banquet and life is a banquet, too, even with a crust, where there is companionship.

We have all known the long loneliness and we have learned the only solution is love, and that love comes with community.

It all happened while we sat there talking, and it is still going on.[1]

These words close *The Long Loneliness*, the autobiography of Dorothy Day. They tell about the beginning of the Catholic Worker movement, which, since its founding during the Great Depression in May 1933, has opened houses of hospitality for the homeless poor across the United States. Modeled on the gospel teachings of simplicity, mercy, and justice, the Catholic Worker movement came to be hailed as the conscience of the church. And at its heart was always love.

Dorothy Day received her calling in December 1932 in Washington, D.C. A free-lance journalist, she was watching a "hunger march" through the capital city and was filled with grief that the church was not responding to such misery and suffering. She went to the crypt of the National Shrine of the Immaculate Conception. Beset by anguished tears, she offered a prayer that she might be able to offer her talent on behalf of the suffering poor. When she returned to her home in New York City, a Frenchman named Peter Maurin was waiting on her doorstep.

Together, Day and Maurin founded the Catholic Worker movement, based on Maurin's philosophy that it should help produce a society "in which it is easier for people to be good."[2] Urban houses of hospitality responded to the devastating needs of people on the streets, while rural communities became the seeds of "a new society within the shell of the old."[3] The Catholic Worker movement was known primarily for its "works of mercy" to the suffering. *The Catholic Worker* newspaper, which sold for a penny a copy, sounded a clear call to nonviolence, community, compassion, and resistance to war and greed. Dorothy Day herself wound up in jail cells frequently for her resistance activities; the first time was in 1917, when she was arrested at the White House with other women demanding the right to vote.

Day based her life on the mandate to serve the "least of these," found in Matthew 25. "Above all, take care of the poor," she said. "It's a life work."[4] Her faith was open, radical, all-consuming. She dared to believe in and stake her life on the words of Jesus. She once said, "If they take your coat, give them your cloak too. If they take your house, well go ahead and camp out someplace else."[5] All that she had, she shared. And she did it joyfully.

Those around her found it easy to label her a saint. She dismissed the idea, firing back at one stary-eyed soul who attempted to idolize her, "Don't call me a saint. I don't want to be dismissed so easily."[6]

Perhaps in her daily two hours of prayer and scripture reading—from six to eight every morning—Day came across the story of Dorcas. They were cut from the same cloth: two women who gave everything in following Jesus; two whose homes and arms were open to the poor.

In scripture, Dorcas, whose name means "gazelle," is called "disciple"—the only occurrence in the New Testament of the feminine form of the word. She lived northwest of Jerusalem at the port of Joppa, an important center of Christianity as the faith spread across the Mediterranean. There, grieving widows looked out longingly at the sea that had claimed their sailor husbands, and the destitute scavenged on the shore for bits of rags.

Dorcas was moved to compassion by their plight. She began sewing clothes for the poor, offering all out of her generosity. She made tunics and coats, which served not only for warmth but as mats for the homeless poor to sleep on at night. Sometimes a tunic was all a widow had. Hebrew law commanded, "You shall not deprive a resident alien or an orphan of justice; you shall not take a widow's garment in pledge" (Deut. 24:17); an outer garment represented survival.

Dorcas's home was a center for mercy and hope. When she died, the grieving was widespread and heartfelt; a beloved saint had been lost. The widows prepared her for burial and laid her in an upper room. The disciples sent for Peter, who was nearby in Lydda. It was high tribute that the leader of the church came immediately; he must have known of the deep faith of this generous woman. Weeping, the widows grasped at the symbols of Dorcas that were left them, showing Peter the tunics and other beautiful garments that she had made.

Kneeling by her in prayer, Peter called her by her Aramaic name Tabitha and beckoned her to arise. What a poignant moment when she opened her eyes and Peter offered her his hand. She must have blinked several times, clearing away any doubt or fear in her vision—or in her heart—graciously receiving this most rare blessing. He gently lifted her up and called in "the saints and widows" to see her restored. Tears of joy and disbelief must have flooded that upper room, as her sisters in the faith rushed to embrace her.

When Dorcas came back to life, word spread quickly. The rejoicing was as ardent as the mourning had been for this beloved sister, the only person recorded to have been raised from the dead by a disciple of Jesus. So well known was her rising that many came to faith through this miracle.

Mention is made twice of "the widows" in this story. It is likely that Dorcas herself was a widow. In the New Testament, the term meant more than just a woman without a husband; it carried a different sense from the vulnerability and desolation that often visited the widows of the Old Testament. Women took much of the lead in the early church in caring for the sick and the poor. Some opened their homes as places of prayer and the breaking of bread. Widows were both the receivers and givers of benevolence, taking care of one another and of many others beyond themselves, living joyfully in sisterhood and service, incarnating the gospel.

Evidence suggests that there was an early order of widows, who dedicated themselves to the service of the church. First Timothy 5:9–10 reads, "Let a widow be put on the list if she is not less than sixty years old and has been married only once; she must be well attested for her good works, as one who has brought up children, shown hospitality, washed the saints' feet, helped the afflicted, and devoted herself to doing good in every way." The pastoral epistles (1 and 2 Timothy and Titus) were written as the church moved from charismatic simplicity to a system of doctrine and authority. The group of enrolled widows had a designated ministry within the church, including charitable and pastoral tasks, as well as the primary responsibility for intercession. The widows continued to do what they had always done, but being "put on the list" implied that they were formally recognized by the church. Like today, these women formed the backbone of many congregations.

First Timothy 5:11–16 reflects the sexism that undergirded the establishment of the church, referring to younger widows' uncontrollable "sensual desires" and their proclivity toward being "idle" and "gossips and busybodies." Verse 12 implies that the enrolled widows took a vow, or pledge, which younger widows were assumed to be incapable of keeping.

While the widows were recognized for their role, they were also restricted in their ministry. As the church became established, traditional patriarchal households and conventional gender roles came to represent the preservation of an orderly and stable society. In response, widows, who fell outside the traditional structures, began to claim their own power. They joined together in communities receptive to the freedom of the Spirit, choosing celibacy as an empowered response to the inequalities imposed by marriage. Among these women the gospel remained alive in its purest and most radical form. Their vowed and communal life formed the basis of later religious orders for women. It is likely that the widows who gathered around Dorcas were the beginnings of such an order. And from such orders came some of the most outstanding women in the church.

Dorcas was resurrected, and the gospel came to life anew because of her faith. Her name remains synonymous with generosity to the poor. Her spirit lives on in other women who have heard her call to give all in service. It flamed alive in Dorothy Day. And it lives on in each of us as we offer ourselves in service to "the least of these."

NOTES

1. Dorothy Day, *The Long Loneliness* (New York: Curtis Books, 1952), 317–18.
2. Ibid., 194.
3. Jim Forest, "There Was Always Bread," *Sojourners* 5, no. 10 (December 1976): 14.
4. Dorothy Day, "Exalting Those of Low Degree" (Interview by Jim Wallis and Wes Michaelson), *Sojourners* 5, no. 10 (December 1976): 19.
5. Ibid., 16.
6. Forest, "There Was Always Bread," 13.

39 Mary, Mother of John Mark: A Haven for Faith

Scripture: Acts 12:1–17

[Peter] went to the house of Mary, the mother of John whose other name was Mark, where many had gathered and were praying. (Acts 12:12)

It was a time of persecution of the church, when Herod the king "laid violent hands" on believers. James the apostle was dead by the sword, and Peter had been thrown into jail. The believers prayed for Peter's release and safety. They gathered in homes, in the dark and quiet, to lift their petitions to God.

One of those homes, considered by some historians to have been the center of the Jerusalem church and perhaps the first "house church," was that of Mary. She is identified only as being the mother of John Mark, who accompanied Paul and Barnabas on their first missionary journey and is considered by some biblical scholars to have been the author of the second Gospel. Her home had an open door for the early Christians, and it is believed by many that she led the church gathered there.

As the prayers were being offered, there came a knock at the gate. Rhoda, a young servant of the household, went to answer it. She heard a familiar voice; certainly, Peter must have been around the house often before his imprisonment to be so recognized. This house was his first destination when he was released, a place of comfort and familiarity, where friends could offer welcome and support after his ordeal.

Rhoda was so flustered with joy at Peter's appearance that she left him standing outside the gate. We can imagine her running back into the house, speaking rapidly and gesturing wildly, to the point that the others considered her mad. "It is only his angel," they insisted. But Peter—himself probably flustered at having been left at the gate— continued patiently knocking. And finally, they came again to him. The recognition was instantaneous, and they were all amazed, overjoyed, incredulous. He told them of his miraculous escape: of the angel who tapped him on the side and the bright light in the cell, of chains that fell off his hands and an iron gate that opened itself. The prayer of the faithful had come true.

The early Christian widows were known for their hospitality, generosity, and compassion. Like Mary, many offered their homes as havens for faith and fellowship in a time of intense persecution and fear. In those homes, at the risk of the lives of the believers, prayers were offered, songs were sung, and bread was broken. They were places of true communion, where women and men gathered together as one to worship and be strengthened.

The tradition of offering sanctuary is at least as ancient as the gesture of the Shunammite woman who said to her husband of the prophet Elisha, "Look, I am sure that this man who regularly passes our way is a holy man of God. Let us make a small roof chamber with walls, and put there for him a bed, a table, a chair, and a lamp, so that he can stay there whenever he comes to us" (2 Kings 4:9). And the tradition has found recent expression in the twentieth-century sanctuary movement for Central American refugees.

In the early 1980s, in the wake of increased persecution of the church in El Salvador—including assassinations of priests, lay leaders, missionaries, and an archbishop—Salvadorans surged in a tide of flight to the United States. Church people in Tucson, Arizona, began to hear tragic stories. Afraid to seek help, a woman who had been shot in El Salvador was in hiding in Tucson, with the bullet still in her. A *coyote* (smuggler) had abandoned twenty-five Salvadorans in the desert, where about half of those fleeing died of dehydration. Hundreds of refugees picked up by the border patrol were suffering in isolated Immigration and Naturalization Service (INS) detention centers, fearing deportation to El Salvador, where they faced almost certain death.

Fully aware that church members could face up to five years in prison for each refugee they took in, Tucson's Southside United Presbyterian Church voted to offer sanctuary to people their government had labeled "illegal aliens." Before long, they had in place an underground railroad—patterned after the network of sanctuary that took slaves to freedom in the previous century—carrying refugees from the border to safety.

Members of the church wrestled with how to handle government threats, harassment, and evidence that INS informants had been placed in church worship services and Bible studies wearing wiretaps and bugs. "We couldn't stop," the Reverend John Fife, pastor of Southside at the time, said to me. "We'd already made the decision when we got involved that the life-and-death needs of the refugees overrode any other set of risks that we might encounter here in the United States." They decided to become not more covert but more public. On March

24, 1982, the second anniversary of the assassination of Salvadoran arch-bishop Oscar Romero, the members declared Southside Presbyterian a sanctuary (as indeed was the original intention of churches) and publicly received a refugee family into the sanctuary of the church. Other churches from Seattle to Los Angeles, from Chicago to Washington, D.C., and Long Island, New York, followed their example. Thus the sanctuary movement, based on an ancient church tradition and in direct opposition to the policies of the U.S. government, was born.

By January 1985, seventeen sanctuary workers had been indicted on a variety of charges, including conspiracy and harboring and transport-ing illegal aliens. Tapes from INS informants were used as evidence against the workers. Stacey Lynn Merkt, one of those indicted, worked at Casa Romero, a hospitality house for Central American refugees in San Benito, Texas. "My faith is my work, and my work is my faith," she told me of her experience there. "I have learned about the nitty-gritty of seeing Jesus reflected in the face of my brother and sister. That is the essence of what faith is to me.

"For me to start responding to the cry of the people of Central America meant that I had to start living and working and touching these people. They became more than names and numbers and faces and events. They became María, and José, and I put living flesh onto statistics.

"I just seek to be a person who lives what I believe and who lives what God has asked me to live," she continued. "It's clear to me that God asks me to love. The greatest commandment is to love the Lord your God with all your heart, soul, and mind, and to love your neigh-bor as yourself. And my neighbor is a world community of persons. That means I have to offer food to the person who's hungry, clothes to the person who has no clothes; I have to welcome the stranger in my midst, and I have to work for the day when those needs, when those deprivations, those injustices won't be. It's an outpouring of myself more than anything else."

Stacey paid for the risks she took on behalf of her faith. She served 78 days of a 179-day jail sentence. Then she was released to house arrest—three months before she gave birth to her first child. She talked openly about her fears:

"We as people of faith need to examine our fears in light of the stories of why the refugees come to us. If we don't take that small step and act regardless of our fears and regardless of whether or not we have courage, we'll never know what courage is. It is step by step and inch by inch that we struggle in our process to live out our faith.

"In contrast to the word 'fear,' I try to look at hope. We are a community of people that God has mandated to act in a certain way—for the best interest of others and also to proclaim that we are a faithful people."

Like Mary, Stacey Lynn Merkt and her companions claimed courage in the face of persecution, offering safe havens for faith. They made a choice to take risks despite their fears, to heighten their resistance to efforts aimed at killing their faith and their love, rather than to back down or hide. In so doing, they have continued a "conspiracy of compassion" that has spanned centuries.

40 Lydia: A Hunger for the Gospel

SCRIPTURE: Acts 16:11–40

A certain woman named Lydia, a worshiper of God, was listening to us. . . . The Lord opened her heart to listen eagerly to what was said. (Acts 16:14)

A mollusk and her own imaginative creativity provided Lydia her livelihood. From the veins of a particular shellfish came a substance that, when exposed to light, took on hues ranging from indigo to dark crimson. With it, Lydia made a dye and turned plain-colored cloth into an exquisite purple. It was the color of royalty, of dignity.

Philippi, a city on the major overland route from Asia to the West, was an ideal location for an artisan and merchant as skilled as this woman. It is likely that Lydia—who bears the unique honor of being considered Europe's first convert to Christianity—presided over the breaking of the bread in her home in Philippi. She was clearly a woman of respect and influence. When she converted to Christianity through the teaching of Paul, her entire household was baptized with her. So enflamed was she with a hunger to learn the gospel that she compelled Paul and his companions to stay at her home and share their knowledge in return for her hospitality.

A friendship solidified between Lydia and Paul. When Paul and Silas were released from prison in a most earthshaking manner, they headed straight for Lydia's house. They must have known that the sisters and brothers gathered there had been in fervent prayer for their safety ever since they had been dragged into the marketplace and flogged. Later, Paul showed his special love for those companions in Christ in his warm and heartfelt letter to the Philippians, referring to the church there as his "joy and crown" (Phil. 4:1). The seeds of that great church were found among a group of women praying on a riverbank. They first took root in Lydia, whose home eventually became the center of the church.

On more modern riverbanks, great-granddaughters of Lydia still gather to pray and hone their crafts. Like Lydia, these women are the heads of their households—in their case, because their husbands or fathers are among the *desaparecidos* (disappeared) in Chile.

Dina Loagos's husband, who was active in a trade union, was sur-

rounded by plainclothesmen and shoved into a car. He was never seen
or heard from again. The youngest of Dina's seven children was two
years old at the time. At two o'clock in the morning, a knock came on
the door where Victoria Diaz Carro lived. Her father, head of the
graphic workers union, was taken by twenty-five members of the militia to the torture chambers of Grimalde Prison. He too was never
heard from again. Both Estele Hildalgo's husband, director of the construction workers union, and her son, a university student, also disappeared. Twenty-five members of her family have been exiled.

The *desaparecidos* were never charged or brought to trial. Their only
crime was organizing workers to protest exploitative working conditions, poverty wages, and brutal repression in Chile. Most were
snatched in the first few years after the 1973 CIA-engineered coup that
killed reform-minded Chilean president Salvador Allende and installed
ruthless dictator Augusto Pinochet.

Dina, Victoria, and Estele are among many women who began creating *arpilleras*—"embroideries of life and death"—in response to their
tragedy. With sorrow as warp and hope as woof, these women have
woven the stories of their lives out of fragments of cloth and thread.
Dina created a tapestry depicting hunger, and Estele a picture of the
agony of unemployment. Victoria made an *arpillera* related to the dis-
covery of the bodies of fourteen *desaparecidos* in a furnace in an isolated
rural area dotted with abandoned calcium mines. It portrays the memorial service for the bodies, attended by fifteen hundred people. A
large cross dominates the scene, and embroidered in the corner is a
poem by Pablo Neruda: "Even if a million footsteps pass over this site
for a thousand years, they will not erase the blood of those who fell
here. Even if a million voices pass over this silence, the hour that you
fell will never be forgotten."[1]

Without any training or employable skills, these women at first
began creating their colorful artwork as a means of supporting their
families. But their work took on political and spiritual significance as
well. The women lost their sense of isolation. The repression, they say,
has made them stronger. They organized themselves into artisan workshops and cooperatives. Now, two decades after they first began working, women of Chile still meet once a week, learning new skills from
one another and augmenting their confidence and pride.

Their work is considered dangerous. They are disturbing the fabric
of the country with cloth and thread. A woman taking suitcases full of
arpilleras to the United States was apprehended at the Santiago airport.
She was taken to the police station, blindfolded, and interrogated

throughout the night before being released. The *arpilleras* were confiscated.

But the work goes on. Hands continue to craft stories of faith and hope. Words from Paul to Lydia and the faithful Christians in Philippi could well be addressed to these sisters:

> I thank my God every time I remember you, constantly praying with joy in every one of my prayers for all of you, because of your sharing in the gospel from the first day until now. I am confident of this, that the one who began a good work among you will bring it to completion by the day of Jesus Christ. . . . All of you share in God's grace with me, both in my imprisonment and in the defense and confirmation of the gospel. . . . And this is my prayer, that your love may overflow more and more with knowledge and full insight to help you to determine what is best, so that in the day of Christ you may be pure and blameless, having produced the harvest of righteousness that comes through Jesus Christ for the glory and praise of God (Phil. 1:3–11).

NOTES

1. Betty LaDuke, *Compañeras* (New York: City Lghts Books, 1985), 4.

Part 8. Questions for Reflection

1. Which biblical woman in this section is your favorite? Why?

2. Do generosity and gratitude come easily to you, or are they a challenge?

3. Dorothy Day believed that relationships with and service to the poor—"works of mercy"—are an essential part of faith. Do you agree?

4. Is your home a "haven for faith"? Why or why not?

5. Why do you think women did—and still do—most of the hospitality and service work of the church?

PART 9
Women Touched by Jesus

Women in biblical times had marginal status. If they were considered sick, strange, or sinful, so much the worse.

The Gospels resound with stories of women who overcame their shame and fear to claim their right to healing and wholeness. Reaching out to Jesus, they were touched, loved, and forgiven. These women asserted their humanity and dignity, receiving the promises of faith. And they invite us all to accept the healing touch of Jesus and the gift of grace.

41 The Woman with a Flow of Blood: Courage That Heals

SCRIPTURE: Mark 5:21–34 (Matt. 9:18–22; Luke 8:40–48)

She had heard about Jesus, and came up behind him in the crowd and touched his cloak, for she said, "If I but touch his clothes, I will be made well." (Mark 5:27–28)

This story of the woman healed would be my choice for the most poignant in scripture. All three Synoptic Gospels carry it, indicating its importance. Its deepest significance can be understood only if we try to put ourselves in this anonymous woman's world. Constantly losing blood, she was chronically weak and weary. Much of her time was spent taking care of her personal needs, washing out garments, dealing with a flow of blood from her body that had not slowed in twelve long years.

People shunned her and doctors abused her. She may have tried the many remedies for her condition outlined in the Talmud: drinking a tonic made from a compound of rubber, alum, and garden crocuses dissolved in wine; eating a dose of Persian onions cooked in wine; taking an infusion of sawdust from the lotus tree, mixed with the curdled milk of a hare, calf, lamb, or deer, to coagulate her blood; wearing the ash of an ostrich's egg in a linen bag around her neck for months; rubbing herself with foul-smelling salves; obtaining a barleycorn found in the dung of a white she-ass.[1]

She had spent all her money, but still the bleeding continued—and grew worse. She was a desperate woman. Not a day went by that she did not realize that she was seen as cursed and contagious. Jewish purity laws made clear that a woman was unclean during the time of her menstruation; and anything or anyone that she touched was also unclean. This woman lived under a harsh sentence: "If a woman has a discharge of blood for many days, not at the time of her impurity, . . . all the days of the discharge she shall continue in uncleanness" (Lev. 15:25–27). She was not allowed to enter any of the holy places of worship as long as her bleeding continued. She was considered ritually impure, a threat to the holiness of the entire community, a constant source of pollution among the people. She was destined to live her life on the edges of the society, untouched, unloved, an outcast judged guilty by her body.

This unnamed woman is the ultimate symbol of woman's biology despised. Unfortunately, she has millions of sisters; women who have suffered at the hands of insensitive doctors or in medical care systems that have deemed women's health concerns a low priority. One of them is Mary Stone.

Mary Stone was eighteen in 1970 when her physician implanted an intrauterine contraceptive device called a Dalkon Shield. Stone soon developed pain and heavy bleeding, which she said her doctor dismissed as "normal." More than a year later, he performed exploratory surgery and discovered that she had a severe pelvic infection. His treatment did nothing to relieve her chronic pain, and finally, in 1977, Stone consulted another physician. He hospitalized her immediately and performed a total hysterectomy. Mary Stone was twenty-five and childless at the time. Now, twenty-four years since she first got her Dalkon Shield, she still experiences physical pain—and anguished grief over a loss that can never be recovered.[2]

Between 1970 and 1974, physicians inserted 2.4 million Dalkon Shields into American women, and another 2 million were sent abroad. In March 1971, the quality control supervisor of the shield discovered that the multifilament string attached to the shield conducted, or "wicked," bacteria into the uterus. Officials of the A. H. Robins Company, manufacturer of the shield, were more concerned about the "male sensitivity" issue (a safer monofilament string would be stiffer and more problematic, they argued) and rejected the supervisor's urgings to change the string. The supervisor was eventually fired, and all documents related to the "wicking effect" were incinerated.

The A. H. Robins Company's falsehood and greed created a nightmare for hundreds of thousands of women. Many suffered uterine perforations or contracted pelvic inflammatory disease, suffering constant hemorrhaging, pain, and eventual scarring and blockage of the Fallopian tubes. Women by the thousands suffered abnormal pregnancies, spontaneous abortions, and sterility. At least twenty deaths have been attributed to the Dalkon Shield.

An alarming number of marriages disintegrated when husbands found that their wives were unable to meet their sexual desires or bear their children. Many women were sent to psychiatrists as "chronic complainers" or hypochondriacs. Most had no idea that the source of their problems was the small, crab-shaped device inside of them that had been touted as "the Cadillac of birth control."

Physicians around the country eventually began to lodge complaints with A. H. Robins. The company's response was to hire a public relations firm in New York to plant favorable stories about the shield in the media and a $500-a-day-plus-expenses consultant to promote it. Lawsuits began to pour in from shield victims. One of the company's defense strategies was to have lawyers publicly accuse women in court of poor hygiene and wanton sexuality.

In June 1974, under pressure from the federal Food and Drug Administration, A. H. Robins suspended marketing of the Dalkon Shield in the United States, although it continued to sell the device in other countries. Not until October 1984—ten years later—did A. H. Robins recommend that women wearing the shield have it removed.

In November 1989, the Supreme Court ended a bitter fifteen-year legal battle, clearing the way for the establishment of a $2.4 billion trust fund to compensate Dalkon Shield victims. Lawyers, seeing a potential bonanza, moved in to reap a large share of the claimants' benefits. One Baltimore attorney representing fifteen hundred shield cases became infamous among claimants for his comment "They tell you they've gone through hell for years, but often it's pain and bleeding and nothing more."[3]

After many long years of waiting, Dalkon Shield claimants are finally receiving compensation. But those who are responsible for their misery not only have so far gone unpunished but, through a series of corporate maneuvers, have made a profit from their crimes. And Dalkon Shields continue to be put into women around the globe, especially in the Third World.

Many victims will never receive a penny, particularly poor women, thousands of whom were given Dalkon Shields at inner-city clinics that either have not kept the necessary documentation or have since gone out of business. And even for those women who will receive compensation, there is little sense of justice. As Gloria Manago, who suffered two spontaneous abortions and gave birth to two stillborn children and another who lived for only one hour, said, "All the money in the world isn't going to bring back my babies."[4]

Women around the country have come together to form the Dalkon Shield Information Network. The network is a self-described "kitchen table movement" of women who are determined to educate themselves and other shield victims about its dangers. The movement is one of many among women who are empowering themselves through education and mutual support to deal with women's health issues and to hold medical establishments accountable for sensitive care.

But when the biblical woman with the twelve-year hemorrhage stepped forward to claim her healing, she did it alone. Each moment in the story required tremendous courage on her part. It was a violation of the purity laws for her even to go among the crowd. She must have moved slowly, keeping her head down, hoping not to be recognized, praying not to faint from the heat of the sun or the press of the crowd.

Jesus had already been interrupted once. A man of importance—a synagogue leader, Jairus by name—convinced Jesus to leave the crowd behind and follow him to where his daughter lay dying. Jesus was on an urgent mission at the request of an imposing man. She was a bleeding, anonymous, no-account woman in a crowd of thousands. But she pushed ahead. It was a particularly grave risk for her deliberately to touch another person—and this was a holy man. But she had come this far, and she had nothing to lose. She reached out and gently took hold of Jesus' clothes.

At that moment, the sun must have shone a little brighter. She felt a rush of healing power surge through her body. Jesus felt it, too, as that power escaped him and entered her. He turned around among the crowd and asked who had touched him. His disciples scoffed at the question; what did it matter in this massive mob that someone had gotten too close? But Jesus kept looking, the question still written on his face.

Frightened, yet astounded at her sudden recovery, the woman came forward. Trembling, she fell down before him and told him "the whole truth." To this stranger, she made a very public confession of what should have been a very private agony. Fearful perhaps that her healing might be undone when Jesus found out what she had done—how she had jeopardized his holiness by her touch—she hesitantly recounted the endless days of bleeding and isolation. His face was gentle in response. He smiled at her. He called her "daughter" and commended her faith. He told her to go in peace.

With one look, Jesus removed the woman's shame. With one gesture, he shattered the purity laws that enslaved women to their biology. With one blessing, he proclaimed female bodies holy. By healing one woman, he touched us all—all of us who have been taught that our body's rhythms are shameful and unclean, rather than a celebration of connection to life's cycles and seasons, to fertility and abundance and hope.

The woman who touched Jesus understood what many of us still struggle to understand: incarnation, the word made flesh. In Jesus' body lies power and healing and peace, if we only have the courage to reach out and touch it. She saw the power of God embodied, and she knew that it could heal her—*even* her. She understood in her being that it required her own powerful courage to draw out and receive the power of God.

A survivor of incest once told me that this is her conversion passage. Her voice cracked and tears came to her eyes as she said, "Jesus was willing to empty himself—to let go of his power in such a dramatic way that he felt it draining from him—for this woman. It took an immense emptying to heal her immense shame. And he's willing to do that for me, too."

NOTES

1. Helen Bruch Pearson, *Do What You Have the Power to Do* (Nashville: Upper Room Books, 1992), 108.
2. Information provided by Karen Hicks, Dalkon Shield Information Network (P.O. Box 53, Bethlehem, PA 18016).
3. Ibid.
4. Ibid.

42 The Bent-over Woman: Standing Tall in Faith

SCRIPTURE: Luke 13:10–17

When [Jesus] laid his hands on her, immediately she stood up straight and began praising God. (Luke 13:13)

It was Christmas Eve at an overnight shelter for homeless women in Washington, D.C. A frigid wind buffeted the city that night, and the shelter, located in the fellowship hall of a church, was crowded. Shopping carts and paper bags loaded with years' worth of collected string, cans, broken umbrellas, and other street items had been dragged in out of the snow and were parked in the church's foyer.

Dinner progressed smoothly. Dozens of sugar cookies had been donated by the church for a Christmas Eve treat; a full turkey dinner would be served the next day. After the meal, the soup bowls were washed and neatly stacked away. In a corner of the fellowship hall, a small circle of women sang "Joy to the World" and "Silent Night," slightly off-key, while others pulled sleeping mats onto the floor. The singing had awakened the memories of the women, some of whom had not sung carols for years; some had cried. There was a warm spirit at the shelter, and I hoped for a quiet night.

When the lights were finally turned out, I took a chair in a corner next to Doris, whose head slumped forward as she nodded off. She suffered from an asthmatic condition that forced her to sleep sitting up. She was like so many of the women there that night—crushed by forces beyond her control.

Many of the women suffered from severe psychotic disorders, victims of governmental deinstitutionalization policies that had ejected them from crowded institutions even though they had little capacity to fend for themselves. Some wound up homeless due to a history of neglect or abuse that had spanned generations. Some women came to the shelter frightened, needing a place of safety for the night away from a battering husband or boyfriend. Many of the older women seemed tough, having learned over the course of years on the streets how to survive in a world inhabited mostly by men. But they were still vulnerable to the street's particular dangers for women.

Rachel spent most of her nights in a downtown park. This fifty-seven-year-old woman who had lived many of her years on the street had been raped in an alley a few nights before. She had been in that alley in a dark, hidden corner because all of the downtown public restrooms closed at midnight and she had need of one.

Groups of homeless people could always be found in winter months huddled around grates that belch steam from Washington's great halls of power: the Congress, the Department of State, and, ironically enough, the Department of Justice. In a city where powerful hands literally shape the world, other hands—homeless hands—rub themselves raw for warmth. Those who sleep on the grates are extremely vulnerable to scalding burns, pneumonia, and other illnesses as a consequence of the wet heat. That winter, five homeless people froze to death on Washington's streets. Another man was doused with gasoline and set on fire by teenagers while he was sleeping on a park bench.

Almost all of the people on the streets urgently need medical care. Many battle alcoholism. Most have bruised and calloused feet, some severe foot ailments and infections, from spending their days walking on hard pavement, often in ill-fitting shoes secured from church grab bags. Frostbite attacks many feet and hands during the winter months.

The arms, legs, and feet of the homeless take a constant beating from the elements. But even stronger is the beating that comes from constant rejection and a life lived without home, family, or security. Many who try hardest to change their situation are victims of deeply entrenched racism, a lack of jobs, and a severe shortage of affordable housing. Most people on the streets get knocked down again and again when they try to get up, battered by poverty, lack of education, lack of support, lack of opportunities.

In some cities, sharp wire cages have appeared over steam grates to keep the homeless poor from sleeping there. Atlanta launched a campaign for a "vagrant-free zone" as a step toward a "clean and safe" environment for new business and downtown redevelopment. Phoenix passed a law declaring all garbage city property, so that people found scavenging for food could be arrested; people have gone to jail for breaking and entering a city dumpster, for a loaf of outdated bread or a piece of bruised fruit. In biblical times, at least a few stalks of grain or ears of corn were left to be gleaned by the poor. But even the crumbs are being denied to the poorest of our citizens. Discarded by a society that despises them, many spend their days bent over by despair.

That Christmas Eve, a disturbance erupted in the far corner of the women's shelter. The voices began quietly, but they escalated before long into a shouting match. The argument was over a coat. Sheila accused Mary of stealing her coat while Sheila was asleep. Mary jumped to her own defense, accusing Sheila of being a liar and calling her a string of creative synonyms for "prostitute."

Then Sheila told Mary she was a "no-good good-for-nothing." And Mary responded, "Oh yeah? I'm better than you'll ever be. I'm an aristocrat of the highest order—with the Rothschilds on my mother's side and the three Wise Men on my father's!"

End of discussion. Sheila couldn't top that one. I smiled to myself. Things quieted down quickly, and both women joined the others in sleep. I was left to ponder the exchange, as Doris nodded and wheezed beside me.

Faced with life in a society that tells her every day that she is nothing, Mary was asserting her "somebodyness." Out of homelessness and powerlessness and brokenness issued forth a claim of power, of dignity, even of royalty.

I picture the bent-over woman of the Bible as being like Mary. She was nameless, outcast, trapped in infirmity. She is symbolic of all women bent by illness or oppression, by the burdens of daily life or the fear of violence and violation. She is also a sign that all women can be made whole by faith, by the touch of Jesus.

In the prevailing understanding of the day, the woman's sickness was perceived as divine punishment for sin. Her infirmity meant that she was considered disobedient, demented, and demon-possessed. According to the dictates of the law, she had been cast out to the margins of the community, so that her "unclean spirits" would not taint the righteousness of the rest. It was an act of courage for her simply to appear in the synagogue. She slipped in, grotesque and shadowlike, moving slowly with her eyes riveted to the ground. She took her place behind the grillwork in the back, which separated the women, children, and slaves from the men.

It is hard to imagine what it must have been like for this woman who had not stood straight for eighteen years, broken in spirit as well as body. Every day, for 6,570 days, she woke up bent with pain, with her field of vision restricted to the ground, knowing that those who saw her saw only a pathetic, crippled woman.

At Jesus' call, she hesitated, wondering if he really meant her. Then she slowly shuffled toward him, afraid. All eyes were on her. She could not move very fast, and the seconds must have felt as agonizing as days. The crowd parted to let her through. Jesus reached out.

What joy broke forth when she was cured! Her life was suddenly flooded with hope. She was able to look Jesus in the face. What tender looks and gentle glances must have passed between them. It is no surprise that her immediate response was to sing the praises of God. Perhaps she even danced a little.

The leader of the synagogue and his cohorts were upset. They called this despised woman unworthy. Jesus, breaking several laws to heal her, was not playing by their rules. Contrary to rabbinic law, he called to a woman in public—in the synagogue, during his teaching, no less—and invited her out of the shadows. Then he touched her. And he did it on the Sabbath.

Jesus called this woman a "daughter of Abraham." The Bible speaks frequently of "sons of Abraham," the "seed of Abraham," and "children of Abraham"; but nowhere else in the scriptures is a reference made to "daughter of Abraham." It was a title of honor. Jesus was telling the healed woman—and those around her—that she was part of the family of Israel, a member of the community, a recognized human being—over the objections of those who would discard her humanity, who would place her a little below the oxen and donkeys.

Jesus' response to her is a paradigm for how to address individual suffering as well as restore a divided society such as our own. He met her immediate need by touching and curing her. Then he confronted the unjust laws and societal assumptions—and the people in power who perpetuated them—that kept her bent and broken. And finally, he affirmed her humanity and her vital part in the community.

It was clear to Jesus then, as it should be to us now, that whenever one of God's children is bent over by injustice, hatred, sickness, or fear, we are all stooped and diminished. Simple charity will not change the structures that keep so many bent to the ground. It is not enough to offer a handout and then push the poor out of sight and mind.

The synagogue leaders were furious at Jesus because he had taken away their scapegoat. The woman's suffering had allowed them to feel superior and holy. But in truth, she bore the mark of *their* sin, not her own; she suffered under their failure to be compassionate rather than her own failure to be righteous. She had been hated and kept on the margins because if they looked too closely, they would have to see themselves.

The religious leaders "were put to shame" over this encounter, "and the entire crowd was rejoicing" (Luke 13:17). Jesus was on a collision course with the powers that be. He minced no words in his continuing encounters: "Woe to you, scribes and Pharisees, hypocrites! For you tithe mint, dill, and cummin, and have neglected the weightier matters of the law: justice and mercy and faith. . . . You strain out a gnat but swallow a camel!" (Matt. 23:23–24).

When Jesus resumed his teaching, he spoke about the realm of God being like a mustard seed or like a speck of yeast in dough: small things with great potential; ordinary things; seemingly insignificant things. Like a marginalized woman suddenly included. Like a homeless woman asserting her humanity. To such belongs the realm of God.

Is not this the fast that I choose:
to loose the bonds of injustice,
to undo the thongs of the yoke,
to let the oppressed go free,
and to break every yoke?
Is it not to share your bread with the hungry,
and bring the homeless poor into your house;
when you see the naked, to cover them,
and not to hide yourself from your own kin?
Then your light shall break forth like the dawn,
and your healing shall spring up quickly. (Isa. 58:6–8)

43 The Forgiven Woman: A Gift of Mercy

Scripture: John 8:2–11

And Jesus said, "Neither do I condemn you. Go your way, and from now on do not sin again." (John 8:11)

I met Tanya in 1985 in a holding cell in the D.C. jail. She was there for stealing to support a drug addiction; I was there for protesting U.S. policy in Nicaragua in front of the State Department.

"Doesn't this hurt your heart?" Tanya asked Millie, a friend sitting next to me, who had also been part of the demonstration at the State Department. As she spoke, Tanya pointed at Millie's scar from open-heart surgery, visible above the edge of her prison jumpsuit. Being processed into prison is a grueling routine, one in which it is difficult to maintain even a semblance of dignity, and I was touched by Tanya's compassion for a stranger.

Tanya was a beautiful and gentle woman, with scars of her own: needle marks running the length of her arms. She listened raptly as Millie talked about her brush with death and as she declared her gratitude to God for the gift of life.

"Yes, God knows your heart," Tanya said gently. "God is giving me a second chance, just like he gave you a second chance." Stating her determination to beat her drug addiction and get her life together, Tanya added, "God always gives us second chances."

Tanya was like so many of the women I met behind bars—abused as children, forced into desperate situations as adults that pushed them to pass bad checks or sell illegal drugs or peddle their bodies. Shirley, who had been arrested for prostitution, told me that as a young child she had squeezed a tube of toothpaste into her baby brother's ear. She concluded, "I guess I've just always been bad."

Ruby had been thrown out of her home by her father when she was fourteen. She got the attention of the cell block with her story of finding a check written to a Sally Harvey. She described the scene when she tried to cash it at the bank: "The bank teller told me that Sally Harvey was a tall Caucasian with blonde hair. . . . I told myself, 'Uh-oh.' "

Wanda always looked down and kept her arms folded, trying to hide cigarette burns on her face and hands. Her father had burned and sexually abused her as a child. She was trying to make a living on the streets. Wanda sucked her thumb when she slept at night on her bunk.

Sylvia, three months pregnant, was addicted to heroin. Her cell was a few doors down and across the corridor from mine. Her hands were all that I could see of her. They alternately dangled limply and trembled as she spoke about her abusive father, her escape from home and into drugs, and how much she wanted this baby. She spent a night moaning and pounding the walls, overcome with the agony of heroin withdrawal, while the rest of us tried futilely to get the attention of the prison guards by shouting and rattling our cell bars.

In lives fraught with tough talk and tougher choices, there was a core of vulnerability in these women, a point where the tears came and the pain and fear spilled out. For most, it was when they talked about their children.

With few exceptions, these women had committed crimes in which they themselves were the primary victims, most often prostitution and illegal drug use. Of those rare few who had commited extremely violent crimes, their targets were frequently abusive boyfriends or husbands. The women were victims of sexism and racism, of sorely lacking financial and emotional resources, of government priorities that excluded them, and of politicians and bureaucrats who wished they would go away (as some of their families had wished since the day they were born). And they were victims of their own bad choices.

But they taught me about God's forgiveness and about being given second chances—and third and fourth. They knew, like the woman caught in adultery, what Jesus' message is really all about.

It is telling that only one partner in adultery was brought before Jesus by the scribes and Pharisees. Hebrew law was clear that the punishment for adultery for both the man and the woman was death (Lev. 20:10; Deut. 22:22). But here, the man was allowed to escape, while the woman stood before the crowd alone, put forward as an example of sin and fallenness.

Adultery was illegal not primarily because of a sense of sexual morality or fidelity but because it was a violation of a man's property rights. A clear double standard was in place: women were required to be faithful to their husbands, but no such requirement was laid on men—as long as they did not violate another man's property by sleeping with his wife. A woman also could be a victim of her husband's jealousy in a most appalling manner, whether or not she was guilty of adultery. Numbers 5:11–31 describes the "ordeal of jealousy," which could be called for at a husband's whim. The death penalty for adultery required witnesses, but if a husband suspected his wife, he could take her to the Temple for this bitter ritual.

The priest was required to take holy water, mix it with dust and dirt from the floor of the Temple, then "dishevel the woman's hair" and make her take an oath before drinking the concoction. If she was innocent, she was allegedly immune from its effects. " 'But if you have gone astray while under your husband's authority,' " the priest would state, " 'the Lord make you an execration and an oath among your people, when the Lord makes your uterus drop, your womb discharge; now may this water that brings the curse enter your bowels and make your womb discharge, your uterus drop!' And the woman shall say, 'Amen. Amen' " (Num. 5:20–22).

Then the priest was to make the woman drink, "and the water that brings the curse shall enter her and cause bitter pain. . . . This is the law in cases of jealousy, when a wife, while under her husband's authority, goes astray and defiles herself, or when a spirit of jealousy comes on a man and he is jealous of his wife. . . . The man shall be free from iniquity, but the woman shall bear her iniquity" (Num. 5:24, 29–31).

Whether or not the woman's womb "dropped," meaning that she could not bear children, the pain in her intestinal tract would have been intense. And the ritual itself was a humiliation. Even if the woman was vindicated, the husband was free from any responsibility for having brought false charges against her.

It is difficult to imagine what the woman "caught in the very act" and brought before Jesus was put through. Yanked away from her lover, disheveled and half-naked, she was dragged into the Temple and made to stand before all the people. She was an object lesson in the efforts of the legalistic scribes and Pharisees to snare Jesus. Perhaps she had even been set up for their trickery.

The synagogue leaders put Jesus in an apparently no-win situation. Jewish law stated that the woman should be stoned to death. Roman law made it illegal for Jews to enforce the death penalty. The leaders were forcing Jesus to choose, ready to bring a charge against him for violating one law or the other.

But Jesus did not fall for the trap. He quietly turned from the spectacle and began writing with his finger on the ground. Conjecture about what he wrote has occupied scholars for centuries. Perhaps he was just scribbling aimlessly, thinking through his answer and buying time while the scribes and Pharisees watched, letting them know he was not rattled. Or maybe he was writing words such as "pride," "lust," "hypocrisy," and "unforgiveness." Maybe the obsessive keepers of the law were being forced to read a list of their own sins traced in the dust. Meanwhile, the unnamed woman waited as this drama unfolded. As an object of shame and condemnation before the crowd, she likely stood with head hung, trying to cover herself, feeling exposed and fearful, expecting the worst. A few in the crowd picked up stones, and she began to imagine the blow of them hitting her flesh, the sting of their judgment. She was staring into the face of a brutal and humiliating death; and neither the law nor the mob was on her side.

But with one statement, Jesus took the vengeful wind out of the accusers' sails: "Let anyone among you who is without sin be the first to throw a stone at her." There was a pregnant pause. No one moved. Then, slowly, one by one, the stones dropped, the crowd walked away, the elders leading the way.

Jesus turned the religious leaders' own trap around on them. If they threw a stone, they committed blasphemy by claiming they were sinless. Not to throw a stone meant admitting their guilt. And in fact, they were guilty—of using this woman as a scapegoat, an object, a pawn. Jesus treated her as a daughter of God. There was a moment of awkward silence as the two were left alone standing in the dust. Jesus spoke first. Making a point for emphasis, he invited her to look around and see for herself that no one remained. "Woman, where are they? Has no one condemned you?"

"No one, sir," she answered, still trembling in disbelief that she had been pulled back from the edge of death.

"Neither do I condemn you," said Jesus, his gentle eyes riveted on hers. It was a balm of reassurance. No one is perfect. Now go, forgiven, and live a new life.

In 1981, I spent a night stretched out on the concrete floor of a large holding cell beneath the Washington, D.C., courthouse. This time fifty-one of us had blocked a driveway during a nuclear arms exposition at a Washington hotel, an offense that was officially entered on our records as "incommoding."

The cell across from ours was filled with women swept up in a raid on a local house of prostitution. Sometime in the middle of the night, I heard a loud racket. In the dim light, I saw a large woman dressed in a sequined skirt and halter top, with bright purple eye shadow caked on her eyelids and a huge, red heart tattooed on her left arm, being let into the cell. She looked over at us and asked loudly, "What did *they* do to get in here?"

A young woman named Gloria in her cell said with a giggle, "They *incommoded!*" and then added, "At a *hotel!*"

Singing had been an important part of our protest, and very early the next morning it began again. A few voices started it, and as other women began to shake off a stiff drowsiness, they joined in. Gloria shouted over to our cell, "Hey, do you all know 'Amazing Grace'?" Soon the two sides of the cell block were trying to outsing each other, and strains of the hymn thundered through the long corridor.

Gripping a contact lens in each fist, as I had throughout the night, I groped blindly toward the chrome contraption that served as drinking fountain, sink, and toilet for our cell. Searching for water for putting my lenses back in my eyes, I pushed what I thought was the tap for the sink. The deafening roar of the jail toilet immediately silenced the singing. Gloria glared at me from across the corridor, pointed a finger, and hollered, "Now, *that's* incommoding!"

The entire cellblock erupted in laughter, with Gloria laughing the hardest. Then she started up again with "Amazing Grace." Before long, a brusque male guard came back to find out what all the commotion was and to silence us. Gloria jumped up, pressed her face against the bars, and said to him, "It's only the *gospel.*"

And indeed it was. Women who understood forgiveness and mercy were teaching me about the grace of God. "Amazing grace, how sweet the sound, that saved a wretch like me; I once was lost, but now am found, was blind, but now I see."

44 The Canaanite Woman: Extending the Reaches of Faith

SCRIPTURE: Matt. 15:21–28 (Mark 7:24–30)

Then Jesus answered her, "Woman, great is your faith! Let it be done for you as you wish." And her daughter was healed instantly. (Matt. 15:28)

Many followers of the faith have found the story of the Canaanite woman unsettling. Clearly, Jesus' response to her was harsh, and then insulting. He first ignored her, then equated her people with dogs. It is understandable why many readers of the gospel wish that this particular interchange had been left out of the canon.

But I find it comforting. It shows both the humanity of Jesus and the radical power of a woman. It allows us to see that Jesus too had bad days and did not always have the clarity of call that we would like to attribute to him. Even the Son of God (like the rest of us) was occasionally less than perfect.

Jesus was living through a rough stretch of days at the time. The people of Nazareth, his hometown, had rejected him. Then word came that John the Baptist had been beheaded. In his grief, Jesus took off in a boat to be alone. But the crowds followed him, and long into the evening he cured their sick. The people hung on past the dinner hour, so Jesus fed them miraculously with the five loaves and two fish. "Five thousand men, besides women and children" (deemed unnecessary to be counted), ate that night.

Again, Jesus went off by himself, this time to a mountain to pray. The disciples took off in a boat, which was battered by a storm through the night. Jesus walked on the water to them and calmed the sea—but not before Peter had tried to walk and sank for his lack of faith.

Once more, the crowds came and brought their sick, crying out, reaching, grabbing for his hem so that with a touch they might be healed. Before he could catch his breath, the scribes and Pharisees arrived to confront and test him.

We can imagine that Jesus was exhausted. Faced with rejection from home and the gruesome assassination of a beloved friend, the constant clamor of the crowd and the testy confrontations of the Jewish leaders, the doubt and confusion of his own disciples, it is no wonder that he withdrew to the borderlands of Tyre and Sidon. His growing reputation was bringing out both the crowds and the threatened religious establishment; things were definitely heating up. He was likely looking for rest and a little peace and quiet.

But then a woman started shouting at him. Spent and weary, Jesus' first response was to ignore her. Certainly, the man who asked at the edge of the cross that the cup be taken from him must have had other moments of doubt and anguished frustration, wondering whether he could bear all the demands, wishing all these clamoring, needy people would just go away.

It does not diminish Jesus that he experienced such human emotions. On the contrary, his responses in the face of such feelings speak to his deep compassion and integrity. If he were simply perfection personified, there would be little of ourselves to see in the One who was God made flesh—and little from which to draw inspiration.

The disciples were annoyed when the woman approached. They could see that Jesus did not want to be bothered. And the pesky woman just kept shouting. Like biblical bodyguards, they urged Jesus to send her on her way. I picture exhaustion in his eyes as he looked at them and justified his lack of response: "I was sent only to the lost sheep of the house of Israel." It was burden enough. He had already sent the Twelve on their mission with these words: "Go nowhere among the Gentiles, and enter no town of the Samaritans, but go rather to the lost sheep of the house of Israel" (Matt. 10:5). His and their mission was to bring salvation to the Jews.

This woman was clearly no Jew. The term *Canaanite* refers to the tribe that occupied the Promised Land that God had given to the Jews, according to Hebrew tradition. It conjured ancient images of idolatry and strange religious rituals, as well as a long-standing tension between the two peoples that erupted often in wars. Mark's account of the same story calls her a Syrophoenician woman, an indication of her nationality rather than her religious affiliation. In any case, she was a foreigner, a pagan, and outside the realm of the designated mission.

But she was also a woman who wouldn't take no for an answer. She too was weary, with the hours of constant and vigilant care for a daughter in deep distress. And she bore the frustrating loneliness of being the mother of a child whose disease was seen by all around her as the consequence of sin. Her daughter was suffering, and she knew that Jesus had the power to do something about it. So she persisted. When he dismissed her, she stopped shouting and knelt humbly before him, saying simply, "Lord, help me." When he insulted her people, she let the offense go and came back with a quick retort: "Even the dogs eat the crumbs."

I imagine a pause in the conversation then; a split second to let the words sink in. Perhaps a look of incredulity—maybe a faint smile of humility as the truth dawned—came over the compassionate face of Jesus. She was right. She had won him over. "Woman, great is your faith!"

Without ever seeing or touching the woman's daughter, Jesus healed her. So deep was the woman's belief that she called forth an instantaneous, long-distance healing. But the implications of her encounter with Jesus reach far beyond the moment. She is the only person in the New Testament who sparred verbally with Jesus and won; even the learned scribes and Pharisees could not claim that. She was a bearer of truth to the Son of God. She opened his eyes, broadened his perspective, changed him and his mission forever. She—a woman—had taught him.

By the end of the Gospel of Matthew, the mandate of mission is quite different: "Go therefore and make disciples of all nations" (Matt. 28:19). Through one marginalized, bold, persistent woman, Jesus understood that he had come to bring good news to *all* people. And perhaps he also understood that he too needed God's grace. The message turned universal.

Mary Williams knows some of the frustration and weariness of the Canaanite mother. Her daughter Rolveatta disappeared in May 1990. A year later, Mary found her in a local Washington, D.C., hospital. The diagnosis was acquired immunodeficiency syndrome—AIDS.

Mary quit her job and took Rolveatta home to care for her. "When people talk about AIDS, they're scared," says Mary. "They treat them like they're nothing. I didn't want that to happen to her." With virtually no resources, Mary cared for Rolveatta and Rolveatta's eleven-year-old daughter, Kimberly. There were days when Mary did not eat, when she knew there was only enough food for two. Rolveatta died the following November on her thirtieth birthday.

Moved by her experience of caring for Rolveatta and refusing to let her daughter's death be in vain, Mary extended her compassion to Joseph's House, a home for previously homeless men who have AIDS. A ministry of the ecumenical Church of the Saviour in Washington, D.C., Joseph's House was founded in June 1990. The name of the house was chosen to reflect the story recorded at the end of Genesis, in which Joseph, rejected and despised by his brothers, was chosen by God to be a prophet to the powerful through his gift of interpreting dreams; it was Joseph who saved the people from the ravages of famine.

"We envision Joseph's House as a place where the ostracized and hated of society are protected, where their dreams and visions are nourished," David Hilfiker, a physician and a founder of the house, explained to me. "As the years of American domination and plenty come to an end, an American famine is coming. The culture now needs the visions of those whom it has marginalized."

Mary Williams offers a listening ear to the devastating stories from the men at Joseph's House. John "Pee Wee" Williamson slept in apartment halls after he tested positive for HIV (the human immunodeficiency virus, which causes AIDS); he did not want to endanger his family. Eventually, a mechanic friend let him sleep in his van at night, curled up on his tools. "My family was afraid of me when they found out I had the disease," Pee Wee told me. "My mother would bring me food and stand three feet away. 'You stay in that van and talk to me,' she would say, 'or I'm leaving.' It really hurt me. I didn't want to live."

Pee Wee ended up in the hospital with double pneumonia, his weight having dropped from 260 pounds to 89. The doctor told him, "Son, you're lucky. You're supposed to be dead."

For many of the men, the diagnosis of AIDS, heard first as a death sentence, became the source of new life. It prompted courage to face the multitude of societal assaults and internal sufferings that come as a result of being homeless, poor, black, gay, and/or addicted. The house's life is marked by a struggle between the forces of despair and the power of forgiveness and grace—for the formerly homeless residents as well as the caregivers who live there.

"One thing that is so therapeutic here for me," David Hilfiker said, "is to see my own weakness and vulnerability so honored and accepted. The men all know what it's like not to be doing well. AIDS is a wake-up call; you have no future unless you do something now. That offers an enormous opportunity for conversion. The disease destroys the fantasy of our independence, which is a problem for all of us. When we get rid of the fantasy, it allows for community."

The walls of Joseph's House reverberate with "resurrection stories." Men who could barely walk up the front steps when they arrived—some, in fact, believed themselves to be dying—have thrived. Hardened exteriors from years on the streets have softened in the safety of an accepting home.

Mary Williams dishes out unconditional love in the form of leg rubs and massages, as well as card games and made-to-order breakfasts.

Speaking of the men and the disease, she explained, "The virus is different. They need understanding. They need love. They need to be touched. People are afraid to touch them; they look at them as 'hands off.' " She paused and added quietly, "And nobody needs to die alone."

Indeed, AIDS has become the "leprosy" of our age. Its sufferers are often marginalized, shunned, labeled sinners of the highest order. Instead of compassion, they are often met with harsh judgment rooted in ignorance and fear. More and more, as the epidemic grows, many are simply being consigned to a solitary death. It used to be that if he advocated persistently enough, David Hilfiker could always get care for his patients, even the most indigent. But with the privatization of health care and the entrepreneurial spirit that dominates the medical system, hospitals increasingly refuse to give care to the very poor. They get not even the crumbs from the table.

Robert Jones moved into Joseph's House after an infection that had gone untreated while he was in prison spread to his bones. A month after he moved in, he was hospitalized. Though he was new to the house, every one of the residents went to visit him, each telling the nurses on duty, "I'm Robert's brother."

One evening, Robert began struggling for breath. Dixcy Bosley-Smith, a nurse at Joseph's House, went to stay by his side. Robert began singing, quietly and with great effort, "Jesus loves the little children, all the children of the world; red and yellow, black and white, they are precious in his sight." And then he said, "I want to go home."

Dixcy held him through the night. They sang hymns together and talked about forgiveness until the morning light. Robert struggled to hang on while arrangements were made for an ambulance. He had a seizure, and Dixcy thought he was gone, but he came back. "Help me," he said. "Take me home."

At 2:30 in the afternoon, an ambulance was finally available. Robert's breathing was labored. As they rode through Washington, D. C., Dixcy told him where they were, how close they were getting to home. As he was being carried up the front stairs of Joseph's House, Robert lifted his head slightly, with some help from the other men. "When he looked up, it was like he was risen," Dixcy told me. "It was the most amazing sight."

"I survived" were Robert's words as they settled him into his bed. Pee Wee offered to spend the night by him. In the early hours of the morning, Robert Jones went to his final home. Lois Smith, also a nurse at the house, removed the oxygen mask he was wearing. She saw a smile develop as he moved from this world into the next.

Robert had wrestled long and hard with guilt about his incarceration and his AIDS, had felt unworthy of God's love. But in the end, said one of the men at Robert's memorial service, "He had the look of one of God's children that has been forgiven and accepted into his kingdom."

The Jesus who heard the Canaanite woman's plea heard Robert Jones's as well. No one is beyond God's healing grace. Red and yellow, black and white—all are precious in God's sight.

45 The Woman of Samaria: Receiver of a Revelation

SCRIPTURE: John 4:1–42

The woman said to him, "I know that Messiah is coming." . . . Jesus said to her, "I am he, the one who is speaking to you." (John 4:25)

He should not have been talking with her. Jesus should not have been talking with that woman at the well. In those days, there were some things that were very clear. One was that Jews did not talk to Samaritans.

After the political split that divided Israel, there was a great rivalry between Jerusalem and Samaria. When Samaria fell to the Assyrians, the Assyrian king deported many Jews and repopulated the city with conquered peoples from distant lands. They intermarried and formed a mixed race known as Samaritans. Jews generally considered Samaritans impure and inferior, religious apostates. It was no coincidence that Jesus told a parable about a Samaritan helping a wounded Jew at the side of the road to make a point about inclusion and neighborliness. To Jews, the concept of a "Good Samaritan" was an oxymoron.

When Jewish exiles began returning and started to rebuild the Temple at Jerusalem, the Samaritans felt threatened, and hatred grew on both sides. Samaritans and Jews were mortal enemies. They did not mingle, they did not talk, and they certainly did not share a jar of water together.

Another thing that was clear in those days was that men did not speak to women in public. Rabbinic law stated, "Who speaks much with a woman draws down misfortune on himself, neglects the words of the law, and finally earns hell!"[1] The Pharisees, who made a career out of following the letter of the law, were known to walk into walls and other obstacles just to avoid having to look at a woman or talk with one.

The disciples, scripture says, were "astonished" to see the conversation taking place (though they were smart enough this time not to ask). Even the woman herself wondered about Jesus' initiation of a conversation with her.

There is a third thing that was odd about this conversation. It happened at noon.

I remember being in Soweto, South Africa, one evening just as the sun was setting. As splashes of crimson and violet deepened the sky, women came from all corners, walking down the dusty streets, some with babies tied on their backs with wide strips of cloth, all with huge water jars perched on their heads. They were all heading to one place: the central water spigot. As they gathered, it became a social time. They filled up their jars with water and chatted about the day's happenings. They came to the spigot in the early mornings and late afternoons, knowing better than to haul water during the most intense heat of the day.

There seems to be only one reasonable explanation for why the Samaritan woman went to the well at noon: she wanted to avoid the other women, to avoid their eyes and their conversation. As a notorious sinner (she had had five husbands and was living with a man to whom she was not married), she was not part of their circle.

Surely, she had little financial security in her life, to have been cast aside by so many men. A foreigner, a woman, a sinner, and poor—she was a paramount outcast of her time; which is why Jesus' conversation with her was so astounding. He chose this most unlikely of candidates, this most unbelievable of persons, to reveal that he was the Messiah, the Christ, the Savior. He did not pick the emperor or the chief priest or even one of his disciples. He chose a simple, marginal woman, who is not even named in her own story.

Jesus took her very seriously. Their dialogue is the longest recorded conversation Jesus had with anyone. While the religious leaders tried to trap him with their theological questions, she hungered simply to understand—and believe. She wanted to know where people should worship: on the mountain where the Samaritans had kept their rituals and celebrations or in the Temple at Jerusalem.

Jesus explained that such sites of worship were unimportant. "God is spirit," he told her, "and those who worship him must worship in spirit and truth" (John 4:24). The message was clear. It does not matter where you worship, what race or gender you are, how much money you have, how many times you have fallen or failed; what matters is what is in your heart. What matters is that you thirst for living water.

But getting that thirst quenched places a responsibility on the one who drinks. It means passing the cup on. It means telling the story, offering a testimony, becoming a witness. In the searing heat of midday, a weary woman longing for a different life drank deeply of all that Jesus offered. She was released from an existence defined by hauling water and pleasuring men, to an oasis of faith and truth. Refreshed in soul and spirit, she abandoned her heavy water jar and dashed unencumbered into the city.

She ran to her neighbors, breathless with excitement. She gathered them together, insisting, "Come and see. Come and see!" The ripple of living water washed over them, and the people who had once scorned and shunned her "believed in him because of the woman's testimony" (4:39). Because of this one woman, the Samaritans invited Jesus—a Jew, an enemy—to spend a couple of days with them.

She really was the best witness possible. It is those who seem the most unlikely who offer the strongest testimony. If we do not need to be saved, there is not much to tell. But if we know that Jesus has touched us, forgiven us, healed us—has reached a place of longing and thirst in us—then we can be witnesses to his power.

In 1858, in the Western Ghat Mountains of India, a girl named Ramabai was born into a Hindu family. Her parents had fled to the mountains years before because her father—then forty-four years old and a teacher of Sanskrit scriptures—had dared to educate his nine-year-old wife. Opposition from relatives and townspeople forced their exodus.

Before Ramabai was six months old, her family began a wandering life, with her being carried for a time in a woven basket on the head of a servant. As she got older, Ramabai's mother, Lakshmibai, passed her knowledge of the sacred language on to her daughter. By the time she was twelve, Ramabai had learned eighteen thousand verses of the poetic scriptures of the people and four vernacular languages, which she had picked up in her travels. The family moved from shrine to shrine, bathing in sacred rivers and lakes, hoping to cleanse themselves from sin.

When Ramabai was sixteen, both her parents and her sister died in a famine. In 1878, she and her brother took a pilgrimage to Calcutta, where they gave lectures and astounded scholars. Ramabai was bestowed with the title Saraswati, meaning "divine embodiment of language, literary expression and learning."[2]

Ramabai's brother died three years later, and being all alone in the world, she decided to marry. Contrary to Hindu tradition, which required her father to arrange a marriage for her when she was between the ages of five and eleven, her father had told her she could choose a husband for herself when she was ready. Her marriage to a lawyer lasted only nineteen months, when he died of cholera. She gave birth to their daughter, Manoramabai, whose name means "heart's joy." Her daughter seemed like her only consolation in a life full of grief. Ramabai became particularly moved by the tragic status of women in

Indian society and began to have serious doubts about Hinduism. She read more deeply into the sacred scriptures. "My eyes were being gradually opened," she said. "I was waking up to my own hopeless condition as a woman."[3]

A Hindu proverb declared, "Woman is a great whirlpool of suspicion, a dwelling-place of vices, full of deceits, a hindrance in the way of heaven, the gate of hell."[4] Women, considered "worse than demons," could find salvation only in the worshiping of their husbands and the bearing of sons. Sacred Hindu law stated, "Though destitute of virtue, or seeking pleasure elsewhere, or devoid of good qualities, yet as a husband he must be constantly worshipped as a god by a faithful wife."[5] Widowhood was considered punishment for sin, and a widow was often accused of being disobedient and the cause of her husband's death. It was popular belief that a man would die if his wife learned to read or write.

In her husband's library, Ramabai had come across a Bengali translation of the Gospel of Luke. A Baptist missionary came to visit and began to explain the Bible to her. But her husband forbade a return visit. After her husband's death, Ramabai formed a women's society to work for the liberation of women from child marriage, religious oppression, and ignorance. She learned English and began to study the New Testament with Church of England missionaries.

In 1883, Ramabai and her daughter sailed to England, where they lived with a community of religious sisters who did mission work among London's prostitutes. It was the story of the Samaritan woman at the well that motivated the sisters' compassion. When Ramabai heard it, she said she realized that "Christ was truly the Divine Saviour He claimed to be, and no one but He could transform and uplift the down-trodden womanhood of India and of every land."[6]

Ramabai and her daughter were baptized into the Christian faith and returned five years later to India. She founded the Sarada Sadan, the "home of wisdom," for child widows in the town of Poona. In 1896, Ramabai went out and gathered hundreds of girls who had been widowed during a famine that year, placing them on some farmland she had acquired outside the town. There, at the farm mission—named Mukti, "home of salvation"—the well never went dry and the crops never gave out.

Although she already had 1,900 girls at Mukti, Ramabai took in 1,350 more during the famine of 1900. The mission developed into a sophisticated cooperative with weaving sheds, a blacksmith shop, a bookbindery, a tin shop, a cobbler shop, a tannery, and a carpentry

shop where the girls worked to support themselves. Ramabai conducted Bible studies and formed prayer circles, calling for an outpouring of the Holy Spirit. Many of the girls became baptized in the
Christian faith—twelve hundred in December 1901 alone. Their witness spread throughout India.

Ramabai devoted her last fifteen years to translating the Bible into
Marathi, in a style that even poorly educated women could read and
understand. She mastered Hebrew and Greek for the task. Printing of
the Bible was under way at the mission when Ramabai fell ill. She
asked God for ten more days to complete the proofreading. She got
exactly that, and she died peacefully in her sleep on April 5, 1922.

Ramabai's thirst for justice was quenched by the living water she
found in the gospel. She passed the cup around, becoming a witness to
the power of God in India and the world. "And many believed because
of her testimony."

NOTES

1. Helen Bruch Pearson, *Do What You Have the Power to Do* (Nashville: Upper
   Room Books, 1992), 144.
2. Nancy A. Hardesty, *Great Women of Faith* (Grand Rapids: Baker Book
   House, 1980), 125.
3. Ibid., 126.
4. Ibid.
5. Ibid., 125–26.
6. Ibid., 127.

Part 9. Questions for Reflection

1. Which biblical woman in this section most deeply touched you?

2. Why do you think the women in these Bible stories all remained anonymous?

3. If you are a woman, have you ever been made to feel ashamed of your womanhood? When? How?

4. In the story of the forgiven woman, with whom do you relate most easily: the woman, the Pharisees, or Jesus? Do you find forgiveness and grace easy to accept? To extend to others?

5. When in your life have you claimed the power to be healed? Was it easy or difficult? Are you persistent in having your needs recognized and working to get them met?

PART 10
Witnesses to Life and Resurrection

Although the biblical record has not counted any women among the Twelve, women were faithful disciples and part of Jesus' intimate circle of friends. Mary Magdalene was among the most beloved of those who followed Jesus, and he was a frequent guest in the home of Mary and Martha. Mary, his mother, and Elizabeth understood Jesus' mission even before he was born. And at the end of his life, an unnamed woman with a jar of nard humbly showed that she was one of the few around him who understood the meaning of his impending death.

While the twelve male disciples fell away in confusion and fear, the women stayed close to the cross and the tomb. They were witnesses to new life. And they beckon us still to live in the hope of resurrection.

46 Mary: Mother of God

Scripture: Luke 1:26–39, 46–55; 2:1–20; Matt. 1:18–20; 2:1–18; Luke 2:34–35, 41–52; John 2:1–11; Mark 6:1–6; Luke 8:19–21; John 19:25–27; Acts 1:14

Then Mary said, "Here am I, the servant of the Lord; let it be with me according to your word." (Luke 1:38)

It was the Saturday before Palm Sunday. The older women in bright purple garb were just ending their prayer meeting in this famous living room as we walked in the open front door. They were members of the Anglican Mothers Prayer Union. They met often in this home in the black township of King Williams Town in South Africa. A woman with a smile that beamed across her broad face graciously welcomed us. The pastor who had brought me there said, "I'd like you to meet Mrs. Biko, Steve's mother." It was a rare privilege.

Steve Biko was a well-known anti-apartheid leader and a leading proponent of "black consciousness." In 1977, while he was in the custody of the South African police, he was brutally tortured and murdered. His death became a rallying point for many in the freedom struggle.

Alice Biko talked openly about both the anguish and the hope that have been part of being the mother of such a son. Her home was frequently searched, and she lived every day, she said, with "the fear of a mother whose son could be shot at any time." One morning he left and never came back. She phoned everywhere, trying to find him. She eventually received a call from the security police, assuring her that her son was fine. Two weeks later, they called to tell her he was dead. She said of the agony that they forced her son to endure and the anguish with which she must live, "I am a bit bitter, but I must forgive."

In one of her last conversations with her son, Alice Biko told him how difficult it was to be always worried about him being arrested and put in jail, how she never slept at night until she knew he was home. He had responded by reminding her that Jesus had come to redeem his people and set them free.

"Are you Jesus?" she had asked impatiently.

Steve had gently answered her, "No, I'm not. But I have the same job to do." After that, she said, she never asked him any more questions.

She told me that she now understands so much more about what he was saying to her then. He had once said to her, in words not unlike Jesus' to Mary, "I am not your son only; I have many mothers. And you have many children." Steve Biko gave his life so that those many mothers and their children might not suffer.

Alice Biko finished her poignant reflections with thoughts about the week we were about to enter: Holy Week. "It seems as if during Lent, the suffering of Jesus becomes very acute," she said. "It is not unlike the suffering my own son went through."

As I sat in Alice Biko's living room, I felt that I got a glimpse of what Mary, the mother of Jesus, must have been like. She was not the ivory-skinned, pious, submissive, halo-encircled image that I grew up with, but a woman who wept and doubted and cried out to God and pleaded for the life of her son.

My favorite Christmas card bears the inscription "A few days later the angel of Mary appeared unto the Lord." This modern angel, dressed in high-top sneakers and holding a trumpet, is saying, "Do not fear, Lord! Mary is still considering it." Indeed, this was something to consider, being the mother of God. Mary was a willing vessel for the will of God, but still she had her misgivings. She was "perplexed" by the announcement of the angel about her pregnancy. Could she believe it? How would she ever explain it to her family? And what about Joseph, whose first response was to "dismiss her quietly"?

It is astounding how many times the phrases "Do not fear" and "Be not afraid" appear in the stories surrounding the birth of Jesus. The angels said these words not only to Mary but also to Joseph and Zechariah, as well as to the shepherds quaking in the field. Fear surrounded the visit of the Wise Men, whose return was anxiously awaited by Herod. Fear attended the wrenching massacre of the children.

This was no ordinary birth. And this was no "ordinary" Messiah. The Jews, suffering under the brutality of Roman occupation, expected a valiant warrior who would arrive on a thundering steed and break the chains of their oppression with a sweep of the sword. What they got was a vulnerable baby, born in the straw in a drafty stable.

Mary herself must have had doubts about whether all was going according to plan. Was she really supposed to give birth to the Son of God in a stable and lay him in the feeding trough of the animals? Was he supposed to be welcomed by these scruffy, smelly shepherds who had just left their flocks? And who were these strange visitors from the East, who brought gifts most inappropriate for a baby? She pondered all these things in her heart.

She must have trembled in fear and pain as she gave birth, attended only by her new husband, in a cold stable in a strange town. What terror must have gripped her as she fled to the strange land of Egypt, an exile. What anguish seared her soul when she discovered that the birth of her son caused the death of so many others.

Mary often misunderstood this son, who at age twelve lagged behind at the Temple and put the scare of a lifetime into her when she discovered his absence. A proud mother, she was anxious for him to show his miraculous powers at the Cana wedding; she was rebuked by a reluctant Jesus, who then relented and turned water into wine. She lived with the shame of his rejection by her neighbors and relatives. She was informed that he had many mothers and many concerns.

Mary must have had some bitter days and tearful nights. But a common thread of faithfulness ran through her life. Long before anyone else understood—while Jesus was still in her womb—Mary knew what this birth would be about. God had entrusted her with the message of the radical social upheaval that was to come, when the rich and powerful would be put off their thrones, the poor would be uplifted, and the hungry would be fed. It had already come true in her. She was a poor Jewish woman, a victim of oppression by class, race, and gender. You could not get much lower in those days than to be a woman in a patriarchal society, a Jew under Roman occupation, and a peasant in a land of plenty. But Mary was the chosen vessel of God's incarnation; God's promises had already become truth in her flesh.

She wove her story into faith history. Her Greek name was rooted in the Hebrew "Miriam," meaning "rebellion," and she drew strength from the example of her sister liberator of the exodus. She understood that Jesus had been spared a ruler's massacre, just as Moses had, in order to free his people. She caught the echoes of Hannah's song of praise and justice as she sang her Magnificat.

Although Jesus was often busy about his work—from the time he was twelve years old on—he never flagged in his love for his mother. The exchange between them at the foot of the cross is one of the most poignant in the Bible. Jesus was making sure that, after his death, she would be taken care of. He was repaying her for years of care and devotion.

She stood by him to the end. The prophet Simeon had been right; her soul was pierced to the core. She wept a mother's tears as she watched him hanging in agony on the cross. She did not always understand him, but she loved him with all the fervor of a mother's love. And after he was gone, she stayed among his friends, praying and hoping and remaining faithful. God had chosen well.

47 Elizabeth: Joyful Friend

SCRIPTURE: Luke 1:5–25, 39–45, 56–66

When Elizabeth heard Mary's greeting, the child leaped in her womb. And Elizabeth was filled with the Holy Spirit. (Luke 1:41)

Elizabeth is joy incarnate. It is not surprising that the angel Gabriel's announcement came with the words "You will have joy and gladness, and many will rejoice at his birth" (Luke 1:14). Some of the joy, of course, was related to an elderly, barren woman conceiving, and some to the fact that the son would be a prophet. But there was more. It seems likely that Gabriel knew that Elizabeth was a woman capable of joy. She had borne much disgrace due to her inability to bear children; but now, because she had always been faithful and devout and full of gratitude to God, she would rejoice.

When Elizabeth's cousin Mary received the announcement that she herself would conceive by the Holy Spirit, she was willing but frightened. And so Mary set out "with haste" to see Elizabeth. It was the natural response. When afraid, go to see a friend who will listen and make it all feel a little less lonely and overwhelming.

The account of their greeting is one of my favorite passages in all the Bible. What a blessed moment for womanhood when Mary, still trembling with the news of what was to be fulfilled in her, ran to the elderly Elizabeth and embraced her. At Mary's greeting, Elizabeth's womb came to life, and the child "leaped for joy" within her! Mary's song of praise and hope flowed forth in this setting, and two miraculously pregnant women basked in the secret of the quiet revolution that was to be accomplished through them.

What a wonderful weaving together of hopes and lives. As Miriam Therese Winter writes, "The joining of both stories, women's stories whose central theme is the salvation and liberation of all people, occurs through the deliberate intervention of God who weaves a storyline through women's wombs against all human odds."[1] Two women incarnated the truth that, with God, nothing is impossible.

We can imagine what their days together were like. They must have been filled with shared secrets, laughter and tears, and dreams of a future unlike any they had conceived before. They watched their wombs swell, felt their sons growing within, probably rubbed each other's aching backs and sore feet at the end of the day.

Elizabeth, in her experience and wisdom, had much to share with her younger cousin. She understood the requirements of faith and the challenges of marriage. She knew that some would point with scorn at Mary, pregnant before her wedding, just as some had spoken of her own barrenness with reproach. She knew how to live proudly despite the whispers behind her back and how to be grateful to God no matter what her circumstances. Mary, for her part, encouraged Elizabeth with her youthful eagerness. And she likely helped with a variety of tasks around the home as Elizabeth's time to deliver came closer and closer.

A tremendous respect grew between them. It began with Elizabeth's first words to Mary on her arrival: "Blessed are you among women, and blessed is the fruit of your womb. And why has this happened to me, that the mother of my Lord comes to me?" (Luke 1:42–43). She was not envious that Mary had been chosen to bear the Messiah, only grateful for her own role in history and for being chosen a witness to Mary's miracle.

In the birth stories, Mary and Elizabeth carried the faith. Hearing of Mary's pregnancy, Joseph wanted to "dismiss her quietly." And Zechariah was struck dumb for the duration of Elizabeth's pregnancy because of his doubt—all the more reason that Mary's visit was well-timed.

When Elizabeth's baby was born, all the neighbors and relatives "rejoiced with her." Elizabeth insisted, at his circumcision, that the child be named John. Puzzled, the neighbors looked to Zechariah for some indication that perhaps Elizabeth was mistaken, to see if he would override her wishes; no one in the family was named John. But in a moment of poignant dignity, Zechariah took the tablet and wrote simply, "His name is John." Without any explanation, he affirmed Elizabeth and her understanding of God's will.

The people grew fearful, and news of the birth was talked about all over the mountains. And they wondered what this child would become. John, of course, became one of a kind—living in the wilderness, wearing camel skins, eating locusts and wild honey, and preaching repentance. He minced no words, calling the unfaithful a "brood of vipers," confronting those who lived by sin.

John and Jesus exhibited the same mutual respect for each other that had marked the relationship between their mothers. Jesus presented himself to John for baptism and said of his cousin, "Truly I tell you, among those born of women no one has arisen greater than John the Baptist" (Matt. 11:11). John acknowledged his place in salvation history: "Among you stands one whom you do not know, the one who is coming after me; I am not worthy to untie the thong of his sandal" (John 1:26–27). The Messiah and the one who prepared the way for him learned respect from mothers who passed it on to them.

Both sons confronted the oppressive power arrangements of the day, calling political and religious authorities to account. And both died terrible deaths at the hands of those authorities—one crucified, one beheaded. Certainly, Mary and Elizabeth must have had an inkling, even while these sons were in the womb, that they would stir things up and suffer for it. What strength the two women must have drawn from their relationship. It is not hard to imagine that at the foot of the cross, Mary thought of her cousin Elizabeth and the wondrous days they had spent together when they were pregnant, drawing on that long-ago memory for strength in her grief.

The friendship of Elizabeth and Mary is a story of tenderness and wonder. But most of all, it is a story of joy.

I think again of the witness to faith that comes from Central America. Several years ago, in a Salvadoran refugee camp in Honduras, preparations were under way for Christmas. A few days before, national guard members had come to the home of a young lay catechist, bound him by the thumbs, and taken him away. When he tried to escape, they mowed him down with machine-gun fire. Later, his pregnant wife and five children gathered around his coffin as a single candle burned in the darkness.

In another part of the camp, a group of women had surrounded an infant and sung to him in a dark tent, lit only by the light of a candle. Between the verses of the song, the anguished cries of his mother filled the air. She had fed her son through the night from an eyedropper, trying to coax some nourishment into his starving body. The child now lay in the center among them, his eyes and mouth open. He did not cry. One of the mothers marked the sign of the cross on the child's forehead while he looked at them fervently, as if expecting an answer to a question he could not ask. Then the singing stopped. The child was dead.

These were the events that preceded Christmas. But when Christmas Eve came, the camp burst into joyful celebration. Women baked sweet cinnamon bread in an adobe oven while men butchered hogs for the making of special pork tamales. The children made figurines for the nativity scene out of clay from the riverbed, adding local touches to the usual characters: pigs, an armadillo, and baby Jesus sleeping in a hammock. They painted beans and kernels of corn in bright colors and strung them into garlands. They made ornaments from small medicine boxes and shaped figures from the tinfoil that wraps margarine sticks, and they hung these on a tree branch. The children dressed as shepherds and passed from tent to tent, recounting the journey of "José and María" in search of shelter. "This Christmas we will celebrate as they did," said one mother, "looking for a place where our children can be born."

The Christmas story is their story. They know the special love of a Savior who was also a refugee, and of a mother who fled with her child to escape Herod's slaughter of the innocents.

Yvonne Dilling, a church worker from Indiana in the camp, told me the story of a refugee woman who once asked her why she always looked so sad and burdened. Yvonne talked about the grief she felt over all the suffering she was witnessing and her commitment to give all of herself to the struggle of the refugees. This woman gently confronted her: "Only people who expect to go back to North America in a year work the way you do. You cannot be serious about our struggle unless you play and celebrate and do those things that make it possible to give a lifetime to it."

Every time the refugees were displaced and had to build a new camp, they immediately formed three committees: a construction committee, an education committee, and the *comité de alegría*—"the committee of joy." Celebration was as basic to the life of the refugees as digging latrines and teaching their children to read.

I remember one evening sitting around a bonfire during a service of welcome to Salvadoran refugees who had made it safely to the United States. A woman who had witnessed the murder of her husband and three sons sat on a log next to me. She clapped as we sang a hymn of praise. Then she jumped up, the first to begin a dance around the bright flames shooting toward the sky. She encouraged others, grabbing hands, widening the circle. I was in awe of her capacity for joy.

In times of suffering such as the world faces today, despair can easily threaten to take up residence in our hearts. But those who suffer most remind us of how tragic and arrogant it would be for us to lose hope on behalf of people who have not lost theirs. They are teachers of joy. Like Elizabeth, they believe the promises of God. They pour their love into their children with a hope that the world will be better for them. And like the infant John in the womb, they have learned to leap and swirl and dance in the presence of God.

NOTES

1. Miriam Therese Winter, *WomanWord* (New York: Crossroad, 1990), 3.

48 Mary and Martha: Living in Freedom

SCRIPTURE: Luke 10:38–42; John 11:1–3, 17–45

The Lord answered her, "Martha, Martha, you are worried and distracted by many things; there is need of only one thing. Mary has chosen the better part, which will not be taken away from her." (Luke 10:41–42)

[Martha] said to him, "Yes, Lord, I believe that you are the Messiah, the Son of God, the one coming into the world." (John 11:27)

A bent-over woman with a mantilla draped over her head slowly makes her way down the aisle of the small church. She pauses before a large picture of Mary and the baby Jesus, who is tied to his mother's hip with a colorful Mexican serape. Votive candles and a statue of a saint draped with beads have places of honor in this simple, white-stucco church filled with wooden benches. There is one stained-glass window, an image of Jesus praying in the garden of Gethsemane. A bell outside rings to beckon people in the surrounding barrio to the Sunday morning service.

This is Dolores Mission Church in East Los Angeles. *Dolores* means "sorrows" in Spanish, and indeed, this corner of the city has its share. Poverty, illegal drugs, and gang violence are rampant.

The service begins with prayer for a woman who has been a leader in one of the barrio's active *comunidades de base*. She had helped to organize Bible studies and nonviolent acts of defiance against the drug trade. Earlier in the week, her home was shot up by drug dealers, and she fears for the lives of her young children.

The church provides a haven of hope. The garage of the parish house has been turned into a meeting place and gym for young gang members, who consider it a home. At night, several homeless people sleep in the sanctuary. A school and temporary shelter for women are housed in the parish hall. In this hall, after the service, tortillas and *menudo* will be served to the congregation and visitors. The *menudo*—a pungent soup made of entrails and hominy, served with slices of fresh lime, onions, dried red chili peppers, oregano, and fresh cilantro—is a mainstay of life here. Every woman has her recipe.

The Gospel passage for this Sunday morning is the story of Jesus' visit to the home of Mary and Martha. The priest, Father Greg Boyle, hopes to use it as an illustration of freedom from prescribed gender roles, emphasizing Jesus' affirmation of Mary's choice to listen and learn rather than to get caught up in the flurry of meal preparation that occupied Martha.

Boyle offers his sermon in base-community style, asking questions and encouraging reflection and discussion. At one point he asks the congregation, "Why do you think it is that only men sat at Jesus' feet to listen and learn?"

Seven-year-old Miguel has his hand up in a flash. Boyle calls on him, and Miguel answers confidently, "Because the men don't know how to make *menudo.*"

An unsuppressable laugh travels through the congregation, and Boyle grins and shouts, "*¡Lo último, Miguel!*" It was the ultimate answer. Miguel got it, even if he didn't know he did.

In a corner of East Los Angeles, women are throwing off the patriarchal shackles of their cultural heritage, leading Bible studies and the fight against illegal drugs. And perhaps the day is coming when the men will learn to make *menudo*. Both activities require courage.

Jesus' choice to teach Mary was an act more radical than it may at first appear. It was prohibited under Jewish law to instruct women, particularly in matters of the faith. Once again, Jesus violated all expectations of discourse between women and men, strongly affirming Mary's right to sit and learn and question.

But he also affirmed Martha. The Gospels mention three occasions on which Jesus visited the home of Martha, Mary, and Lazarus. Clearly, there was a bond of friendship and intimacy between these four.

Jesus partook gratefully of Martha's gracious hospitality. His retort to her was not a denigration of her generous gift but a response to her criticism of Mary for not joining her in the activity of preparing the meal. He refused to corner these women into prescribed roles, acknowledging that there is need for both vigorous caregiving and quiet listening. He made clear that there is room in the faith for the servant activist as well as the contemplative. By his love for these two very different sisters, he affirmed the breadth of gifts and temperaments that women possess.

Jesus also knew that Martha was more than a generous hostess.

Their poignant encounter over the death of Lazarus shows Jesus' deep trust and respect for her. It was Martha, strong and energetic and involved, who ran to Jesus while Mary stayed at home. She began their conversation with a gentle confrontation and an affirmation of Jesus' power: "Lord, if you had been here, my brother would not have died. But even now I know that God will give you whatever you ask of him" (John 11:21–22).

Jesus met her honesty with honesty of his own. It was to Martha that he revealed the secret of his authority: "I am the resurrection and the life." He spoke about the mystery of eternal life and then asked her simply, "Do you believe this?" She responded with more certainty and truth than he had asked for: "Yes, Lord, I believe that you are the Messiah, the Son of God, the one coming into the world."

It is one of the strongest affirmations of faith in the Bible, matched only by Peter's declaration "You are the Messiah, the Son of the living God" (Matt. 16:16). The church was built on Peter's confession. But a similar acclamation came from the lips of a woman, all but forgotten in church history.

Mary too had a poignant encounter with Jesus over the death of Lazarus. Her tears moved Jesus to weep with her. She knelt before him as they wept together for the loss of a dear brother and friend. How comforting that moment must have been for Jesus as well as for Mary. Scripture records, just verses before, that the Jews "took up stones again to stone him" (John 10:31). And the verses following the raising of Lazarus recount the stir that the event created. Many Jews believed in Jesus as a result, but some went and reported it to the Pharisees. The chief priests and Pharisees, seeing their authority threatened, called a meeting of the council. "So from that day on they planned to put him to death" (John 11:53).

How much it must have meant to Jesus to have friends with whom he could rest, break bread, laugh, weep, and share the deepest truths of his life. Even the disciples often did not comprehend. But there in Bethany, in the home of friends, he knew he could always find a wonderful meal, intimate companionship, and the love of two sisters who understood for what purpose he had come among them.

49 The Anointing Woman: Prophetic Service

SCRIPTURE: Mark 14:1–10

Jesus said, "She has performed a good service for me. . . . Wherever the good news is proclaimed in the whole world, what she has done will be told in remembrance of her." (Mark 14:6, 9)

Each of the four Gospels has a story of a woman anointing Jesus, but the details vary. All agree that the incident happened in Bethany, but from there the stories diverge considerably.

Luke's version, set near the beginning of Jesus' ministry, is about "a woman in the city, who was a sinner" (Luke 7:36–50). Jesus' host, Simon the Pharisee, took offense at her anointing and kissing of Jesus' feet because of the type of woman she was. Jesus used the occasion to tell a parable and preach about forgiveness and grace.

John attributes the anointing of Jesus' feet to Mary, the sister of Martha and Lazarus (John 12:1–8), six days before the Passover. In this account, it was Judas Iscariot who took offense at the pouring out of the nard, because of the waste of money.

Matthew's version most closely resembles Mark's, with an anonymous woman anointing Jesus two days before the Passover feast (Matt. 26:1–13). The key difference between these two accounts and the others is that the woman anointed Jesus' head. It is the kind of detail that can be easily overlooked, but it is crucial to understanding the woman's action.

The image of the scene that remains most common in Christendom is that of a sinful, sensual woman weeping at Jesus' feet, wiping up her tears with long and tangled hair. She is needy and subordinate, a receiver of mercy at the feet of her Lord. Although no scriptural evidence exists to support the theory, some interpreters have concluded that the woman was Mary Magdalene, stereotyped throughout faith history as an archetype of woman's sexual sinfulness.

A woman standing over Jesus, pouring ointment on his head, is quite a different matter. Kings were anointed in Israel with the pouring of oil over the head, always the task of a male leader or prophet specially chosen. This woman acted boldly, radically, and prophetically.

Two days before the betrayal, the male disciples still did not understand that Jesus had to die. They had not yet grasped that salvation was going to come by way of a cross. But this anonymous woman understood. Wrenched to the heart by the suffering that lay just ahead, she performed an act of loving-kindness. She was a prophet, announcing a death, preparing a body for burial. She was telling all the world that this Jesus was indeed the Messiah, the "Anointed One." She had done the honor. She had come not to receive but to minister to him. She alone among the disciples at the table understood that power in God's kingdom came through servanthood.

What a balm it must have been to Jesus' soul and heart to be so lovingly anointed. His loneliest hour was approaching, his closest friends were turning away in confusion, his agonizing death was in view. An unknown woman let him know that she understood, that he was not alone. She offered reverence and consolation.

She had boldly entered Simon's home, uninvited, interrupting the fellowship of men. She carried a jar of pure nard, a luxurious ointment made from the flowers of the spikenard, a plant growing on the slopes of the Himalaya Mountains, likely carried by caravan on a long journey to Jerusalem. Nard was expensive—worth a year's wages for a laborer—and was never used more than a drop at a time. What extravagance to have broken open an entire jar! That fact did not go unnoticed by the men present. It could have been sold, the money given to the poor, they argued. Jesus' response was swift: "She has performed a good service for me."

Jesus was not in any way denigrating the importance of caring for the poor. Justice and compassion were so central to the message of his ministry that no one who took him seriously could have mistaken his point. He was pointing a finger at the self-righteous, the narrow, the ones who had no capacity to celebrate and appreciate beauty, who put a politically—or spiritually—correct measure up against any move.

The men at the table missed the point. They took offense at the woman's gesture, unable to see love at work, unwilling to grasp the deeper meaning of her extravagance. Certainly they missed the fact that she was a prophet who had an understanding deeper than theirs. She had done a thing of beauty.

She is the poet who whispers of life's generosity, even while looking into death. She is the weaver transforming strands of color into tapestries exalting the interconnectedness of all things. She is the host who makes a meal a celebration of sight and smell and taste. She is the dancer who breathes delight into movement. She is the singer whose joyous melodies rival all the praises of creation.

She is a standing rebuke to all those who believe that faithfulness means joylessness, that justice and beauty must be rivals. She has been largely forgotten, but Jesus has given us a command: Wherever the good news is being proclaimed in all the world, what she did must be told in remembrance of her.

50 Mary Magdalene: First Witness to Resurrection

SCRIPTURE: Luke 8:1–3; Mark 15:40–47; John 19:25; 20:1–18

Mary Magdalene went and announced to the disciples, "I have seen the Lord"; and she told them that he had said these things to her. (John 20:18)

She was at Jesus' side as he preached and healed. She was at the foot of the cross when he died. Keeping watch even as his body was laid in the tomb, she never let him out of her sight during those last days of his life.

We do not know much about Mary Magdalene. Her surname comes from her hometown of Magdala, a bustling port on the Sea of Galilee. We are not told what "demons" possessed her. Perhaps she had a physical infirmity or suffered from a form of mental illness. Or maybe her "demons" were the resentment, anger, and envy that take root in a gifted and charismatic woman when a society denies her an opportunity to give and lead.

She has been labeled a prostitute, the greatest of sinners, the ultimate "fallen woman." Scripture makes no such claim. But charging her with sexual immorality was the easiest way for biblical interpreters to discredit her. She was a problem, after all—a woman who clearly shared a deep intimacy with Jesus and a passion for his teaching and example. In noncanonical Gnostic writings, she is portrayed as a spiritual companion of Jesus, the only follower who truly understood the mysteries and profundities of the faith, which she interpreted for the male disciples.

Resentment and envy may well have played a part in the effort to paint her as a sexually sinful woman. She got too close to Jesus for comfort, from the perspective of all those men who wanted the inner circle to include only Peter and James and John.

But it was the women who stood by the cross; the women who kept vigil through silent tears and came with spices at dawn to anoint the body. Judas had betrayed him, Peter had denied him, and the rest had fallen asleep in the garden when Jesus most needed their vigilance and companionship. As the tragic drama unfolded, the men kept their distance, safely huddled behind closed doors; but not the women. The women were there, present, watching and weeping and waiting. Some of their names have been lost to history, and those whom we know were never counted among the Twelve. But that was true of women's fate from the beginning.

Dinah, Jacob's only daughter, was left out in the reference to his "eleven children" on their journey home. The five property-owning daughters of Zelophehad were the only women counted in the census in the wilderness. When Jesus did his miracle of multiplication with the loaves and fishes, those who ate were "four thousand men, besides women and children." Women were always present and unaccounted for.

Joanna, Susanna, Salome, the mother of James and Joseph, and many unnamed "other women" surrendered all to follow and support Jesus through their prayers and resources. It is not surprising, given the biases of the biblical writers, that the female disciples were never given the attention that the male disciples received. But truly, the women were fervent followers. Their persistent presence, especially during Jesus' last days, could not be ignored.

The Gospel versions vary as to which women stood by the cross and went to the tomb. But all agree that Mary Magdalene was there. Her name often appears first in the lists of women who surrounded Jesus. She was their guide and example. She was the paramount disciple and friend, faithful to the bitter end. She could not leave him. She had known love and mercy, healing and empowerment, through his voice and touch. There was no choice for her but to stay as close as she could, whatever the cost. No other disciple, male or female, surpassed her in ardent devotion to Jesus and the way of God.

Jesus rewarded her love and faith. He showed through his friendship with her that his scandalous acceptance of women was more than just a series of chance encounters at wells, on hillsides, and in temples.

He revealed himself first to her. A woman was the first witness to the resurrection, a truth made more astounding by the fact that the testimony of women was not considered valid in a court of law at the time; women were deemed unreliable witnesses. Luke's resurrection account places Mary Magdalene, Joanna, and Mary the mother of James at the tomb. When these women went to tell the disciples about the resurrection, they considered it "an idle tale" (Luke 24:11). But in John's version, Peter and the "other disciple," considered to be John, ran straight for the tomb on Mary Magdalene's word. They saw the linen wrappings and believed that what was promised had come true. Then they went home.

For Mary Magdalene was reserved the special grace of seeing the risen Christ. The tender beauty of the garden scene is all hers. For her, grief disappeared at the sound of a voice. Jesus' first word out of the tomb was "Woman." He spoke it gently. Then he spoke her name, and everything changed. The tears of sorrow became tears of unspeakable joy. She wanted to rush to him, to hold fast now that she had him back. But as with all love, there are times to hold on and times to let go.

The calling of Mary Magdalene is the calling of us all. She is an example of injury healed, spirit empowered, and life bestowed with grace. She lived out a fervor, rooted in her love for Jesus, that moved heaven a little closer to earth. She is all of us at our passionate best, when we refuse to live in the broken present and dare to dream of a future full of promise. We commune in intimacy with Jesus, as Mary Magdalene did, when we accept the gift of abundant life and live as joyful witnesses to the resurrection.

Part 10. Questions for Reflection

1. Does joy come easily in your life? Why or why not?

2. How do you think you have conformed to or broken gender stereotypes?

3. How do you feel about the woman who anointed Jesus?

4. Why do you think no women were included among the twelve disciples recognized by the church? How does that make you feel?

5. Given all the suffering in the world today, is it unrealistic to live with "resurrection hope"?

Epilogue: The Woman Clothed with the Sun

A great portent appeared in heaven: a woman clothed with the sun, with the moon under her feet, and on her head a crown of twelve stars. She was pregnant and was crying out in birthpangs, in the agony of giving birth. Then another portent appeared in heaven: a great red dragon, with seven heads and ten horns, and seven diadems on his heads. His tail swept down a third of the stars of heaven and threw them to the earth. Then the dragon stood before the woman who was about to bear a child, so that he might devour her child as soon as it was born. And she gave birth to a son, a male child, who is to rule all the nations with a rod of iron. But her child was snatched away and taken to God and to his throne; and the woman fled into the wilderness, where she has a place prepared by God, so that there she can be nourished for one thousand two hundred sixty days.

And war broke out in heaven. . . . The dragon and his angels . . . were defeated, and there was no longer any place for them in heaven. . . .

So when the dragon saw that he had been thrown down to the earth, he pursued the woman who had given birth to the male child. But the woman was given the two wings of the great eagle, so that she could fly from the serpent into the wilderness, to her place where she is nourished for a time, and times, and half a time. (Rev. 12:1–8; 13–16)

We have known the dragon. He is apartheid and war, hunger and sexual violence, poverty and patriarchy. He is all that lurks nearby, ready to devour that which we long to bring to birth. He is the enemy of justice and compassion and community, the destroyer of peace.

Several years ago, I preached at a college in Pennsylvania just before Christmas. The chaplain's four-year-old son, Kyle, had memorized the Christmas story that year, and his parents were proud to show him off a little the first time there was a guest in the house. Kyle started out strong. He did just fine until he got to his favorite part, when the angels proclaimed to the shepherds, "Glory to God in the highest, and on earth, peace." He got the "Glory to God" part right, but then his mind went blank.

His parents urged him on. Suddenly, Kyle's little face brightened and he started out again with confidence: "And the angels appeared to

the shepherds and said, 'Glory to God in the highest . . . and I'll huff
and I'll puff and I'll blow your house down.' "

I smile when I picture Kyle and the angels. But his version of the
story often feels closer to the truth. It is hard to trust the promise of
peace on earth. The gale-force winds of oppression, violence, and
greed lay waste to homes and hopes. We can feel the dragon breathing
down our necks.

But Revelation offers us a beautiful portrait of a woman empowered.
She is clothed in sun, upheld by the moon, crowned with stars—
swathed in the power of Creator and creation. Her womb is brimming
with life, vibrant with possibility. The world is hers.

The waves of pain begin—the agonizing end that ushers in a bold
beginning. She weeps, cries out, holds on, lets go, submits to a force of
life beyond herself. And all the while the dragon waits; a monster so
large his tail can take out a third of the stars in one swipe. He stands
there, by her side, jaws open and ready to devour the thing she loves
most.

Her son is to rule by the power of justice. But he is snatched away—
not by the dragon but by the bearers of children to God. He is safe,
and so is the woman. In the wilderness, far from all that is comfortable
and known, there is a place for her. Nourishment waits. She can rest.

But the dragon is not through. He pursues the woman. And this
time, she is given the wings of an eagle to soar away and back to the
wilderness to her place, to be nourished for "a time, and times, and half
a time." She can stay as long as she likes.

This woman is considered by some to be a symbol of Mary or of the
church. She reflects each of us as well. We all know the joyful agony of
giving birth to something, whatever it is we are bringing to life, whatever our longing and labor. The monsters lurk, threatening to devour
our creativity, our confidence, our life.

But the monsters do not win. The dragon loses in the end, while the
woman soars in glorious freedom on eagle's wings. The creativity and
compassion of God cannot be stopped. The woman cannot be subdued.

The woman's son will rule, but it is she who is robed in glorious
splendor, she who stands face to face with the dragon, she for whom
God has prepared a place. It looks like a wilderness, but it is a place of
rest and nourishment. In the most desolate places, God nurtures and
provides.

She is a woman of power. If she were not, the dragon would not
have bothered. But he persists. Her power is a threat to all that he
stands for. But her trust in a God of light and love saves and sustains

her. God bears her up on wings. A dance that God began with Eve continues through time. God and the woman soar like one being.

God dances still. The spirit is in the wings, and we are all invited to soar; for each one of us is clothed with the sun, bearing glory and honor—created in the image of God.

Building an Altar:
A Ritual of Closure

The following ritual can be used at the conclusion of the year. Have a member of your group gather up stones, three or four for every participant. Prepare a simple altar base, such as a small table covered with a colorful cloth, with a lit candle on one end.

Have participants sit together in a circle around the table, with the stones on the floor beside it. You may want to have some quiet music playing. Read the story of Jephthah's daughter (Judg. 11:29–40), and have one member share briefly with the group about the importance of grieving, remembering, and honoring, as the daughters of Israel did for their sacrificed sister.

Build an altar to the memory of Jephthah's daughter, the other women in the book who have been part of the yearlong journey, and all the women who will be named. Invite all the participants to come forward in turn, as they feel moved to do so—to pick up a stone, name a woman and speak briefly about her, and place the stone on the table. Participants should be encouraged to name women who have been saints, mentors, and heroines to them, as well as victims and survivors of discrimination or sexual abuse.

One woman should be named for each stone. Participants can come forward as many times as they wish to add another name and stone. After the altar is completed, spend a few moments in silence.

You may wish to close the time together with the prayer below or another of your choosing.

We gather today remembering that, at the dawn of creation, God made woman and proclaimed her good. God danced at the marvel of her beauty and wisdom and strength. We celebrate that goodness within each of us.

At the same time, we confess our capacity to hurt others and ourselves. We acknowledge our need for God's forgiveness and grace. We accept these gifts so freely offered.

We remember our sisters who have suffered.

Daughter of Jephthah, you dance among us with timbrels, innocent again, remembered for claiming a few months of your own to wander the mountains with your sisters before he took your life away. We call you Strength.

Slave of a Levite, victim of unspeakable abuse, here you are remembered as strong enough to run away and claim your own life. Here you are remembered whole. We call you Dignity.

Women of Midian, spoils of war, handed over as property, we see your young, frightened faces. We picture you clinging to one another, finding strength in bonds that could not be broken by war or abuse. We call you Sisters.

We remember those who showed us how to walk our journey with dignity. Ruth and Naomi, we thank you for modeling the strength of true sisterhood. Vashti, we applaud you for refusing to be exploited. Dear Puah and Shiphrah, we commend your courage and compassion.

We give thanks for the gift of mother love that moves mountains and hearts. We remember the widows who teach us about gratitude and generosity. We think of all the women—bent, bleeding, afraid, ashamed—who asserted the power of faith, claimed their healing, and learned to walk tall.

Jochebed, Miriam, Abigail, Dorcas, Priscilla, Mary Magdalene— thank you all. Prophets, teachers, mothers, widows, we invite you all here and enfold you in our circle. We remember your pain, and we thank you for your witness to life and the power of resurrection.

We lift up all our sisters named here today—and those unnamed. By the grace of God we claim their strength and dignity and courage—and ours.

Amen.